A Platonic Theory of Education

Discussing Plato's views on knowledge, recollection, dialogue, and epiphany, this ambitious volume offers a systematic analysis of the ways that Platonic approaches to education can help students navigate today's increasingly complex moral environment.

Though interest in Platonic education may have waned due to a perceived view of Platonic scholarship as wholly impractical, this volume addresses common misunderstandings of Plato's work and highlights the contemporary relevance of Plato's ideas to contemporary moral education. Building on philosophical interpretations, the book argues persuasively that educators might employ Platonic themes and dialogue in the classroom. Split into two parts, the book looks first to contextualize Plato's theory of moral education within political, ethical, and educational frameworks. Equipped with this knowledge, part two then offers contemporary educators the strategies needed for implementing Plato's educational theory within the pluralistic, democratic classroom setting.

A Platonic Theory of Moral Education will be of interest to academics, researchers, and post-graduate students in the fields of ethics; Plato scholarship; moral psychology; educational foundations; and the philosophy of education. This book would also benefit graduate students and scholars in teacher education.

Mark E. Jonas is Professor of Education and Professor of Philosophy (by courtesy) at Wheaton College, US.

Yoshiaki Nakazawa is Assistant Professor of Education at University of Dallas, US.

Routledge International Studies in the Philosophy of Education

For more information about this series, please visit: www.routledge.
com/Routledge-International-Studies-in-the-Philosophy-of-Education/
book-series/SE0237

A Platonic Theory of Moral Education

Cultivating Virtue in Contemporary Democratic Classrooms

Mark E. Jonas and
Yoshiaki Nakazawa

Routledge
Taylor & Francis Group

NEW YORK AND LONDON

First published 2021
by Routledge
605 Third Avenue, New York, NY 10017

and by Routledge
2 Park Square, Milton Park, Abingdon, Oxon, OX14 4RN

First issued in paperback 2022

Routledge is an imprint of the Taylor & Francis Group, an informa business

Publisher's Note
The publisher has gone to great lengths to ensure the quality of this reprint but points out that some imperfections in the original copies may be apparent.

Library of Congress Cataloging-in-Publication Data
Names: Jonas, Mark E., author. | Nakazawa, Yoshiaki M., author.
Title: A Platonic theory of moral education : cultivating virtue
   in contemporary democratic classrooms / Mark E. Jonas and
   Yoshiaki Nakazawa.
Description: 1. | New York, NY : Routledge, 2021. | Series: Routledge
   international studies in the philosophy of education | Includes
   bibliographical references and index.
Identifiers: LCCN 2020018234 (print) | LCCN 2020018235 (ebook) |
   ISBN 9780367226572 (hardcover) | ISBN 9780367556525 (paperback) |
   ISBN 9780429276255 (ebook)
Subjects: LCSH: Moral education. | Education—Philosophy. | Plato—Influence.
Classification: LCC LC268 .J58 2021 (print) | LCC LC268 (ebook) |
   DDC 370.11/4—dc23
LC record available at https://lccn.loc.gov/2020018234
LC ebook record available at https://lccn.loc.gov/2020018235

ISBN 13: 978-0-367-55652-5 (pbk)
ISBN 13: 978-0-367-22657-2 (hbk)
ISBN 13: 978-0-429-27625-5 (ebk)

DOI: 10.4324/9780429276255

Typeset in Sabon
by Apex CoVantage, LLC

This book is dedicated to Henry and Pearl, and to Christa, Augustine, and Vivienne.

Contents

Acknowledgments

The authors wish to thank the publishers of the following articles and book chapters for granting permission to use portions of these publications in this book: "Education for epiphany: The case of Plato's Lysis," *Educational Theory*, 65(1), 39–51; "Appetite, reason, and education in Socrates' 'city of pigs'," *Phronesis* 57(2012), 332–35"; "Plato on Dialogue as a method for cultivating the virtues," in T. Harrison and D. Walker (Eds.) *The theory and practice of virtue education*, London: Routledge; "Plato on the Role of Political Leadership" in J. Arthur (Ed.) *Virtue in the Public Sphere*, London: Routledge; and we would like to thank Hackett Publishing Company for letting us cite from J. Cooper and Hutchinson (Eds.) *Plato: Complete Works*, Indianapolis: Hackett.

The project would not have been possible without the help of countless people with whom we have discussed the ideas and theses defended in this book over the years. These include but are not limited to (in alphabetical order): Drew Chambers, John Fantuzzo, Matthew Farrelly, Kevin Gary, David Hansen, Róbert Jack, Ryan Kemp, Kristján Kristjánson, Megan Laverty, Alexander Loney, Mason Marshall, and Avi Mintz, Julian Rome, Douglas Yacek, as well as countless participants of conferences (especially those at the Jubilee Centre for Characters and Virtues, the North American Association of Philosophy and Education, and the Philosophy of Education Society of Great Britain) who offered comments on drafts of several of the chapters found in this book. We would like to extend special thanks to our research assistants Alicia Mundhenk and Misheel Batzorig for their invaluable help in preparation of the manuscript. Finally, we would like to thank Douglas Yacek for reading the penultimate draft in its entirety and offering invaluable comments.

Introduction

Plato the Teacher

Can Plato provide pedagogical guidance to moral educators in contemporary democracies? Judging from the almost complete absence of books or articles that advocate for a retrieval of Plato's ideas, the answer seems to be "no." While educational theorists and practitioners occasionally analyze one or more of Plato's dialogues,[1] and are interested in the figure of Socrates[2] and the way Socratic dialogue can be used to help students think about ethical ideas,[3] there have been no recent attempts to advocate for a thoroughgoing Platonic theory of moral education.[4] Interestingly, during the same period of time Aristotelian theories of moral education have abounded. There have been countless articles and book-length treatments on Aristotle's usefulness to contemporary moral education.[5] Why is it that Aristotle's philosophy has experienced a dramatic renaissance while Plato's has not? The answer at least partially lies in the belief that Plato's metaphysics are far too otherworldly, his epistemology far too intellectualist, his ethics far too elitist, and his politics far too totalitarian. While his use of Socratic dialogue might be employed as a method of teaching, the philosophical content of his dialogues seems distinctly unsuited for contemporary, pluralistic democracies, because it seems Plato's ideas and contexts are too far removed from our own. Even Lawrence Kohlberg (1981), the last significant educational figure to advocate for "Socratic" principles in education, distanced himself from Plato, claiming that he was too "indoctrinative and hierarchical" (p. 29).

The question is whether Kohlberg and other interpreters are right about the unsuitability of Plato's ideas to pluralistic, democratic classrooms. In this book, we argue that Plato's interpreters are incorrect, and that Plato's views are far more suitable to contemporary democratic classrooms than is commonly believed. If we correctly understand Plato's ideas, we can see them for what they are: potential foundations for a theory of moral education that could improve the moral lives of students living in democratic societies. Even though Plato offered ideas on how to cultivate virtues in *his* time and place, we can use his ideas to cultivate virtues in *ours*.

In order to understand the significance Plato's ideas and their relevance for contemporary education, we need to understand first the renewed interest in Aristotle's theory of moral education. Educational practitioners and theorists have been increasingly looking to Aristotelian-inspired approaches to moral education. The reason for the growing interest in Aristotle is because of a recognition that cognitive approaches to moral education have not proved sufficient to change students' moral behaviors. Generally speaking, cognitivist approaches to moral education focus on how students *think* about moral behaviors and activities. The idea is that if we can help students cognitively understand that certain actions are immoral and other actions are moral, and if we help them see that the former are more just than the latter, then students will choose the former. These kinds of approaches carry with them an intuitive plausibility. We can often change our behaviors when we are motivated by intellectual reasons to do so. However, this is not always the case. Frequently, we encounter situations in which we are intellectually convinced that some behavior is more moral than another, and yet in spite of our intention to act on that conviction, we behave in the less moral manner. This *all too human* fact about our lived experiences undermines purely cognitivist approaches to moral education. The reality is that children and adults often act immorally not because they have the wrong beliefs or convictions but because they do not have the "will-power," or "strength of character," or "courage," or other ways of expressing the inability to do what we know is the right thing to do. This fact about human nature is what makes Aristotle an attractive guide for moral education. Unlike cognitivists, Aristotle believes that knowing what the right thing to do is insufficient for morally good actions.

Somewhat surprisingly, Plato holds the same views on the centrality of the *affective* and *conative* dimensions of moral behavior as Aristotle does. It is surprising because Plato has often been considered to be an intellectualist regarding virtue—meaning he believes that proper cognition (knowledge) alone will lead to virtuous behavior. This is simply not the case. Like Aristotle, Plato believes that humans must not only *know* what the right thing to do is, but must also *desire* to do that thing, and have the *strength of character* to follow through on those desires. For Plato, behaving virtuously requires the *cognitive, affective*, and *conative* aspects of the soul to be functioning in concert with one another.

In order to illuminate the relevance of Plato's ideas for contemporary moral education, we examine some of the most important educational themes in Plato's corpus. In Chapters 1–5, we discuss Plato's views on knowledge, recollection, habituation, dialogue, and epiphany, respectively. These five chapters offer a systematic analysis of these themes and illustrate the ways they have been misunderstood. In Chapters 6, 7, and Conclusion, we connect these four themes of Plato's philosophy with the ways educators might employ them in the classroom.

General Interpretive Issues

How to Interpret Divergences Among the Dialogues

Before moving into the central argument of this book, it is necessary to address two important issues regarding how to interpret Plato's corpus. The first has to do with the fact that Plato's dialogues differ, at times significantly, with respect to style and content. Some of these differences are so stark that certain dialogues seem philosophically inconsistent with other dialogues. This has caused difficulties for interpreters who want to provide an overarching interpretation of Plato's philosophy. The problem is: one dialogue appears to articulate a particular philosophical position, while another dialogue appears to articulate a different position.

There are two general strategies in dealing with the apparent inconsistencies between the dialogues. The first, which has been dominant in the twentieth century, is the *developmental thesis*, which argues that Plato's philosophy *develops* over time. This thesis posits three stages of development in Plato's dialogues: the *early*, the *middle* and the *late*. According to developmental interpreters, in the *early* dialogues, Plato had not yet developed his own philosophical position and had been content to lay out the philosophy of his teacher, Socrates. Thus, the ideas in the early dialogues represent Socrates' theories more than Plato's. (Of course, Plato might have believed these theories at the time as well, but either way the ideas originate primarily with Socrates.) In the *middle* dialogues, by contrast, Plato began to express his own original philosophical ideas. Famously, the middle period is marked by some of the most indelible philosophical ideas ever discussed in the history of Western philosophy, like the theory of recollection, the Forms, the tripartite structure of the soul, and the rule of the philosopher-kings. These ideas and many others are so profound and provocative that it would seem strange that Plato never mentioned them in the early dialogues if he had been thinking about them at the time. The fact that they appear in the middle dialogues rather than the early dialogues leads naturally to the supposition that, when writing the early dialogues, Plato had not yet conceived of these ideas. Therefore, to developmental interpreters, it is natural to think that those ideas occurred to him some years later in the middle period. These interpreters also appeal to the late dialogues as evidence his ideas change again, and that he no longer believes what he believed in the middle dialogues. In the late period, affirmations of the Forms and the philosopher-kings disappear, and ideas that are inconsistent with these arise. In sum, the developmental thesis argues that Plato's ideas developed over the three periods and philosophical inconsistencies between the early, middle and late periods reflect these changes in his beliefs. This interpretation has become so established in the last 100 years that it has become a kind of *de facto* orthodoxy that many interpreters of Plato merely take the developmental reading of Plato for granted. As Julia Annas (1999) argues, "[The Developmental] assumption goes so deep that its operation is pervasive and often unnoticed, and it is often assumed to be the only sensible interpretive assumption" (p. 12).[6]

The other interpretive strategy, in contrast to the developmental thesis, is the *unitarian thesis*. According to the unitarian reading of Plato's corpus, the apparent inconsistencies are just that, only apparent. The unitarian reader argues that Plato's works are part of a larger philosophical and literary whole that, when taken together, can be shown to be consistent. Unitarians argue that it is naïve to read one dialogue in isolation from other dialogues and draw conclusions as to what doctrines Plato held at the time of its writing. According to these interpreters, had Plato written in an expository form the developmental approach would make sense. But the reality is that Plato wrote in dialogues, and nowhere in the dialogues does he speak in his own voice. Thus, we cannot know whether the doctrines that Socrates or other interlocutors articulate in one dialogue represent Plato's exact philosophical position which he held at that time, or whether they are supposed to serve some other purpose that can only be determined when one surveys his corpus in its entirety.

The Unitarian hermeneutic is the same approach used to interpret novels and plays. It is quite common for novels and plays to be written with no single character that represents the views of the author or playwright. Rather, the views of the author are found, if it can be found at all, in the drama as a whole, not in the words of a particular character. To look for the playwright's personal philosophy in one of his or her characters would be, in many cases, to miss the playwright's philosophical point of view. It is the same way when we interpret the entire body of work of a particular playwright. Certain texts may not be properly understood on their own; rather they may require the context of the author's entire corpus for a proper understanding. To read just one text and assume that the point of view offered in that text is what the author thought at that time is to have a far too narrow view of the author's larger literary project. Unitarian interpreters claim that Plato's dialogues are more similar to novels or plays than they are to discursive philosophical treatises, and thus the responsible interpreter must seek to understand Plato's broader literary-philosophical project if she hopes to genuinely understand a single work by Plato.

While most twentieth-century commentators were developmentalists, there have been several well-respected and influential analytic interpreters who have offered unitarian interpretations of Plato's corpus (Shorey, 1933; Kahn, 1996; Annas, 1999; Clay, 2000). Moreover, prior to the twentieth century, most readers, beginning with members of Plato's *Academy* immediately following Plato's death, were unitarians.

In this book, we offer a unitarian interpretation of Plato's dialogues, but we nevertheless rely on the developmental strategy of separating the dialogues into the early, middle, and late periods. For reasons that will become clear in the following chapters, we argue that the unitarian interpretation is the correct one and that the seeming *philosophical* inconsistencies between the early and middle periods disappear if we understand them in the context of Plato's whole corpus. Yet, we consider the grouping of the dialogues into the early, middle, and late periods to accurately reflect the differing ways Plato *expresses* his philosophical ideas. For example, in the middle dialogues Plato is much more inclined to use rich metaphysical descriptions of his ideas, whereas in the early dialogues Plato expresses his ideas without the same metaphysical imagery. Developmental interpreters have assumed that the use of metaphysical imagery reflects a change in Plato's *beliefs*, whereas we argue that it reflects a change in Plato's way of *describing* his beliefs. As Kahn (1996) argues: "because of his acute sensitivity to the seductions of language, Plato never likes to repeat himself exactly, and we must always be ready to find him expressing old thoughts in a new form" (p. 390). Plato's beliefs remain, in the most important respects, the same whether he relies on metaphysical imagery or not. Thus, while the philosophical ideas in the early, middle, and late periods are largely consistent, the way Plato expresses them differs (sometimes significantly) between periods.

In both the early and middle periods, for example, Plato offers ideas on how people become virtuous. For the most part, in the early period his dialogues are full of practical examples and discussions of human beings in everyday situations, whereas in the middle and late periods his dialogues are full of inventive philosophical metaphors and discussions of human archetypes in imaginary and otherworldly situations. These changes do not represent changes in his philosophical beliefs, however, but merely in the way he expresses them. Nevertheless because his ideas are expressed differently in the so-called early, middle, and late periods, we use the developmental language to talk about the dialogues.

The Status of the *Republic*

The second interpretive issue is with the *Republic* and its role in Plato's corpus. The *Republic* is, by any measure, one of the greatest works in the history of political, ethical, and educational theorizing. In it, Plato describes an elaborate political community as well as an educational program that makes the community possible. Because of its scope, rigor, and inventiveness, the *Republic* has dominated the horizon of scholarship concerning Plato's political, ethical, and educational thinking in the twentieth century. The problem is the *way* it has dominated that horizon. It is customarily assumed that the *Republic* represents the ultimate expression of Plato's political, ethical, and educational philosophy. As such, it is thought that Plato wants to establish a political community in which philosopher-kings rule with unchecked authority, while common citizens are given only the most basic education: Being taught to regard themselves as inferior human beings who need others to shape and guide their behaviors (Vasiliou, 2008). It is similarly believed that the educational program outlined in the construction of the *kallipolis* (the elaborate city described in the *Republic*) is the highest expression of Plato's educational philosophy (Barrow, 2008). This standard reading of Plato's *Republic* has led to the belief that Plato's values in the *Republic* are inconsistent with the values of contemporary democratic education. This is one of the reasons Kohlberg (1981, p. 29) distances himself from Plato of the middle period, and relies instead on what he takes to be the ideas of Socrates in the early period.

Unfortunately, this is a misunderstanding of the *Republic* and of its political and educational ideas Plato aimed to put forward. As we have argued elsewhere (Jonas, Nakazawa, & Braun, 2012), the *kallipolis* does not represent Plato's preferred political ideal; rather, it is meant to be just what Socrates claims it is: a metaphor for the human soul. Because the *kallipolis* is a metaphor and not meant to represent Plato's ideal city, it is wrong to assume that the educational program that stands at the center of the *kallipolis* represents Plato's ideal educational philosophy either.

While we cannot reconstruct the entire argument we made in 2012,[7] it will be helpful to briefly outline a few of its main points. The first is the sometimes acknowledged, but rarely examined fact that when Socrates, Glaucon, and Adeimantus set out to describe a city with justice in it, their reason for doing so is not because they want to create an ideal political community for its own sake, but to help them "see" justice in the soul (368c–369a). Socrates says, "So, if you're willing, let's first find out what sort of thing justice is in a city and afterwards look for it in the individual" (368e). In the most fundamental sense, the point of their dialogue is not to create a city because they *want* to establish an ideal political philosophy but to discover what sort of thing justice is *in a soul*. Socrates claims that it will be easier to see justice in a city because a city is a larger thing, whereas a soul is a much smaller thing. Moreover, after creating the *kallipolis*, Socrates never once claims that it is the best city, or even that it is his preferred city; rather, all that is said about the city is that it meets the formal requirement for justice—namely, that each social group in the city performs its own function and does not attempt to perform the functions of the other groups. The fact that Socrates never once calls the *kallipolis* a virtuous city, or a healthy city, or his preferred city, and the fact that the whole point in creating the city in the first place was to illuminate justice in the soul, suggests that interpreters ought to exercise caution in assuming that the *kallipolis* represents Plato's preferred political arrangement.

The need for caution becomes even greater when we recall that there is a different city in the *Republic* that Socrates *does* praise as "true" and "healthy" (369d–373b). When Socrates, Glaucon, and Adeimantus first begin to discover justice in a city (before they create the *kallipolis*) they come up with a very simple city, which is often referred to as the "First City" or the "City of Pigs." This city embodies justice, and Socrates refers to it as the "true" and "healthy" city. Importantly, this first city is an egalitarian city where every individual is provided for and has an important social vocation. Moreover, the citizens of the city practice moderation and the rest of the virtues—they do not give into their appetitive desires (372a-d). Based on Socrates' unmitigated and un-recanted praise of this city, it makes far more sense to interpret the First City as Plato's preferred political arrangement rather than the *kallipolis*, which he at first negatively refers to as a city with a "fever" (372e). Even after the *kallipolis* has been purged of its fever and embodies justice, in that each part does its own job, Socrates never once praises it as true or healthy.[8] Indeed, the *kallipolis* is founded on the principles of acquisitive war, giving in to appetitive desires, the need for potential lawsuits, and the promotion of unhealthy dietary habits (373b–374a): All of which are the hallmarks of a city whose citizens lack moderation and wisdom.

Of course, it might be claimed that although the *kallipolis* was founded on these principles, Plato makes it clear that the city is eventually purged of injustice and becomes a just city. This is true insofar as the city eventually meets the formal requirement of justice—that each part does its own job—but the injustice that is done away with is not the injustice found in acquisitive war, appetitive desires, potential lawsuits, and poor eating habits. Although there are limits that protect them from going to extremes, the auxiliaries still go to war to protect and acquire wealth (537a), the class of producers are still encouraged to give in to their appetitive desires (465b–466c), are given provisions to sue one another in court (464d-e; 405a-b), and still eat unhealthy meals (404e–405b)—to name just a few behaviors that Plato believes are vicious and conducive of unhappiness. Moreover, these individuals are never given an education that would help them develop the virtues to overcome these vices. Instead, they are given laws that prevent them from indulging in these vices to extreme degrees (465b), but they are given opportunities and even encouraged to live lives rooted in the satisfaction of unnecessary desires.[9]

Why then does Socrates still consider the *kallipolis* a just city if the vast majority of its citizens lack the moderation and wisdom and must depend on philosopher-kings to protect them from a headlong descent into vice? There are two answers to this question. The first one is that the *kallipolis* meets the *formal* criterion of justice—namely, that each of the three groups in the city performs its own role and does not attempt to perform the role of the other two groups. In other words, justice can still be seen in the city because of its formal harmony between the three parts, even though the individuals of the city are not living just and harmonious lives themselves.

The second reason Socrates acquiesces to Glaucon's wish to allow appetitive desires to flourish is because he claims that allowing them to flourish will help Glaucon "see" the nature of justice in the soul. After creating the First City, Glaucon rejects it because it does not have the luxuries and conveniences to which he has become accustomed. The inherent desirability of justice that is found in the First City is lost on Glaucon, and so he rejects the city as a political ideal. He does not realize that an ideal city would require the moderation of appetitive desires, and therefore believes that a city without the resources to satisfy its citizens' appetitive desires could never be a desirable city. Socrates acquiesces to Glaucon's desire to create a city with a "fever," not because he thinks luxuries and conveniences are compatible with an ideal political community but because adding them might make it easier for Glaucon to see the difference between justice and injustice. Socrates claims that creating such a feverish city "may not be a bad idea, for by examining it, we might very well see how justice and injustice grow up in cities" (372e). Here we see that the point of abandoning the First City is not because Socrates wants to create a superior city, but, on the contrary, to create an inferior city.

The upshot of this brief analysis is that since there is no evidence in the *Republic* that the *kallipolis* is intended to represent Plato's preferred political arrangement, we should be wary of assuming that the educational program found within the *kallipolis* represents Plato's preferred educational program. Interpreters have been too willing to assume that the best place to look for Plato's ultimate views on education is to look to the *Republic*. While there is much to find there that, properly contextualized, can shed light on Plato's philosophy of education, it should not be assumed that the *Republic* is where his definitive ideas on politics and education are found. The political and educational ideas expressed in the *Republic* need to be compared with the political and educational ideas expressed in the other dialogues. Where there are divergences, the *Republic* should not be the standard by which the other dialogues are judged, but the other way around. If anything, in the case where several dialogues diverge from the *Republic*, we ought to assume that they more likely represent his philosophical views.

For example, the *Laws* and the *Statesman*—Plato's most significant political treatises beyond the *Republic*—mention neither the philosopher-kings nor the other classes of citizens, the auxiliaries and producers. In these dialogues, Plato advocates for the teaching of virtue to all citizens, and he expects all citizens to willingly choose to live virtuously. In the *Laws*, the Athenian Stranger indicates that older, more distinguished citizens ought to show respect for the younger and try to persuade them to be virtuous rather than force them to be so (729b-c). Connected to this, the Athenian claims that all children can be persuaded to live virtuously, so long as the entire community participates in their education (664a-c). He also believes that simpler people of the past are actually wiser and more virtuous than contemporary citizens (679e). While Plato makes distinctions between individuals and their respective chances of becoming virtuous, he does not claim that some individuals are innately vicious but rather that the combination of their natural temperament and upbringing is a matter of fact. For Plato, not all people will achieve the same level of virtue; thus, both laws and education need to be put in place in society in order to ensure a measure of virtue in it. Similarly, in the *Statesman* Socrates claims that *every* citizen ought to be taught "to share in a disposition that is courageous and moderate, and whatever else belongs to the sphere of virtue" (308e–309a), and only those who act unjustly will be excluded from full citizenship in the city. The same goes for public offices, which have the same criteria for participation—namely, having the capacity to be governed by the proper amount of courage and moderation as the situation requires (310e–311e). The goal of the society in both the *Laws* and the *Statesman* is to achieve, to the best possible degree, an ethical equality between citizens. As Bobonich (2008) puts it,

> First, as we saw in the *Statesman*, Plato suggested a new conception of a good city as an association in which all citizens aim at leading virtuous lives and at fostering virtue in the other citizens. In the *Laws*, Plato is much clearer and more emphatic in building on this conception of a good city and, as we have seen, restructures the citizens' education accordingly. Second, since the citizens are more capable of exercising good, ethical, and political judgment and engaging in rational discussion, they will be able to hold office and exercise political authority.
>
> (p. 331)

To summarize, there is wide agreement across the dialogues that Plato thinks that all people are capable of achieving virtue if they are properly educated—and not merely in the *Statesman* and the *Laws* but, as we will show, across many other dialogues. Unfortunately, interpreters have tended to overemphasize the *Republic*, without sufficiently appreciating the metaphorical character of the *kallipolis*, and assume that Plato's educational philosophy and the politics it was supposed to support was radically anti-egalitarian. In this book, we argue otherwise showing that Plato's philosophy is not anti-egalitarian, and as such can provide insights to contemporary educators in democratic contexts.

Plato's Ideas on Education vs. a Platonic Theory of Moral Education

Before we move into the body of the book, we need to distinguish between Plato's ideas on education and the Platonic theory of education we are offering here. Concerning Plato's ideas on education, we are not advocating a complete revival of all of his ideas. As we have suggested earlier, and as will become clear in the pages that follow, Plato's ideas are not as radical as they are assumed to be in their metaphysics, epistemology, and politics. Nevertheless, they come from a particular conception of the way the world is and how human beings interact with that world. Plato is an

Ancient Greek and therefore he held many beliefs that would not be shared by contemporary educators and theorists. As such, there will be aspects of his thought which would have no place in secular pluralistic classrooms. Nevertheless, we think that he offers a methodology for moral education that could be used in contemporary contexts, even though those contexts are different from Plato's.

Our Platonic theory of moral education rests on two foundational principles. The first principle concerns the role that *moral epiphanies* can play in the moral development of students. For our purposes, epiphanies are dramatic internal events in which a student suddenly comes to realize that what they have pursuing is not the happiest life and that pursuing a life of goodness and virtue would make their lives better. The kind of moral epiphanies we are concerned about in this book are the kind that are so powerful and dramatic that when students have them, they see them as a turning point in their lives and have a strong urge to live differently. We argue that it is possible and desirable for teachers to attempt to produce these epiphanies in their students, and we argue that Plato helps us see the importance of the epiphanies in the moral development of students, and he also provides readers with hints about how to create these epiphanies. Plato believes that all human beings have the capacity to see that living a virtuous life is superior to living a vicious life. Unfortunately, he also believes that most people will never exercise this capacity on their own; they need a guide to help them appreciate the value of living virtuously. The problem is that while all people have the capacity to see the value of virtue, the vast majority have been trained by their parents, their friends, or popular culture to believe that the most important things to pursue in life are careers, fame, power, money, luxuries, conveniences, and so on. When people are systematically taught by everything and everyone around them to prioritize careers, power, fame, etc., they find it difficult to appreciate the value of the virtues. This is where epiphanies come in. Plato believes that trying to reason with students about why pursuing virtue is more attractive than pursuing fame, fortune, and luxury is nearly impossible—as evidenced by the countless failures that happen in the Platonic dialogues. However, he believes that if we can somehow lead students to *see* that virtue is better than vice, where they briefly transcend their previous upbringing, their desires can be temporarily reoriented, and they can come to *want* to pursue virtue. These epiphanies are not logical conclusions entailed by a series of rational arguments but are seemingly spontaneous moments of recognition that include a cognitive dimension (knowledge), an affective dimension (desire), and a conative dimension (commitment). When a person has an epiphany they feel transformed; they do not just come to believe different things, but want to be different people. According to Plato, moral epiphanies of this sort rarely happen accidently but require tremendous forethought and careful execution. The Platonic conception of moral education that we are promoting prioritizes a mode of dialogue which takes seriously the need for moral epiphanies in students and offers ideas on how teachers might learn to hold classroom dialogues that promote these epiphanies of a very particular kind of dialogue in the classroom. "Socratic dialogue," as it is called, is already a staple of many K-16 classrooms. Many teachers from around the world and across all grades use this form of dialogue (Schneider, 2013). In Socratic dialogue, teachers ask students questions in order to help the students discover their own beliefs and also help them appreciate the perspectives of others. We think that these kinds of dialogues are important and can improve students' abilities to think deeply about moral issues. However, from Plato's point of view, and from ours, what passes as Socratic dialogue in contemporary classrooms is not as transformational as it could be. Dialogues have the potential not only to deepen students' thinking on moral issues, but can actually create epiphanies which serve as transformative catalysts in which students become inspired to live virtuously.

However, we believe that dialogues are not the only way to induce epiphanies in the classroom. Indeed, there are several other ways teachers might induce epiphanies that, depending on the teachers personality and teaching style, might work as well, or even better than dialogues. In the second part of this book—in Chapter 6, Chapter 7, and the Conclusion—we examine these methods and make suggestions about how teachers might employ them.

The second foundational principle that our Platonic theory rests on is Plato's insistence on the essential role habituation plays in the development of the virtues. Although habituation is recognized as a hallmark of Aristotle's educational philosophy, it is equally a hallmark of Plato's educational philosophy from the "early" dialogues to the "late" dialogues. For Plato, human beings have very little chance of becoming virtuous unless they have been rigorously habituated in the virtues. We hope to shed light on the role contemporary teachers could play in helping students to rehabituate their ethical selves. Currently, while some teachers think of themselves as helping students establish intellectual habits, far fewer think of themselves as helping students establish habits in the moral realm. The problem is, whether they want to or not, teachers *are* helping to establish moral habits. As Kohlberg (1981) rightly says:

> Although *moral education* has a forbidding sound to teachers, they constantly practice it. They tell children what to do, make evaluations of children's behavior, and direct children's relations in the classrooms. Sometimes teachers do these things without being aware they are engaging in moral education, but the children are aware of it.
>
> (p. 6)

Every decision teachers make in the classroom has a moral component to it. To simply ignore the impact of these decisions does not make them go away. We hope that this book will inspire teachers to be more deliberate in the habituation or rehabituation they provide for their students. If they are going to habituate their students one way or another, it makes sense to habituate them in ways that make students more moral.

The Structure of the Book and a Summary of Its Chapters

Part I

The first chapter addresses Plato's claims in the "early dialogues" (expressed through the character of Socrates) that knowledge of virtue is all that is necessary to make individuals virtuous. It is tempting to assume, as Kohlberg and others do, that the knowledge Socrates has in mind is a purely cognitive knowledge that is gained through dialogue, disputation, and ratiocination. We demonstrate the falsity of this standard view by examining Socrates' famous craft-analogy and his repeated exhortation to his interlocutors to *act* virtuously. We argue that Socrates considers virtue a craft because he saw practice and habituation as essential to developing the cognitive dimension virtue but also the *affective* and *conative* dimensions. For Plato, having full knowledge of virtue requires not only that we have cognitive knowledge about which actions are virtuous and which are not, but that we also have the desire to perform virtuous actions and the strength of character to follow through on those desires. Without the right kinds of attitudes, dispositions, and desires, people are not capable of having full knowledge of virtue. They might know cognitively that some action is not virtuous, but if they do not desire to perform the action, and if they do not have the strength of character to follow through, they do not have full knowledge of virtue. This makes sense of Socrates' otherwise bizarre exhortations to his interlocutors to practice virtue: If they already know what virtue is, then he would not need to exhort them to practice it; but if they do not know what virtue is, then how would they know what to practice? This paradox dissolves, however, if we understand what Socrates means by knowledge. He believes that people can *partially* know what virtue is insofar as they can correctly and rationally identify virtuous actions but not *fully* know what virtue is. They can only achieve full knowledge of virtue after they develop the right kinds of desires and dispositions towards those actions, which only comes by way of practice and habit.

Chapter 2 expands on Chapter 1 by addressing Plato's supposed belief that knowledge of virtue can be achieved through contemplation alone because of the theory of recollection. According to interpreters like Kohlberg (1981), Plato believes that since all souls existed in the Realm of the Forms prior to taking on human form, they already know all that there is to know about virtue; their souls already contain all knowledge which just needs to be recalled or recollected. Essentially, because Plato believes that all souls contain, deep within them, complete knowledge of virtue, then all teachers need to do in order to access that virtue is ask the right questions. This is a serious misunderstanding of Plato's theory of recollection. While it is true that Plato believes that all souls have the theoretical capacity to recollect knowledge, he also claims that they are incapable of full recollection without radical readjustments of their lifestyles and actions. The body that each soul lives in encourages it to participate in vicious actions, which create what Plato calls "encrustations." These encrustations prevent the soul from seeing the virtue that it should be recollecting, therefore, question-asking through dialogue is insufficient to achieve full recollection because these encrustations prevent the soul from turning itself in the right direction. Thus, while every soul has the potential to recollect knowledge of virtue, it will only be able to achieve that recollection after the encrustations have been removed through practice and habituation.

Chapter 3 builds upon Chapter 2, by explaining the most effective way of dealing with these encrustations: prevention of their formation in the first place. As Jonas (2016) argues, educational theorists have largely ignored the role that habit plays in Plato's thought. We usually think of Aristotle when we think of habituation, but Plato (and Socrates for that matter) are equally insistent on the need for habit. Importantly, it is not the mindless process of mere repetition and obedience that Kohlberg (1981) incorrectly attributes to Aristotle. We show that not only does Plato argue for a process of habituation, but also that it is a process that is far from mindless; it requires personal engagement and reflection. Through an analysis of Plato's promotion of habituation in childhood, we examine his concept of "kinship" and explain how the soul is formed into a shape that can see virtue correctly. In other words, the soul's attitudes, dispositions and desires are aligned with its vision of virtue. Plato describes this becoming akin to virtue as a forging process in which the human being is hammered into the proper shape. This hammering occurs through the performance of certain actions and the imitation of the right kinds of people. However, it is not merely mindless behaviorism or blind imitation. Rather, it is reasoned and reflective action that includes both the body and the full engagement of the mind.

Chapter 4 proceeds from Chapter 3 by addressing the problem of the encrustation of young adults. We argue that dialogue is critical in helping older students overcome bad habits developed in their youth; however, this is not the kind of dialogue typically attributed to Plato. It is tempting to assume that, for Plato, dialogue is a process in which students can be led to the *rational* conviction that certain actions are more virtuous than other actions. In this chapter we show that, in fact, Plato believes that the most important purpose of dialogue with non-virtuous interlocutors is not to produce *rational* conviction but to produce an *affective response* which potentially leads to the desire to live virtuously. Ideally, children would be prevented from becoming encrusted through the process of reflective habituation in which they develop a kinship with virtue. Unfortunately, individuals who were not given the right kind of habituation in their childhood are now incapable of recollecting virtue because their souls are "turned in the wrong direction." They have passed the age where they can be compelled effectively by adults to go through a habituation process. But Plato has a plan for them as well. Rehabituation can occur through dialogue that goes beyond attempting to create rational assent and instead focuses on generating an affective response that transforms the interlocutor's desires. Plato believes that dialogues can be constructed in order to produce this emotional transformation, and we show this through an examination of the *Seventh Letter* in which Plato explains why he uses dialogue with adults in order to begin the process of removing their encrustations. Plato says that dialogue has the power to create epiphanies, where individuals catch a glimpse of virtue, and what it might be like to live virtuously, and are thereby motivated to voluntarily pursue a rehabituation process in the virtues. After examining the *Seventh Letter*, we look at some epiphanies induced in some of the other dialogues like the *Lysis*, the *Alcibiades*, and the *Symposium*.

In Chapter 5 we examine Plato's conception of dialogue in further detail, paying careful attention to the way dialogue is used to produce a transformative epiphany in Glaucon in the *Republic*. As we saw in Chapter 4, this desire is not created through logical inference but through an emotional response that is connected to the arguments found in the dialogues. In other words, it is not the bare inferences that provide the motivation, but rather it is the way the inferences are couched. While it is sometimes tempting to assume that Socrates is primarily concerned with logical arguments in dialogues that are intended to lead his interlocutors to rational knowledge, an analysis of these dialogues reveals that Socrates is far more interested in eliciting emotional responses. In every case we examine, however, it is clear that the dialogue did not achieve the production of *full* knowledge. Rather, it sets the stage for it. *Full* knowledge can only come about as individuals undergo a rehabituation process in which their encrustations are removed gradually under the supervision of mentors who guide them in their actions. As they perform these actions, their souls gradually develop a kinship with virtue and slowly but surely develop full knowledge.

Part II

In Chapter 6 we move into *Part II* of the book, which examines the practical aspects of what a Platonic theory of education might look like. In Chapter 6 we examine the contemporary relevance of Plato's theory of moral education and how secular educators could employ Plato's methods. Drawing on the examples we find in the dialogues examined in Chapters 4 and 5, we discuss methods educators might use in order to create a desire for moral change in their students. It is common for educators to believe that if they use Socratic dialogues to cast doubt upon students' assumptions about ethical issues, they have succeeded in moral education. Plato teaches us that merely causing students to rethink their assumptions is not enough to produce moral change. Instead, teachers should attempt to induce epiphanies in their students whereby the students have a moment of realization regarding what virtue is and why it is desirable. We outline several ways teachers can attempt to create these epiphanies by examining several contemporary examples found in literature and film.

Chapter 7 extends Chapter 6 by discussing the necessary follow-ups to the epiphanies that are achieved in the classrooms. Plato claims that creating an epiphany regarding virtue can lead to the desire for change in students; however, he also claims that such epiphanies are not enough to make students virtuous. In order to develop this desire into a full knowledge of virtue students must begin a rehabituation process. We discuss the contemporary application of this view by describing the way teachers can support a rehabituation process in their students. We offer three different strategies teachers can use, including one-on-one mentoring; creating a classroom culture of mutual rehabituation; and supporting students in developing friendships of excellence or finding communities of rehabituation that students can join. While most teachers cannot be the kind of extracurricular mentors their students will need to complete their rehabituation process, they can help guide students in finding alternatives methods of rehabituation.

In the Conclusion of this book, we first explain the attractions of the Platonic theory of moral education we are offering in this book by comparing it to cognitive theories of moral education and the neo-Aristotelian theories. Both theories have aspects of them that are highly attractive to contemporary educators, but they both have some shortcomings that Plato helps solve. Especially in the case of the Aristotle-inspired theories, we do not need believe that Plato needs to supplant these theories, but he might be able to supplement them in important ways. After outlining what we take to be the attractiveness of the Platonic theory we offer, we end with some general guidelines teachers might consider employing in their classrooms if they hope to bring about the moral growth that Plato thinks is possible for their students.

Notes

1. See, for example: Jonas (2015), Mintz (2014, 2011, 2007), De Marzio (2006), Bruell (1999), Higgins (1994), Hansen (1988), Haroutunian-Gordon (1986, 1987, 1988, 1990)
2. See, for example: Haroutunian-Gordon (1987), Reich (1998), Boghossian (2012), Brickhouse and Smith (2009), Pekarsky (1994).
3. See, for example: Jonas (2015), Wilberding (2014), Smith (2011), Mintz (2006), Scott (2000), Reich (1998), Rud (1997), Strong (1996).

4. There have been two book-length treatments of Plato's philosophy of education (Barrow, 2008; Mintz, 2018), but these are mostly historical and descriptive and do not offer a full-blown Platonic theory of moral education. Barrow's book outlines several ways that Plato's ideas relate to contemporary education, but his book does not advocate a detailed theory concerning the ways Plato's ideas on moral education could be systematically applied to K-16 schooling. This is especially the case concerning the role Socratic dialogues can play in creating moral epiphanies and the role teachers can play in helping to rehabituate students, two topics that will be central in this book).

5. A comprehensive list of publications promoting an Aristotelian philosophy and its relationship to education would be too long to include here, but there have been dozens of books and articles on Aristotle's theory of moral education in the last thirty years. Some of the most prolific contributors to this rapidly growing area of scholarship include Kristjánsson (2005, 2006a, 2006b, 2007, 2014a, 2014b, 2014c, 2015), Sanderse (2011, 2012, 2013, 2015), and Curren (2000, 2013a, 2013b).

6. Annas (1999) further says:

> In the twentieth century, this kind of unifying approach has been very much out of fashion, and one major reason for this is that we have got used to an overall developmental approach to this, as to other difficulties and inconsistencies in the Plato's works. It usually goes so deep as to be unquestioned that the dialogues of negative argument are early, and represent a different stage of Plato's thought from the positive, dogmatic middle dialogues. It goes so deep, in fact, that we tend to forget that it is only relatively recently that Plato's works have been interpreted as though the dialogues marked stages in a developing intellectual biography.
>
> (p. 24)

7. The entire argument, reprinted with permission, can be found in the Appendix of this book.

8. It could be argued that he does just that at the beginning of *Timaeus*; however, a careful examination of that supposed endorsement cannot be maintained. Socrates' seeming praise of the *kallipolis* is thinly disguised irony. That it is ironic is seen in "how he has come to feel about the political structure we've described" (19b). What are his feelings? He is curious to know just how the city would "distinguish itself in the way it goes to war and in the way it pursues the war: that it deals with the other cities, one after another, in ways that it reflects positively on its own education and training, both in word and deed" (19c). Socrates then turns to Critias and asks him to answer this question because he is a "master" of philosophy. Critias' answer shows just how poorly he understands virtue and its relationship to war, for he claims that the goddess that created the cosmos was "a lover of both war and wisdom" and sought out an environment that would produce men and women with similar loves (25c-d).

McDavid (2019) argues that Socrates' praise of the First City, calling it "true" and "healthy," is to be read as comparative praise: that is, it is not true and healthy *simpliciter*, but rather true and healthy compared to the luxurious, feverish city that Glaucon demands. McDavid argues that the First City is an "image of justice" (p. 592), but that it is itself not just, unlike *kallipolis*, which, McDavid maintains along with the standard reading, is just. She goes on to say that the First City does not participate in "the Form of the Justice itself." But McDavid does not explain why Socrates does not assign the same (or more) praise to *kallipolis*. And, like all standard readers, McDavid adduces principles and conditions of justice from the middle books of the *Republic* that belong to *kallipolis* and thereafter retrospectively brings those principles and conditions to bear on the First City, thereby showing that the First City is unjust. This is an order of argumentation, however, that is problematic, the most important of which is that it misunderstands Plato's purpose in designing *kallipolis*, which is to educate Glaucon about justice. See the Appendix for a more detailed argument and analysis.

9. To be clear, the citizens of the *kallipolis* are not completely depraved or licentious—the philosopher-kings and the auxiliaries would never allow that to happen. However, the common citizens are allowed to eat pastries, sue one another in court, and imbibe in a host of unnecessary desires. These desires are expressions of their appetites which Socrates believes decreases the health and happiness of the individuals (373c-e). Moreover, the common citizens are not internally moderate but are externally forced to be moderate by the philosopher-kings and auxiliaries. Were they not so controlled, they would become licentious. Thus, the common citizens of the *kallipolis* are not internally virtuous and are never given an education that would encourage them to become so.

1 The Relationship Between Virtue and Knowledge in the Early Dialogues

Introduction

In order to show the contemporary relevance of Plato's theory of moral education, we must first address his reputation as an intellectualist with respect to virtue. There are two ways Plato might be called an intellectualist. The first is his claim in the so-called "early dialogues" that virtue is knowledge, and that any person who knows the good will always do the good. According to *Protagoras* 352b-e, any person who has knowledge of virtue will always act virtuously and no other psychological force could persuade this person from doing so. According to the early Plato, if a student *knows* that it is wrong to cheat on a test, and yet in a moment of temptation looks over at her classmate's answers to check the correctness of her own, it is not that she is weak-willed, or that she is overcome by temptation, or even that she wants to act immorally, but simply that she did not really *know* that she should not cheat on tests, even if she thinks she "knows." For the "early" Plato, knowledge of virtue is an all-powerful motivational force, and if a person has knowledge there is no possible way any temptation could sway her from following it.[1] The strange upshot of this view is that all immoral actions proceed from ignorance (and therefore are involuntary) and that there is no such thing as weakness of will (*akrasia*). The fact that Plato is supposed to have held this theory makes him seem like a bad guide for contemporary moral educators, since the latter are not inclined to believe that immoral actions are *only* the result of ignorance. Contemporary educators recognize that there are many reasons why people do bad things, and a lack of moral knowledge is often only part of the problem.

The second way Plato might be considered an intellectualist is that in the so-called "middle dialogues" he seems to claim that the only people who are genuinely virtuous are those who have *true* knowledge of virtue which is gained through intellectual contemplation of the Realm of the Forms. According to this interpretation, Plato believes "only philosophers possess real virtue, while non-philosophers have only a 'shadow-painting of virtue that is really slavish and contains nothing healthy or true'" (Bobonich, 2002, p. 322). How do philosophers come to possess this "real virtue?" They are supposed to "make the ascent and see the good" (*Republic*, 519c) and "lift up the radiant light of their souls to what itself provides light for everything" (*Republic*, 540a), and this happens through contemplation. Plato supposedly believes that the only people who are capable being truly virtuous are innately gifted philosophers who, after years of training in mathematics and dialogue, can finally transcend their bodies and achieve the "philosophical ascent to a kind of knowledge that will result in cognitive contact with the Forms" (Morgan, 1992, p. 234). Similar to Plato in the early dialogues, Plato in the middle dialogues seems like a poor choice as a guide to contemporary moral education, since contemporary educators typically do not believe that virtue can only be achieved through intellectual contemplation, and do not believe virtue is available only to an elite caste of "philosophers."

These two forms of intellectualism have led many commentators to wonder at Plato's strange beliefs about moral development. The eminent Plato scholar, George Grote (1875), for example, claims that

> Both Sokrates (*sic*) and Plato (in many of his dialogues) commit the error of which the above is one particular manifestation—that of dwelling exclusively on the intellectual conditions of human conduct, and omitting to give proper attention to the emotional and volitional, as essentially cooperating or preponderating in the complex meaning of ethical attributes.
>
> (pp. 399–400)

Friedrich Nietzsche (1997) argues similarly, claiming that

> Socrates and Plato, in this regard great doubters and admirable innovators, were nonetheless innocently credulous in regard to that most fateful of prejudices, that profoundest of errors, that "right knowledge *must be followed* by right actions" . . . the opposite seemed crazy and unthinkable—and yet this opposite is precisely the naked reality demonstrated daily and hourly from time immemorial.
>
> (p. 72)

What Grote and Nietzsche articulate is the fact that it seems completely implausible to think that cognitive knowledge alone is all that is necessary to act virtuously. Nehamas (1999) argues similarly, when speaking of Socrates in the early dialogues, asks the question: "How could such a supremely intelligent man fail to realize that intelligence is not enough for being good and, as it followed for him, for being happy" (p. 27). That *is* the question. How indeed could Plato, who seems to be so perceptive in other areas of moral and intellectual life, have missed such an obvious fact about human nature? The answer is that he did *not* miss this obvious fact, and that if we rightly understand both his early and later conceptions of knowledge we will see that he is not the intellectualist that he is assumed to be by Grote, Nietzsche, Nehamas, and so many others.

In this chapter we examine Plato's so-called "intellectualism" in the early dialogues, otherwise known as "Socratic Intellectualism," since most scholars purport that Socrates' ideas are found exclusively in these dialogues.[2] In Chapter 2, we will address the "intellectualism" of the middle dialogues.

Socratic Intellectualism

In order to defend the theory of moral education articulated by Plato in the early dialogues, it will be necessary to defend his (in)famous "intellectualism" with respect to virtue. At first glance his intellectualism may, for obvious reasons, seem highly implausible. After all, most of us have had many first-hand experiences in which we *knew* we should do one thing and yet found ourselves choosing to do the opposite. But it is implausible only if we fail to understand what Socrates means by "knowledge." Interpreters like those included here and others have assumed that Socrates is talking about *cognitive knowledge*, which can be acquired through arguments, intellectual reasoning and dialogue alone. Penner (2000), for example, claims, that for Socrates "*only philosophical dialogue* can improve one's fellow citizens" (pp. 164–165); Rowe (2012) argues that "nothing apart from talking and reasoning . . . will be necessary [to facilitate ethical improvement], because there is nothing apart from what we think and believe that is even in principle capable of causing us to go wrong" (p. 166); and Kohlberg (1981) claims that "virtue is knowledge of the good. He who knows the good chooses the good. . . . [And] the teaching of virtue is the asking of questions and pointing the way, not the giving of answers" (p. 30). These passages are indicative of the assumptions interpreters make about what constitutes *knowledge* for Socrates and *how* that knowledge comes about. But, as we shall see, this is not what Socrates means by "knowledge." Socrates has a much richer conception of knowledge than what is normally attributed to him, and that is what he calls *craft knowledge*, which can be acquired only through years and years of practice and habituation. Craft knowledge is not acquired through thinking and reasoning alone, but requires embodied practice and habit which also shapes our attitudes, dispositions, and desires.

Presumably, part of the reason that interpreters make these assumptions is that Socrates seems to prioritize reason and argument in his attempts to persuade his interlocutors to live virtuous lives. Over and over again, Socrates uses arguments to interrogate his interlocutors' claims to knowledge and demands rational arguments from them. It is assumed that Socrates must be a rationalist who believes that the only thing that counts as genuine knowledge is propositional knowledge, that is, the cognitive recognition of the correspondence between some truth claim and the way the world is. A person has propositional knowledge when they affirm that 2 + 2 = 4, when it rains it is also cloudy, and murder is wrong. It is true that Socrates believes that this kind of knowledge theoretically can be gained through dialogue alone. Socrates uses dialogue to examine his interlocutors' conceptions of virtue and through dialogue he demonstrates that his interlocutors do not have knowledge of virtue. Within the dialogues, though, he outlines methods of creating moral knowledge in individuals that go beyond using reason and arguments. We must not be deceived by the argumentative and dialogical form that he uses, assuming that this usage implies that rational argument alone is what produces knowledge. Rather, we should look at what he explicitly says about how moral knowledge comes to exist in a soul if we want to know what his theory of moral education really is—and whether it can speak to contemporary educational concerns. As we will show later, according to Socrates, people do *not* have *full* knowledge of virtue if they cannot consistently act on that knowledge.

In order to establish Socrates' theory, we must first briefly outline Socrates' explicit claim that practice rather than rational argument is necessary for developing moral knowledge. Next, we will examine several instances where Socrates encourages virtuous action in order to show why he believes acting virtuously improves an individual's capacity for moral knowledge. Next, through an analysis of Socrates' famous *craft-analogy*, we will show that acting virtuously does more than merely improve the capacity to gain moral knowledge—it actually *produces* moral knowledge. Finally, we will conclude with a brief discussion of how this connects with Plato's theory of recollection in the following chapter.

Socrates' Claim That Virtue Requires Practice

The standard view of Socrates' theory of moral education is that arguments are all that is necessary for moral development; all the teacher needs to do is use arguments to lead the student to the knowledge that x is virtuous, and they will unerringly do x (Kohlberg, 1981, p. 30; Irwin, 1977, p. 78; Penner, 1992, p. 129, 1997; Benson, 2000, pp. 156–157; Rowe, 2006). If this is the case, we would expect Socrates to use arguments to lead people to the knowledge of virtue or recommend that they discover that knowledge through rational discussion. But this is not what Socrates recommends. Instead, he explicitly claims that if a person is to become virtuous they must *practice* the virtues.

In the *Gorgias* (504d-e), after claiming that a self-controlled and virtuous life is the happiest one, and that an orator should do everything in his power to help make people virtuous, Socrates recounts his discussion with Polus which demonstrated that it is worse to act unjustly than to suffer injustice. Callicles reluctantly agrees, and then Socrates lays a method of how to avoid acting unjustly and suffering injustice. Even though suffering injustice is better than performing an injustice, Socrates acknowledges that one would be happier if one could avoid both. Much of the discussion that follows focuses on whether it is possible to avoid being treated unjustly in a city by becoming an imitator and friend of the ruler. The fact that the discussion of how to avoid being treated unjustly is extensive while the question of how to avoid acting unjustly is left largely unelaborated has, it seems, distracted interpreters from the fact that Socrates does offer a method for guaranteeing the avoidance of acting unjustly.[3] What is Socrates' method? Although the standard interpretation suggests that it is to use arguments to lead a person to the knowledge of justice, this is not the method Socrates recommends. Instead, he argues that two things are necessary to ensure that a person will act justly: learning and practice.

> And what about doing what's unjust? Is it when he doesn't wish to do it, is that sufficient—for he won't do it—or should he procure a power and a craft for this too, so that unless he *learns and practice*s it, he will commit injustice.
>
> (509d-e; emphasis added)

The fact that the person must "learn" justice is consistent with the standard interpretation insofar as learning can often be achieved through argument. But Socrates requires here an additional component of disciplining oneself by practicing what one has learned. Without both of these things, the person will not invariably act justly. Indeed, without practice, Socrates claims that the person "will" commit injustice.[4] Socrates is saying that mere learning is insufficient for knowledge; individuals can be taught (through arguments) that x is virtuous and even believe that they "know" that x is virtuous, but in order to guarantee that they *fully* know that it is virtuous, they must practice it. Socrates makes it clear that if individuals do not practice what they are learning while they are learning it, they will not develop the full knowledge necessary for the avoidance of future injustice.[5] This means that the standard interpretation that Socrates believes that knowledge of virtue can be gained through intellectual means alone, and that once achieved, the person will always act virtuously is false. For them to always act virtuously, practice must go along with intellectual training.

Even though the passage earlier is clear in its requirements concerning the need for practicing the virtues, if one is to become virtuous, it does not explain *why* practice is required. To discover that we must examine further passages where Socrates encourages his interlocutors to practice the virtues.

Socrates' Reasons for Requiring Habit and Practice

To understand *why* Socrates believes habit and practice are essential for coming to knowledge of virtue, it will be helpful to look at specific examples in which he claims precisely this. Take the following claim in the *Crito* where Socrates asserts that the soul of an individual is harmed by bad actions.

> Should a man professionally engaged in physical training pay attention to the praise and blame and opinion of any man, or to those of one man only, namely a doctor or trainer? . . . He must then act and exercise, eat and drink in the way the one, the trainer and the one who knows, thinks right, not all the others? . . . So with other matters, not to enumerate them all, and certainly with actions just and unjust, shameful and beautiful, good and bad, about which we are now deliberating, should we follow the opinion of the many and fear it, or that of the one, if there is one who has knowledge of these things and before whom we feel fear and shame more than before the others. If we do not follow his directions, we shall harm and corrupt that part of ourselves that is improved by just actions and destroyed by unjust actions.
>
> (47b-d)

On first glance it might be argued that Socrates *is* using reason and argument to encourage the development of virtues. But on closer inspection we see that he is not actually offering arguments about the content of virtue but rather how one becomes virtuous. When he says that a person should follow the directions of a virtuous role model, he is not claiming that merely listening to the instructions or being convinced by arguments are what makes the person virtuous. Instead, the person must *practice* what the role model asks her to practice. The change in the person comes not through the listening, but through the doing of the actions. This is why Socrates begins by comparing the learner of virtue with an athlete under the care of a trainer or doctor. A person under the care of these individuals must *do* what they say if she is to become healthy and physically adept.

The same type of exhortation to practice the virtues occurs in the *Gorgias* where Socrates explains "how justice may come to exist in the souls of his fellow citizens and injustice to be gotten rid of" (*Gorgias* 504e). Socrates argues that people who lack justice must develop "self-control" and must "be kept away from [their] appetites and not be permitted to do anything other than what will make [them] better" (505b). These people have desires that run contrary to virtue and thus must be compelled to perform virtuous actions so that justice "come[s] to exist in the soul" (504e). Once their souls are sufficiently improved by just actions, they will no longer require compulsion to be self-controlled. They are self-controlled in the sense that they are no longer unduly influenced by those appetites which lead to vice. They have been made better by the soul-constructing activities they performed, and it is clear that it is the actions that cause this soul-constructing work; not once in either the *Crito* or the *Gorgias* does Socrates indicate that the improvement of the soul is secured by way of argument alone.

It might be objected that this is an anomaly in the Socratic dialogues and that Socrates' discussion with Hippocrates in the *Protagoras*, where he urges Hippocrates not to entrust himself too quickly to the sophist Protagoras, is more representative of the way an individual is corrupted. There, Socrates seems to indicate that corruption of the soul occurs directly through the arguments of a teacher:

> When you buy food and drink from the merchant you can take each item back home from the store in its own container and before you ingest it into your body you can lay it all out and call in an expert for consultation as to what should be eaten or drunk and what not, and how much and when . . . But you cannot carry teachings away in a separate container. You put down your money and take the teaching away in your soul by having learned it, and off you go, either helped or injured.
>
> (*Protagoras* 314a-b)

At first glance this passage appears to support the view that Socrates believes that it is arguments alone that directly improve or corrupt the soul. However, a closer look at the context surrounding the passage suggests otherwise. What Socrates is actually worried about is that Hippocrates has already decided, prior to hearing the arguments, to make Protagoras his teacher and follow his advice. Protagoras is reputed to make disciples in the art of citizenship. These disciples not only listen to the teachings of Protagoras but also act according to them. Protagoras claims in his great speech that *acting* in accordance with the correct teaching is a requirement for learning the art of citizenship. The advice that Protagoras gives is based on his own practice, and his disciples are urged to follow his example. Socrates likens Protagoras' teaching to that of a "music teacher or wrestling coach" (*Protagoras* 312b). His analogy is not accidental. Music teachers and wrestling coaches do not merely offer explanations and arguments—they model specific activities and then demand that their students practice these activities over and over again until they become second nature. This is the corruption that Socrates is worried will corrupt Hippocrates' soul. He is not worried that Hippocrates' soul will be damaged merely by *hearing* the advice of Protagoras; otherwise we would expect to find Socrates apprehensive of listening to Protagoras' arguments. Socrates is worried that Hippocrates' soul will be damaged by *acting upon* the advice of Protagoras. That this is the only plausible interpretation of Socrates' worry is seen in that he does not advise Hippocrates to forego listening to the advice of Protagoras—which is what the earlier passage would seem to dictate if interpreted in the standard way—but to listen to the advice and then subject that advice to the wisdom "of our elders" (*Protagoras*, 314b), which is what Socrates recommends. It is not merely listening to teachings that will help or injure the listener. Rather, the listener is helped or injured only if they actually internalize the teachings and then act on the advice contained therein.

This interpretation is supported in the *Gorgias*, where Callicles promotes oratory over philosophy. Anticipating Callicles' recommendation on how to become an orator, Socrates claims that to be taught by an orator is not merely to listen to his teachings but to "engage in these manly activities, to make speeches among the people, to practice oratory, and to be active in the sort of politics" (*Gorgias* 500c-d). Again, like a wrestling coach, an orator gives his students instructions and then requires that his students practice those instructions. It is only after doing so that they will develop full knowledge of oratory.

If it is true that Socrates believes practice to be essential for the acquisition of virtue, then the following problem arises. Socrates continually demonstrates that his interlocutors lack knowledge of virtue, and he himself often claims that he lacks this knowledge too. Why then would Socrates exhort his interlocutors to practice virtue if they do not have knowledge of it? Why not continue using argumentation to help them know what virtue is first? The answer is that Socrates thinks that our actions affect our ability to acquire knowledge of virtue.

At the end of the *Gorgias*, Socrates offers a myth of what happens in the afterlife: a myth that he acknowledges may not be precisely true in the particulars but is "true" enough "that something like this takes place" (*Gorgias* 524b). In the myth, Socrates claims that souls are separated from their bodies after death and are judged based on how they lived their lives. However, the judge does not know anything about their actual lives because all distinguishing features of their specific place in history have been removed. All the judge has to go on is the "scars" that the person's "actions ha[ve] stamped upon his soul" (525a). What kinds of actions does Socrates have in mind? He mentions "perjury," "injustice," "license," "luxury," "arrogance," and "incontinence [weakness of will]" (525a). The effect of these actions is that the soul appears to have "been thoroughly whipped and covered with scars" (525a). We know that these scars are not from literal, physical punishments meted out by public authorities (Socrates makes it clear that these individuals escaped punishments in their lifetimes); rather they are the metaphysical results of vicious actions. Vicious actions damage the soul. These damaged souls are then forced to undergo "pain and suffering" in Hades, which is the only "possible way to get rid of injustice" (525b-c). Socrates certainly intends the description of the suffering souls will undergo in the afterlife to be a motivator for Callicles to give up his advocacy of following one's unrestrained desires and pursue virtue. But there is an additional purpose—namely, to show that vice leads away from the possibility of knowing virtue.

As the myth continues, Socrates explains what happens when individuals continue to practice vicious behavior. They become incurable (525c–526c). These souls, whose unjust actions were especially plentiful or especially grievous, lose the capacity to become just either in this life or the life to come. Their souls have become permanently damaged. This permanent distortion of the soul is significant because for Socrates the soul is the seat of reason and is responsible for ethical decision-making. When the soul is corrupted, the result is not only an (ontologically) deformed soul but also a soul that loses its capacity to develop knowledge of virtue and the ability to act on that knowledge. Socrates unambiguously states that what causes this distortion is *vicious action*; it is not the motivation of the soul that causes the damage, for we know from 467c–468e and 509e that all people are motivated to pursue the good; they merely misunderstand what the good is. The upshot of this is that every time a person does a vicious action, their soul becomes, to some degree, distorted. As their soul becomes distorted they lose the capacity to reason about virtue; their reason has lost the capacity to see clearly. Brickhouse and Smith (2010) describe the effects that wrongdoing has on the capacity of the soul to act otherwise by depicting a person who becomes increasingly vicious.

> The more "unruly" and "undisciplined" one's appetites and passions become, in Socrates' view, the less capable we become of finding or considering seriously any evidence that may lead us to refrain from pursuing what our nonrational potentials represent as goods. . . . As his appetites and passions increase in strength, making it increasingly difficult for the agent to see reasons to resist them, they strengthen his incorrect beliefs about what is really good for him. Intoxicated by the causal effects of the distortions and misleading appearances his appetites and passions create in his soul, the increasingly habitual wrongdoer is not only less interested in considering alternative goals and modes of living, but is also actually less able to do so.
>
> (pp. 105–106)

At some point, a person's soul can become so distorted that it no longer has the capacity to be epistemically and ethically healed. In these particular instances, talking or reasoning about virtue will be an impossibility. The only way to counteract this distortion of reason, is to encourage the person to begin to *act* differently, which is to say virtuously. This alone seems to be the only hope for reformation.

We are now in a position to understand why Socrates would encourage Callicles and Crito (and the rest of the citizens of Athens, as he does in the *Apology*) to practice virtue even if they do not fully know what virtue is. He wants them to practice virtue so that they can protect themselves from acting viciously and thereby avoid reasoning inaccurately about what virtue is. (This is echoed in the passage quoted earlier from *Crito* 47d, where Socrates claims that our souls are "improved by just actions and destroyed by unjust actions.") He wants them to develop the habit of doing good and to avoid developing the habit of doing bad. If they develop the right habits and thereby avoid developing the wrong habits, then their souls can be more easily led to virtue later in their lives. Thus, habit and practice are important means by which to prepare the soul to know virtue—which is why Socrates is committed to encouraging it.

From the considerations earlier, the view that Socrates believed that virtue is cultivated through arguments alone begins to look less and less plausible. In fact, it seems far more plausible to think that he believes that virtue is cultivated through actions more than through arguments. However, while it is clear that he believes *that* our souls are "improved by just actions" (*Gorgias* 47d), we have not yet seen *how* he thinks they are improved. Put differently, we have learned how *bad* actions distort a person's ability to know what virtue is, but not how *good* actions improve a person's ability to know what virtue is. To understand how good actions produce this, we must turn to Socrates' famous craft-analogy.

The Craft-Analogy and Developing Moral Knowledge

Socrates believes that to become virtuous one must not only learn what constitutes virtue but must also practice acting virtuously. When a person has a teacher who provides instruction about virtue and then requires the student to act on that instruction, the student will eventually gain expert knowledge in virtue. Socrates refers to this expert knowledge as craft-knowledge—his examples include doctors, captains of ships, cobblers, wrestling coaches, carpenters, shipbuilders and so on.[6] Interestingly, Socrates explicitly denies that he has craft-knowledge of virtue. He allows that he has some knowledge about moral matters, but not the expert knowledge of the craftsperson.

For example, in the *Gorgias*, Socrates claims that he has some moral knowledge concerning the comparative value of doing or receiving injustice. He says:

> I affirm that to knock or cut me or my possessions unjustly is both more shameful and worse, and at the same time that to rob or enslave me or to break into my house or, to sum up, to commit any unjust act at all against me and my possessions is both worse and more shameful for the one who does these unjust acts than it is for me, the one who suffers them.
>
> (508e)

After making this claim, Socrates explains that while he knows *that* the claim is true, he does not know *how* it is true. "I don't know how these things are, but no one I've ever met, as in this case, can say anything else without being ridiculous. So once more I set it down that these things are so" (509a). In making the distinction between knowing *that* something is true but not knowing *how* it is true, Socrates affirms that he has partial knowledge of virtue but does not have complete knowledge.[7]

Although it is possible in theory that this more "complete knowledge" that Socrates lacks can take the form of a proposition that he has simply not yet come to grasp—namely, the reason why being treated unjustly is better than committing and injustice—Socrates thinks that complete knowledge of virtue involves knowledge that cannot *fully* be expressed in propositions. Relying on Socrates' use of the craftanalogy, Brickhouse and Smith (1994) explain the distinction between partial and complete knowledge of virtue by comparing the person who has some knowledge of a craft, a shoemaker's apprentice, for instance, with a master cobbler. They claim that a novice cobbler, while she is under the tutelage of the master, will know many things about making shoes; she would be able to follow the master's instructions and put together a pair of shoes with a certain degree of accuracy. She would also be able to identify a well-made pair of shoes of a similar type. Nevertheless, the novice does not have expert knowledge—she cannot be counted on to make an excellent pair of shoes on every occasion without instructions from others.

> The true cobbler is not the one who is able to make one good pair of shoes, or even a few good pairs of shoes. To be a good craftsman, the cobbler must understand *what it is* for a pair of shoes to be a good pair of shoes, and also *be able to employ* that knowledge *in making* and *judging* all sorts of good shoes.
>
> (Brickhouse & Smith, 1994, p. 37)

Ultimately, Brickhouse and Smith claim that the novice cobbler lacks the *wisdom* that characterizes the master cobbler.

> Wisdom, then, consists in the kind of knowledge by the possession of which one is able to perform the right acts and judge the proper instances pertinent to the field of endeavor in which one is wise. One aspect of such knowledge is not propositional: it requires that one have the ability to do the right things at the right times in one's field of expertise. Another aspect . . . has to do with the control knowledge gives its possessor over his or her own inclinations: the wise person never pursues inclinations conflicting with his or her good.
>
> (p. 38)

Another way of saying this is that *knowing how* something is true or an action right cannot be fully captured by the propositional form, i.e., by giving a propositional reason for the action, even when the proposition by itself is formulated accurately. This expert knowledge is "embodied," one might say. The question then becomes, what does Socrates think is the best way for individuals to learn this expert knowledge? According to the standard interpretation, Socrates believes they need only be given arguments to learn it. In light of the craft-analogy, we see that this cannot be Socrates' position. It would be tantamount to Socrates believing that a master cobbler could make a novice cobbler an expert simply by providing arguments regarding the construction of an excellent pair of shoes. This, of course, is not how craft-knowledge works, as Socrates knows well. While exploring what it would take for a person to be an "expert in the care of the soul and . . . caring for it well," Socrates claims that it must be a "man who has studied and *practiced* the art and who had had good teachers in that particular subject" (Laches, 185b-e, emphasis added). Nehamas (1999) argues that Socrates, being the son of a craftsman himself, "must have known that, like any other craft, [virtue] could be learned only through an early beginning and after long training. Such training does not only impart knowledge; it also trains one's habits and dispositions" (p. 46). In order for a novice cobbler to become an expert cobbler, she must be given instruction and then be required to practice that instruction over and over again, which leads to habitual ways of thinking, seeing and feeling.

For Socrates, it is the same with the cultivation of the virtues, which is precisely the reason he insists on using the craft-analogy. As the educational process proceeds, novices in the virtues will begin to gain a rudimentary knowledge of virtue—they will begin to gain knowledge *that* certain actions are virtuous and that other actions are vicious. As they are required to act virtuously and are taught how to discern virtuous and vicious actions, they will begin to gain an appreciation of what makes actions virtuous—the *how* of the matter. All along, the master craftsman will be offering verbal instructions and then requiring the novice to practice those instructions. The novice gains knowledge that is both cognitive and *affective* and *conative*. She develops cognitive memory while simultaneously gaining muscle memory, as it were. In the same way that a master cobbler will explain techniques of judging the quality of the leather while she is requiring the novice to practice stretching that same leather, the master of virtue will explain techniques for judging the quality of a particular virtuous action while she is requiring the novice to practice that action.

For Socrates, it is not enough to have been instructed through propositions or arguments to attain full virtue; such instruction would not be sufficient for a person to act virtuously without error, nor without temptation, at which point an individual can be counted on to act virtuously without error. To have *full* knowledge they must undergo a much more demanding training. Previously, even though her teacher offered arguments during the apprenticeship, the novice simply could not fully grasp them—she did not have the intellectual and experiential context in which to accurately place this knowledge. It is only after countless hours of practice that the instructions are understood in their totality. Previously, the novice may have thought she understood the instructions, but it is only when she has mastered the aspect of the craft for which the instructions were given that she can say: "Ah, *now* I understand what you meant when you explained x. I thought I understood before, but now I *really* understand." This kind of understanding could never come through verbal instructions alone—any more than a child could learn how to swim with verbal instructions alone. Only when the words are combined with practice will it come. In this way, the novice will begin to develop the habit of acting in accordance with their expanding understanding. As virtuous habits develop, the desires and dispositions of the novice will be formed simultaneously—they will find themselves increasingly disposed to act virtuously. And these desires and dispositions are essential to understand what Socrates means by knowledge.

Socrates argues in the *Protagoras* that a fully virtuous person, who has complete knowledge of virtue, would never act viciously because knowledge cannot be dragged around like a slave. We are now in a position to see what he means. A person who has devoted her life to learning and practicing the virtues, under the guidance of a virtuous master, is the only person who has full knowledge of virtue. She has been habituated through instruction and practice to always act according to virtue: her knowledge includes a *cognitive* dimension (knowing the right thing to do), an *affective* dimension (desiring to do the right thing), and a *conative* dimension (having the strength of character to follow through on that desire). It is this person, and this person alone, who can be counted on to act virtuously on all occasions. On the other hand, a person who only has partial knowledge of virtue does not have the expert knowledge that would make her impervious to acting contrary to virtue, precisely because she does not have one or more of the right cognitive, affective, or conative experiences.[8] She may believe that she has knowledge, and she may even be able to offer rational propositions that sound as if she has knowledge, but she does not have full knowledge until she has the right habits and dispositions. Therefore, she will be susceptible to acting viciously.

The importance that Socrates places on having the right habits and dispositions is the key to understanding how he could believe the radical and implausible claim that knowledge is sufficient for virtue. It is normally assumed that all Socrates requires for virtue is deep cognitive knowledge, which is why he has been considered an "intellectualist." As such, his theory seems patently false. But if we consider his thesis rightly it becomes much more plausible and even inspiring. The expert cobbler has the knowledge of what makes an excellent pair of shoes and also the skill in making them, which is gained after years and years of practice. But this is not all—she also loves making shoes and loves making them well. The expert's craft knowledge includes not only skillful artistry, but an appreciation of the special aesthetic and moral goods of the craft. This appreciation means that she is enlivened by her practice but also wary of the things that would close her and others off from attaining its internal goods. To see a bad pair of shoes repulses her enough, but to participate in making a bad pair of shoes would be a denial of who she is. True, there are no doubt many cobblers who, to make more money for example, quit practicing their craft and instead began mass-producing inferior quality shoes. But for Socrates, this is because they were never true craftspeople in the first place. Had they been, they would have never been tempted away from their craft. It is the same for the virtuous person, according to Socrates. Virtuous people are craftspeople who have the cognitive, affective and conative elements that make up full knowledge that is part and parcel of their identity. As such, they would never desire to commit vice and thus would only do so, if ever, by some sort of accident where they lost their minds and their knowledge.

Conclusion

We are now in a position to see why Socrates can make the claim that if people *fully* knows what the right thing to do is, they will always act on that knowledge. It is not because they have rationally assented to a proposition about the correctness of the action but because they have rationally assented to it *and have developed the desire and dispositions* that will provide the motivational impetus to perform the act. Thus, knowledge is not genuine knowledge unless the cognitive, affective, and conative components are in place. A person who claims to know the value of honesty and yet sometimes enjoys telling lies, does not really *know* the value of honesty. How can they learn this knowledge? Not by thinking more about honesty or by talking about honesty, nor by debating more about honesty and taking classes from experts on honesty, but by practicing honesty under the guidance of a mentor who can provide assistance in a rehabituation process. While it is true that Socrates believes that knowledge is an all-powerful force that motivates action, he is not an intellectualist with respect to virtue. For Socrates, knowledge is not a purely intellectual phenomenon. It includes cognitive, affective, and conative components.

Having explained Plato's views in the early dialogues concerning the relationship between knowledge and virtue, we can now examine his views in the middle dialogues. Kohlberg and others have assumed that his theory of recollection means that individuals can be led to the knowledge of virtue through dialogue alone because the knowledge is already in them. We showed that leading people to knowledge requires a much more elaborate program of education, one that includes dialogue but also includes the training of the dispositions and attitudes through habituation. In the following chapters, this program of education will become clearer.

Notes

1. Brickhouse and Smith (2010), Devereux (1995), and Singpurwalla (2006) have recently challenged this standard view of the role of the appetites and passions in Socrates' moral psychology. They argue that Socrates believes that overweening

appetites and passions can influence reason to such a degree that reason will reject the true good in favor of the apparent good. Thus, even though these interpreters deny that Socrates believes the passions can influence behavior directly, they claim that Socrates believes that passions can present themselves so strongly, that reason can be influenced to follow them. This is opposed to variants of the more customary interpretation which either claim that Socrates scarcely acknowledges the existence of the passions (Irwin, 1979; Santas,1979) or claim that Socrates acknowledges the existence of these desires but believes they do not influence behavior at all (Penner, 2000; Rowe, 2006; Taylor, 2000).

2. Because Socrates is the main speaker in the early dialogues, and because he is customarily assumed to hold the ideas that are expressed in the early dialogues, we will use his name rather than Plato's throughout most of this chapter.

3. It is very rare for commentators to acknowledge the force of Socrates' claim. Stauffer (2006), for example, glosses over the passage claiming that "Callicles shows little interest in Socrates' suggestion that it might be necessary to develop a certain capacity and art to avoid doing injustice" (p. 142). Roochnik (1996) makes the even stronger claim that "the notion of a moral techne is so intrinsically problematic that, despite his offer to Callicles of a 'moral technician,' Socrates probably does not consider it to be a realistic possibility" (p. 207). See, also, Hall (1971, p. 216). Those that do acknowledge the force of the passage, such as Irwin (1977, p. 128), claim that it is an anomaly and inconsistency with the rest of the Socratic dialogues. The one interpreter who acknowledges the central importance of the passage for understanding Socrates' moral psychology is Michael J. O'Brien (1967).

4. Citing this passage, O'Brien (1967) is one of the few interpreters who have questioned "the easy assumption that the ethical paradoxes [of Socrates] constitute a sweeping denial of Greek educational experience," which focused on the importance of precisely such practice for attaining virtue (p. 92). O'Brien (1967) argues that, like other fifth-century thinkers, Socrates believed that virtue is a craft and knows that as such it would require instruction and practice.

> Both Socrates and Gorgias assume that justice is an art like carpentry, music, and medicine. But it is Gorgias, not Socrates, who assumes that the art of justice can be imparted by instruction alone, since in fact this is how he teaches it.
>
> (p. 93)

5. While he does not specifically mention the passage concerning the necessity of "learning and practice," Devereux (2008, p. 162) also suggests that the "psychic order" implied by the context around the passage represents an inconsistency with the intellectualism that Socrates more typically affirms.

> The intellectualist conception of the virtues as forms, or a single form of knowledge is clearly dominant in the Socratic dialogues. But there is another conception, virtue as psychic order, which appears in several of these dialogues [*Crito, Apology, Gorgias*] and is developed in some detail in the *Gorgias*.
>
> (p. 163)

Moreover, in an earlier work, Devereux (1995, pp. 381–408) claims that in the *Laches*, Socrates argues that a courageous person must overcome "countervailing fears and desire" that are in conflict with reason. (For similar interpretations of the *Laches*, see, also, Shorey (1903, p. 12), O'Brien (1967, p. 113), and Santas (1979, p. 194)). The question is why Devereux thinks that psychic order is inconsistent with Socratic intellectualism. From our point of view, McPherran

(2012) rightly argues that the notion of psychic order does not entail the rejection of Socrates' thesis that virtue is knowledge: "I therefore deny that the issue of psychic order raised in the later parts of the *Gorgias* is actually at odds with Socrates' view that virtue is knowledge" (p. 24). One can believe that there are desires in the soul that must be "ordered," and also believe that if one has knowledge that "order" will necessarily exist. However, before one has knowledge—and for Socrates developing that knowledge is extremely difficult, such that no one he has ever met has developed it—one must create psychic order through a process of habituation.

6. The craftanalogy is a well-known staple of many of the Socratic dialogues, but there is significant debate about how literal the reader/interlocutor is supposed to take the analogy. The question is whether virtue is a craft in *exactly* the same way that cobbling is a craft or is it merely *similar* to it. Irwin (1977, pp. 6–7) argues that it is identical to a craft. Gregory Vlastos (1978, pp. 232–233), on the other hand, vigorously disagrees with Irwin and argues that it is similar in some respects but different in other respects. A debate in the *Literary Times Supplement* ensued between them for almost six months. What was at stake for Irwin and Vlastos was whether the craft-analogy implied that virtue was identical to happiness or whether it was merely instrumental in achieving happiness. Klosko (1981) and David Roochnik (1992) have also criticized Irwin's interpretation. Roochnik (1992, p. 186) correctly argues that how one interprets the craft-analogy makes no small difference in how one interprets the entire Socratic project. Irwin claims that a craft is always productive of something else—the cobbler produces shoes, and thus if virtue is a craft it must aim to produce something. That something is happiness, says Irwin. Roochnik disagrees with the notion that for Plato all crafts are productive. He claims that Plato considers theoretical sciences like math and astronomy to be crafts as well and yet these do not actually have a concrete product beyond knowledge. Thus the craft-analogy is merely an analogy and cannot be applied literally. For the purposes of this chapter, the question is not on the product of the craft but on how one develops knowledge of the craft. Whether the craft in question is cobbling or mathematics, the knowledge of the craft includes teaching and practice. Master cobblers cannot be produced merely through verbal instructions alone and neither can master mathematicians. Mathematicians, even brilliant ones, must practice what they have learned if they are to understand mathematics to the fullest extent.

7. Interpreters have used a variety of terms to explain Socrates' distinction between knowing that something is true and how it is true. Vlastos (1985, pp. 11–18), for example, makes the distinction between "elenctic knowledge" and "certain knowledge"; Reeve (1989, pp. 37–53) and Woodruff (1992, pp. 90–91) make the distinction between "non-expert knowledge" and "expert knowledge"; McPherran (1992, pp. 230–231) makes the distinction between "fallible human knowledge" and "infallible divine knowledge"; and Brickhouse and Smith (1994, pp. 38–45, 2000, pp. 108–109) make the distinction between "knowing that" and "knowing why."

8. Devereux (1995, pp. 394–396) suggests that such individuals do not have "knowledge" at all; rather they have "true belief," which Socrates does not believe is as stable as knowledge. Thus, on Devereux's conception, "knowledge *that*" is actually just a species of true belief and is not knowledge at all. This means that when someone has knowledge *that* X is a virtuous action and yet does Y instead because Y appears more pleasurable, their knowledge has not been overcome, but only their belief. The (true) belief X has been overcome by (false) belief Y. The question then becomes what makes knowledge so much more powerful than true belief? Why does Socrates consider knowledge less susceptible to being overcome than true belief? Socrates never gives us an answer

to that question, except that knowledge is "tied down," whereas true beliefs "are not willing to remain long, and they escape from a man's mind" (*Meno* 98a). According to Aristotle, Socrates does not offer reasons for his belief but merely thought "it would be strange" (1145b) for knowledge to be dragged around. Devereux's (1995) gloss is that Socrates thought it was "intrinsically plausible" (p. 394) that knowledge was that powerful. On this reading, the fact that knowledge is supreme is apparently self-evident to Socrates—whereas it is not at all self-evident to Aristotle who claims that Socrates' "view contradicts the plain phenomena" (1145a). Now that we have seen the central importance habituation plays in Socrates' educational theory, it seems that Socrates thought that there was something about the habituation process that conditions the learner's desires in a way that gives knowledge its power. Brickhouse and Smith (2010, pp. 80–81) argue that knowledge is not made more powerful by habituation but rather that countervailing desires are made much weaker. As the learner practices virtuous activities over and over again, she is unable to act upon vicious desires. These desires are therefore neglected and thereby begin to lose their strength. Eventually, they are so weak that knowledge has no trouble overpowering them. Their explanation seems both exegetically plausible (considering what Socrates has said about the importance of not allowing individuals' appetites to be allowed to get out of control) as well as psychologically plausible. Considering the craft-analogy, it is also the case that in the same way that a desire for vice is made weaker by neglecting it, a desire for virtue will be made stronger by feeding it. As we practice the virtues we begin to desire them more. If this is the case, then in addition to the generalized desire for the good that Socrates advocates for in the *Protagoras*, there are additional desires (to perform virtuous actions) that are developed when a person practices those actions. These desires significantly augment the desire for the good that motivates all action. In other words, knowledge of virtue is all-powerful not because bare knowledge is omnipotent but because one cannot have that true knowledge without having developed a taste for the actions based on that knowledge. This is why we cannot impart knowledge directly to individuals. They may think they *know* that some action is correct but because they do not have the proper attending desires gained through habituation, they do not really *know* and thus cannot be counted on to perform those actions. Habits are made in the practice, and those habits provide the overwhelming motivational force that makes knowledge all-powerful.

2 Recollection, Wisdom, and the Soul's "Encrustation"

Introduction

In the last chapter, we reconsidered the so-called "intellectualism" of the early dialogues. We argued that while it is true that Plato believes that knowledge is sufficient for virtue, it is not the case that he believes that knowledge can be achieved through a purely intellectual process. Rather, individuals must practice virtuous acts over and over again under the guidance of virtuous mentors if they are ever to develop *full* knowledge of virtue. Merely dialoguing, discussing, or debating about virtue will, at best, produce cognitive knowledge, but it will never produce the affective and conative components that help to make *full* knowledge.

In this chapter, we move on to the middle dialogues and consider the "intellectualism" found in them. The supposed intellectualism in the middle dialogues is different from the supposed intellectualism in the early dialogues because the middle dialogues, unlike the early dialogues, are purportedly founded on strong metaphysical doctrines, whereas the early dialogues are not. Starting with the *Meno*, moving through the *Republic* and *Phaedo*, the intellectualism of the middle dialogues supposedly relies on metaphysical theories about the soul and how it comes to apprehend virtue. The first theory, usually known as the "theory of recollection," asserts that human beings have immortal souls that have always existed, and because they have always existed they contain within them all knowledge. In order to access that knowledge, all a person has to do is be led through dialogue to recollect the knowledge that they already possess. The second theory in the middle dialogues states that certain, gifted individuals (philosophers) have the capacity to be led to unmediated access to the realm of the Forms, "which is attainable by abstract and theoretical thought" (Cooper, 1997, p. xiii). Philosophers access the realm of the forms through *dialectic*—a technical process of dialogical mentoring between a teacher and pupil. The reason to call Plato's stance in the middle dialogues a form of intellectualism is because he supposedly believes that this intellectual apprehension can be achieved only by those who are able to transcend their bodies and achieve contemplation of the

Realm of the Forms. Moreover, he seems to state elsewhere that virtue devoid of complete knowledge is not virtue at all but is something closer to vice (Bobonich, 2002, p. 322).

We argue that the charge of intellectualism in the middle dialogues is as unfounded as it is in the early dialogues, and that, for Plato, in order to achieve the knowledge of virtue one must practice virtuous acts over and over again through a habituation process. The habituation process is actually more important than the intellectual process. It is more important for two reasons: The first is that only people who have undergone habituation will have the necessary desires and volition to act virtuously, and second the intellectual apprehension is not possible without first removing what Plato calls "the encrustations" found within the soul, which can only be removed by rehabituation. These encrustations prevent wisdom from apprehending what virtue requires. Even though individuals are—qua human beings—theoretically capable of apprehending virtue through dialogue, they will be incapable of achieving that apprehension if the vision of their souls is obscured by the "encrustations" that develop during their bad upbringings. They must have their encrustations mitigated prior to being able to turn to the intellectual apprehension of virtue discovered through dialogue. To demonstrate this, we examine three dialogues in the middle period that are often cited in defense of Platonic intellectualism: the *Meno*, the *Republic*, and the *Phaedo*. We argue that these dialogues, rather than supporting intellectualism, actually demonstrate the opposite—Plato believes that the way to achieve full virtue is not to use dialogue to contemplate the Form of the good, but to practice the virtues over and over again.

The Status of *Meno* as a Middle Dialogue

Our analysis of Plato's supposed intellectualism in the middle dialogues begins with an analysis of the *Meno*. In the developmental theory of interpretation, the *Meno* is hard to place. It is usually considered a middle dialogue, but many commentators have argued that it should be considered a transition dialogue since it bears certain resemblances to the early dialogues and certain resemblances to the middle dialogues.[1]

Concerning its similarity to the early dialogues, the *Meno* is *aporetic*, which means that it ends in doubt, with seemingly no conclusive answer to the question raised at the beginning of it. This is a common characteristic of the early dialogues, but it is relatively absent in the middle dialogues. Additionally, the *Meno* articulates the same "sufficiency of knowledge for virtue" thesis that is articulated in the early dialogues. In the *Meno*, Socrates famously claims that knowledge of virtue is sufficient for acting virtuously, and that whenever a person commits an immoral act it is out of ignorance and not out of a genuine desire to act immorally (Meno, 77b-c). In this way, it seems natural to group the *Meno* with the early dialogues.

However, the *Meno* contains an expression of one of the middle dialogues' great metaphysical doctrines: the theory of recollection. The theory of recollection is non-existent in the early dialogues but is found in a variety of forms in the middle dialogues. Thus, it also seems natural to group the *Meno* with the middle dialogues. For most developmental commentators, the fact that the *Meno* contains the theory of recollection means it should be considered a middle dialogue, although many recognize that the dialogue does not fit neatly into the developmental picture.

As Unitarian interpreters, we argue that the fact that the *Meno* contains ideas found in both the early and middle dialogues falls in line with our view that Plato's ideas do not change substantially over time: rather, Plato changes the way he expresses them. In other words, since Plato does not substantially change his philosophical outlook between periods, but only changes the way he *expresses* his outlook, we argue that the theory of recollection should be interpreted as a new, metaphorical way of describing how the sufficiency of knowledge for virtue thesis works (and does not work). Rather than abandon the sufficiency of knowledge for virtue thesis, he merely reframes it in a new evocative and metaphysical way in the middle works.

This new way of articulating the sufficiency of knowledge thesis presents, on the face of it, a problem for our interpretation. The sufficiency of knowledge thesis in the *Meno* is based on a metaphysical doctrine which seems to indicate that habituation is unnecessary for the development of the knowledge of the virtues because every human being already has knowledge of them. According to the theory of recollection, all souls, by virtue of their immortality, know all that there is to know. Therefore, every soul must necessarily already have knowledge of virtue. And if all souls already have knowledge of virtue, then the only process necessary to bring that knowledge into consciousness is recollection, which can be gained through rational dialogue alone. In order to show why this is not the case, it will be necessary to explore the sufficiency of knowledge for virtue thesis in the *Meno* more carefully and to examine its connection with the theory of recollection.

The Sufficiency of Knowledge for Virtue Thesis and the Theory of Recollection in the *Meno*

In the *Meno*, Socrates claims that no person ever desires to do evil, but only desires to do good. Why then do people commit evil acts? Like in the early dialogues, Socrates' answer is that they think these harmful acts are beneficial acts for themselves. The upshot is that if they could see them for what they really are (harmful), they would immediately stop doing them because nobody wants to do what is harmful to herself. Thus, all vicious acts stem from ignorance. The person committing them does not have knowledge of which acts are beneficial and which acts are harmful, which is why she commits bad and harmful acts (77b–78b).

At first glance, Socrates' claim appears completely wrong-headed. It seems perfectly clear that many people know very well that they are acting badly when they commit evil acts and choose to commit them anyway. But Socrates' view seems wrong-headed only if we think that what he means when he says they do not *know* that they are committing evil acts is that they have not experienced and expressed cognitive assent. He thinks it is entirely true that many people would cognitively assent to the rightness or wrongness of certain actions, and in *that* sense they know they are right or wrong; but they do not know in the much stronger sense, outlined in the last chapter, which is characterized by a *cognitive* dimension (a clear, if inarticulable, understanding of the rightness or wrongness of the action), an *affective* dimension (the desire to perform the acts), and a *conative* dimension (the stable disposition to act in light of that desire). Only when cognitive knowledge is combined with the affective and conative can true and full knowledge be obtained. Put differently, people may claim to *know* that certain acts are harmful, and they may indeed have genuine cognitive knowledge that they are harmful, but they do not have the full knowledge found in craft-knowledge unless their cognitive assent is combined with the desires and dispositions to perform the right acts. Thus people who say that they know that some action is harmful and yet do it anyway, do not *fully know* that it is harmful.

So far, this is the same position Socrates holds in the early dialogues. However, the *Meno* presents us with a problem: the doctrine of recollection. In the last chapter we saw that the desires and dispositions necessary for full knowledge can only come through practice and habituation; they cannot come through rational dialogue alone. However in the *Meno*, the doctrine of recollection makes it seem that perhaps, after all, dialogue is all that is necessary to draw out full knowledge.

In the *Meno*, Socrates puts forward a metaphysical theory by which human beings purportedly arrive at knowledge. This theory is given by Socrates in response to the learner's paradox advanced by Meno, which supposedly demonstrates that human beings are incapable of learning anything at all.[2] The paradox goes like this: If a person lacks knowledge of x, then they have no idea of what x is; but if they have no idea of what x is, then they will never know if they have knowledge of it. Since they do not know what x is, even if they believed they had learned x, they could never be certain that they actually learned x, because they have no standard by which to judge whether what they think is x is really x. Thus, a person is incapable of learning anything if they do not have knowledge of that thing. On the other hand, if they have a standard by which to judge that x is really x, then they must necessarily have knowledge of x, and they cannot be said to have learned x. Therefore, according to the paradox, if they do not know what x is, then they are not capable of learning x, but if they already know what x is, then they are incapable of learning x because learning is defined as moving from an absence of knowledge to knowledge. Since there is no absence of knowledge, there is no learning.

The upshot of the learner's paradox is that no one can technically learn anything. But if no one can learn anything how is it that individuals go from having no knowledge of x to having knowledge of x? The answer lies in the theory of recollection. According to the theory of recollection, as expressed in the *Meno*, individuals do not learn anything; they merely recollect what they already know but have forgotten. Socrates claims that "the truth about reality is always in our soul" (86b), which means that all human beings have complete knowledge of all ideas within their souls, but they do not have direct access to the entirety of that knowledge. Because they only have limited access, they think, act, and speak out of ignorance. Fortunately, people can improve their access to the knowledge buried deep in the recesses of their souls, becoming less ignorant as they do so.

In order to demonstrate that his theory is correct, Socrates uses dialogue to draw geometrical knowledge out of Meno's slave boy who had never been taught geometry. Employing the same question and answer style that he uses in the early dialogues, Socrates poses questions to the slave boy, questions that are supposed to draw out knowledge that the slave boy did not previously know he had. The slave boy, like Socrates' previous interlocutors, makes many false starts but simply through questioning Socrates is able to draw out the knowledge that already exists in the slave boy.[3]

Judging from this example, it looks as though we have an open and shut case of intellectualism in the *Meno*. After all, rational dialogue was all that was required to draw the knowledge out of the slave boy.[4] Since "the truth about reality is always in our soul," it seems that all one must do to bring that knowledge into consciousness is to recollect it, which can be achieved through dialogue alone. Therefore, it seems like he is the intellectualist that he is standardly interpreted to be. However, we need to look a little more carefully at Socrates' claims concerning the nature of the virtues.[5] It will turn out that, while it is true that certain virtues can be (theoretically) drawn out through dialogue, other virtues cannot be.

Wisdom and the Other Virtues in the *Meno*

In order to understand why most of the virtues cannot be drawn out of individuals in the manner of the geometric knowledge in the slave boy, we first need to consider a distinction Socrates makes in the *Meno* between wisdom and the other virtues. In some places, Socrates claims that "virtue is wisdom [*phronesis*] . . . either the whole or part of it" (89a). When he says this he appears to be claiming that there is only one virtue—namely, wisdom. And yet at other places he distinguishes between "wisdom and virtue" (91a), which includes "moderation, and justice, [and] courage" (88a). Here, by contrast, he appears to be claiming that there are other virtues besides wisdom.[6] What are we to do with this ambiguity in the *Meno*? The answer lies in the dual quality of virtuous action.[7]

In the *Meno*, Socrates claims that two distinct elements are necessary for virtues like moderation, courage and justice to be exercised. The first is wisdom and the second is what he calls "qualities of the soul" (88a). The qualities of the soul are the basic desires to face one's fears (courage), not to control one's impulses (moderation) and to have regard for others (justice). Socrates says these qualities are neither beneficial nor harmful in themselves and only become so when they are directed by the correct use of wisdom (88b-e). Because they are neither good nor bad in themselves, they are not virtues *per se*. They are just the desire to act in a certain way. Therefore, one cannot be courageous, moderate or just if one does not have wisdom. More specifically, one may have the desire to face one's fears, or the desire to abstain from certain foods, or the desire to treat others fairly; but these desires in themselves are not virtuous unless they are employed in ways that are beneficial. At the same time, if one has wisdom alone, but not the desire to act courageously, moderately, or justly, then, by definition, one cannot be courageous, moderate, or just. The person would know what the courageous thing to do is but may be afraid to do it because he lacks the desire to face his fears. Or he may know that having too much dessert is not beneficial, and yet not have the desire to abstain from overindulgence, and so on.

The question then becomes: How does one cultivate the two necessary parts of virtue, the "wisdom" and the "quality of soul?" Socrates gives two separate answers. In the case of wisdom, it comes through recollection because wisdom is a type of knowledge (88d). But the qualities of the soul such as the desire to act courageously, moderately, and justly are not knowledge and therefore cannot come by way of recollection. This is why Socrates claims earlier that "if virtue is of one kind it can be taught [recollected], but if it is of a different kind, it cannot" (87c). He goes on to use "courage" as an example of something that "is not knowledge but different from it" (88b). Plato claims that the virtues that cannot be recollected are not knowledge because knowledge is always beneficial and yet these non-recollectable virtues are neither harmful nor beneficial in themselves, but become beneficial if properly directed by wisdom. The upshot is that the only virtue that can be recollected is wisdom. Unfortunately, however, a person who has recollected wisdom but does not have the desire to act courageously, moderately, or justly means that they will never be a fully virtuous person. They will know what the right thing to do is but will not have the desire to do it. Thus, wisdom alone is worth very little in the moral sphere since it can never, on its own, produce the other virtues.

But if the desire for courage, moderation and justice does not come by way of recollection, how do individuals develop it? Plato does not give a direct answer to this question in the *Meno*, but, as we have seen, he does give an answer in the early dialogues: habituation. In the early dialogues Plato's theory of moral development operates on the distinction between *cognitive* knowledge of virtue, which can be gained through dialogue, and *full* knowledge of virtue, which *cannot* be gained through dialogue. Plato claims that this latter kind of knowledge can only be achieved through habituation because such knowledge includes *affective* and *conative* dimensions. While he does not explicitly recommend habituation in the *Meno*, it stands to reason that since the *Meno* makes a similar distinction between wisdom and the other virtues, and because he distinguishes between the ways knowledge of them is gained, habituation must be the key to developing the affective component that characterizes the virtues of courage, moderation, and justice. Furthermore, as we shall see shortly, the plausibility that this is his position in the *Meno* is even greater when we consider that in the *Republic* (another middle work), Plato says explicitly that the virtue of wisdom is always present in the soul, whereas the virtues of courage, moderation, and justice "are added later by habit and practice" (*Republic*, 518d).

An added benefit of this interpretation is that it makes sense of Socrates' otherwise completely confusing claim at the end of the *Meno* that "because it cannot be taught [recollected], virtue no longer seems to be knowledge" (99a). This about-face from Socrates' earlier suggestion that "virtue is a kind of knowledge" (87c) would be perplexing, rendering the whole dialogue incoherent. Half of the dialogue proceeds under the assumption that virtue is knowledge and therefore can be taught or recollected, and the second half proceeds under the assumption that virtue is *not* knowledge and cannot be taught or recollected. However, if we understand the dual nature of virtue—that certain virtues are recollectable (wisdom) while other virtues are not recollectable (courage, moderation, justice)—then the incoherence is mitigated. Virtue *as a whole* cannot be recollected or taught, but neither can it be merely habituated. Virtue *as a whole* contains a cognitive component (which can be recollected) and affective and conative components (which cannot be recollected), and therefore it requires a complex training process that uses a variety of methods to produce virtue, which is exactly why Plato ends the *Meno* by describing how difficult it is to create virtue—claiming that anyone who is virtuous has received a gift from the gods.

We are now in a position to see that the charge of intellectualism in the *Meno* is, as a whole, false. Plato seems to affirm an intellectualist position regarding the virtue of wisdom, but he denies an intellectualist position regarding the other virtues. Like the early dialogues, virtue as a whole can only be cultivated through a process of education that includes discussion, dialogue and habituated action. And, as we will now see, it is the same in other middle dialogues, like the *Republic* and the *Phaedo*, which also affirm the need for an educational program that includes dialogue, habit and practice.

The Allegory of the Cave and the Virtue of Wisdom

As in the *Meno*, Plato in the *Republic* distinguishes between the virtue of wisdom, which he claims is always present in the soul, and the other virtues which come by way of habituation.

> It looks as though the other so-called virtues of the soul are akin to those of the body, for they really aren't there beforehand but are added later by habit and practice. However, the virtue of [*phronesis*][8] seems to belong above all to something more divine, which never loses its power but is either useful and beneficial or useless and harmful, depending on the way it is turned.
>
> (518d-e)

Wisdom is always present in the soul and is *not* something that is learned in the sense of being instilled from without. In the *Meno*, the slave boy's knowledge of geometry was present in him, but he was not directing his vision towards it, rather he was directing it to other aspects of his life, to use the "turning" metaphor that appears in the *Republic*. All that was necessary for him to access his geometric knowledge was for Socrates to ask him questions that redirected his sight. Once the slave boy was looking in the right place, as it were, he was capable of seeing what was there all along.

This need to redirect the soul in order for learning to occur is famously expressed in the *Republic's* Allegory of the Cave. Socrates claims

> that the power to learn is present in everyone's soul ... and [education] isn't the craft of putting sight into the soul ... but takes for granted that sight is there but that it isn't turned in the right way or looking where it ought to look.
>
> (518c-d)

Plato argues that all human beings have the ability to "know the good," an ability which he calls wisdom (*phronesis*), but that their souls must be properly turned to discover it. It is different for the other virtues which need habit and practice to be formed.

The problem is that one gets the impression in the *Meno* that all that is necessary to point wisdom in the right direction is to use dialogue to turn the soul, which is exemplified in the example of the slave boy. All that Socrates had to do to "redirect" the wisdom of the slave boy was to have a conversation with him. In the *Republic*, Plato complicates this impression. While a person's wisdom, "which can never lose its power" (*Republic*, 519a), cannot be corrupted at the ontological level, it can be corrupted at the practical level. Just like we saw in the early dialogues, when people regularly engage in vicious behavior their vision can become so distorted that they begin to regard virtue as something to be avoided and vice as something to be engaged in. When this happens a snowball effect can begin; if they are not encouraged to practice virtuous behaviors again they will increasingly desire to do vice and will further lose their capacity to see correctly. In the *Republic*, Plato refers to the corrupting effects of vicious behaviors as "encrustations" that metaphorically weigh down the soul and block its vision under "the shells, seaweeds, and stones that have attached themselves to [it]" (611d). Thus, while the capacity for sight is never lost, it is as good as lost when it is buried under the effects of vicious behavior.

Plato explains that these encrustations are not present in the soul itself and are not part of the virtue of wisdom in its purest form. Rather, they are developed as accretions through a poor upbringing. And, unfortunately, with each subsequent evil action, the encrustations get heavier and thicker, increasing the downward spiral. The only way to free a person from encrustations is to "hammer" on them through a rehabituation process which will eventually liberate their wisdom so that it can be directed in the right way.

> However, if a nature of this sort [whose "sight isn't inferior but [has been] forced to serve evil ends"] had been hammered at from childhood and freed from the bonds of kinship with becoming, which had been fastened to it by feasting, greed, and other such pleasures and which, like leaden weights, pull its vision downward—if being rid of these, it turned to look at true things, then I say that the same soul of the same person would see these most sharply, just as it now does the things it is presently turned towards.
>
> (519b)

Here we see that while souls who regularly engage in vicious actions are, for all intents and purposes, incapable of using their *phronesis* correctly, they have not utterly lost the capacity to see correctly. Their *phronesis* is as powerful as before; it is just directed towards vice instead of virtue. This means that even the most depraved individuals can, in theory, be reformed. All that is necessary is for them to engage in a habituation process that could free their vision from the encrustations developed through a previous bad upbringing.

Of course it might be asked why human beings ever developed these encrustations in the first place. If individuals were born into the world as pure souls their *phronesis* should be free from encrustations. Furthermore, Plato claims that these pure souls long to have intercourse with the good (*Republic*, 611e). So why would they have ever begun focusing their *phronesis* in the wrong direction in a way that developed encrustations? The answer lies in the process by which souls enter the physical world.

For Plato, the myth of the embodiment of souls starts when a soul enters a physical body at birth. As immortal, the soul has no need of physical sustenance, but once it is embodied and becomes a human being it must eat and drink and avoid danger if it is to keep its body alive. This is especially true when the human being is a baby. Food and drink and protection from danger are especially essential for an infant's body as it does not have the physical reserves to live on or resources to protect it. As such it is up to the parents to provide the necessary elements of life if the baby is to survive. Indeed, it is important for a parent to let a child eat as much as it wants—first on its mother's milk and later on solid food—if the child is to survive. The more fat the child develops in its earliest years, the more likely it is to survive and grow into a healthy young person. Thus, from their birth children are encouraged to feast and to demand food whenever they feel like it. The child is encouraged to feast whenever it is hungry. The problem is that this feasting produces the very encrustations to which Plato is referring—the continual imbibing of food habituates the soul to desire it more and more. Additionally, infants are protected from all other privations to the degree possible, which makes them more and more accustomed to getting what they want and being protected from things they fear. This produces further encrustations. Through this process, *all* children are being systematically habituated to prefer feasting and greed because that is what they have been allowed to do since their birth; indeed, they have been encouraged to do so, because it is through such encouragement that children are able to survive. They need fat on their bodies, and to be protected from all dangers in order for their bodies to survive as infants. Their "virtue of wisdom" that started out completely pure and directed towards the good becomes redirected towards vice by the actions of the parents.[9] Thus, the child's wisdom will therefore need to be redirected back towards virtue if it is to learn to avoid immoderation and vice.

This leads to the question: If a habituation process is necessary to exercise one's virtue of wisdom correctly, how is it that Meno's slave boy's vision is able to be turned around through a single dialogue? The answer is that the redirection of the slave boy's wisdom in this context concerns purely rational knowledge, in particular, theoretical geometry. To understand and act upon the axioms of geometry one must merely "see" them. One does not need to have the right desires or strength of will to perform them once they are seen. Put differently, in the case of the slave boy doing geometry, there are no countervailing affects that prevent the slave boy from understanding the truth of the geometry.[10] It would be different if the slave boy's wisdom was directed to a context related to virtue. If his wisdom had been redirected, for example, to see that helping people is more just than harming them (and according to Plato his wisdom could be redirected in this way through dialogue alone), but he had previously been taught to harm people if he can get away with it, he would not have the affective desires to *want* to act upon the virtue towards which his wisdom had been redirected. To recall, full knowledge of virtue includes a cognitive dimension, an affective dimension, and a conative dimension. Without all of these dimensions in play, the person will not act virtuously. Thus, even if the slave boy's wisdom had been redirected towards virtue through dialogue, he would not have the desires to do what wisdom recommended because he did not (in our hypothetical situation) have an upbringing that created these desires.[11] We see this time and time again across the dialogues. Socrates routinely leads a person to affirm a moral truth, and yet the person is not reformed. For example, Thrasymachus is led to see that "a just person is happy, and an unjust one wretched" (*Republic* 354a), yet he does not change his philosophical point of view or live a more just life. Rationally speaking, he came to the right conclusion—and in that sense his virtue of phronesis was pointed in the right direction— but because his motivational state had long been habituated towards vice and away from virtue, his cognitive understanding was not sufficient to motivate him to live differently. Thus, while it is possible to redirect peoples' wisdom through rational dialogue, doing so will not produce virtuous behavior without a reorientation of their affection and conation. One can lead a slave boy to knowledge of geometry through dialogue alone, but one cannot lead a poorly raised adult to virtue through dialogue alone.

Here again, in the *Republic*, we have seen that the intellectualist interpretation of Plato is false. To be sure, Plato does place a premium on cognitive knowledge that can be gained through the redirection of wisdom through dialogue, but it is equally clear, and will be spelled out in detail later, that he places a premium on habit and practice for reorienting a person's affection and conation. Becoming virtuous is not merely an intellectual matter solved by an intellectual apprehension of the knowledge of the good, but is a premeditated, rigorous, practical activity that requires habituation and training for all individuals if they are to have any prospect of becoming good. This fact is especially clear when we examine the *Phaedo*, which is where we will now turn.

Intellectualism and Habituation in the *Phaedo*

The thrust of the claim of intellectualism in the *Phaedo* comes from a common interpretation that in distinguishing between the "philosophers" and "non-philosophers" in the *Phaedo*, Plato affirms the view that only philosophers have the capacity to attain virtue at all because only they have pure, undefiled knowledge of virtue. Put differently, the charge of intellectualism of the *Phaedo* is based in Plato's supposed insistence that the only way for people to be genuinely virtuous is for them to escape their bodies and achieve a kind of beatific vision of virtue through contemplation. This interpretation is usually assumed to be similarly affirmed in the *Republic*, where the philosopher-kings are trained through mathematics and dialectics to achieve unmediated access to the Form of the Good. In the introduction to this book, we suggested that the political structure of the *kallipolis* and the major components that make up that structure should be interpreted metaphorically and not literally. We make an extended argument for this point of view in the Appendix of this book. But even if we grant the metaphorical status of the *Republic*, we cannot do so for the *Phaedo*, which does not depend on a grand mythological society. Instead, in the *Phaedo*, Plato distinguishes between "philosophers" and "non-philosophers," who are categories of people who exist in the world as it stands, not in a perfect society. As such, we need to examine the *Phaedo* to determine if the standard interpretation that "philosophers" actually achieve unmediated access to the Realm of the Forms is true, as is commonly assumed.

In order to understand Plato's views on the acquisition of virtue in the *Phaedo*, we will start with the common interpretation of his distinction between the "philosophers" and "non-philosophers" and the virtues they are capable of attaining. Bobonich (2002) offers a stark but characteristic interpretation in the following way:

> only philosophers possess real virtue, while non-philosophers have only a "shadow-painting of virtue that is really slavish and contains nothing healthy or true". . . . There seems to be very little that a city can do to improve significantly the lives of the vast majority of its citizens; no non-philosopher can have a life that is really worth living for a human being.
>
> (p. 322)

According to Bobonich's interpretation, the non-philosophers' virtues are not really virtues at all but a form of socially affirmed vice. The fact that Bobonich quotes Socrates as saying that the non-philosopher's virtue "contains nothing healthy or true" seems straightforwardly damning.

Importantly, however, when Plato explicitly distinguishes between philosophers and non-philosophers in the *Phaedo*, he does not do so at the level of innate qualities. Rather he takes pains to explain that *all* human beings have complete knowledge of all things—by virtue of their soul's immortality—but all human beings forget that knowledge at birth (76a-c). They only recollect that knowledge (or some of that knowledge) later (73d-e). This knowledge includes the knowledge of the "Beautiful and the Good and all that kind of reality" (76d). Thus, every person is equal with respect to the innate knowledge in their souls. Socrates claims that every human soul is "divine, deathless, intelligible, uniform, [and] indissoluble" (80b). Why then does Socrates distinguish between the philosophers and non-philosophers if both of their souls are equal with respect to latent knowledge? The answer lies in how the philosophers and non-philosophers were raised.

Socrates claims those individuals who are brought up poorly will live unhappy lives and have unhappy afterlives, while those who were brought up well will live happy lives and have happy afterlives. Describing those who were brought up poorly, Socrates explains the state of the vicious who "are not the souls of the good but of inferior men [who] are paying the penalty for their previous bad upbringing" (81d). The reason the individuals are inferior is not because they are innately inferior but because they had a "bad upbringing"; they were not educated in the proper habits and practices. As we saw earlier, the soul of every child begins pure, but as soon as it is placed in a body and physically birthed into the world, the soul begins to develop bad habits because its parents allow it to feast, protect it from all privations, mollify its fears, etc. This means that all children start with bad habits, but virtuous parents begin to change those habits as early as possible once the child's body has gained the proper strength to live on its own. As early as possible, these parents start to encourage the moderation of their child's appetites, and help their children begin to face their fears, and make them treat others justly. According to Plato, it is otherwise with most parents, who continue to encourage bad habits in their children. As they do, their children's souls become covered in the scars and encrustations that Plato says happen when we engage in vicious behaviors. The souls of people who are raised this way habitually learn to desire the wrong things and continue to pollute their soul. As we saw in the last chapter, when these souls leave the body at death, they are corrupted. Plato says the same in the *Phaedo*.

> The soul is polluted and impure when it leaves the body, having always been associated with it and served it, bewitched by physical desires and pleasures to the point at which nothing seems to exist for it but the physical, which one can touch and see or eat and drink or make use of for sexual enjoyment. . . . [D]o you think such a soul will escape pure and by itself[?]. . . . It is no doubt permeated by the physical, which constant intercourse and association with the body, as well as considerable practice, has caused to become ingrained in it.
>
> (81b-c)

It is the repeated vicious behavior that is initiated in childhood and continually practiced through adulthood that makes some non-philosophers especially vicious. Plato claims that these individuals lack virtue altogether and suffer the consequences both in this life and the life to come.

However, this is not to say that *all* non-philosophers will suffer such a fate. Indeed, there are other classes of non-philosophers who Plato thinks are substantially virtuous and whose souls are not nearly so corrupted. Socrates describes the experiences of non-philosophers who had a different upbringing—one in which they were trained in the virtues of moderation, courage, and the like. "The happiest of these, who will also have the best destination, are those who have practiced popular and social virtue, which they call moderation and justice and which was developed by habit and practice" (82a). While it is true that even these individuals could be happier if they become "philosophers" by coupling philosophical reflection with habit and practice, they are far from the "slavish" lives that Bobonich (2002) describes. Now, Bobonich is correct that Socrates claims that "all" individuals who do not practice philosophy will live lives that are less fulfilling than those who do practice philosophy, but we should not conclude, as Bobonich does, that "there is very little that a city can do to improve significantly the lives of the vast majority of its citizens." On the contrary, Socrates suggests that the city can do a great deal in the improvement of its citizens, namely to habituate them in virtuous practices and encourage them to think critically about those practices. When we carefully examine the passage that Bobonich pulls from to substantiate his interpretation, as well as the context immediately surrounding it, we discover that the distinction between the virtues of philosophers and non-philosophers is not as sharp as Bobonich suggests.

The same refrain about giving all human beings a chance to become virtuous is reinforced in later dialogues, like the *Laws* and the *Statesman*, where Plato advocates for the teaching of virtue to all citizens, and he expects all citizens to willingly choose to live the virtuous life. In the *Laws*, Plato indicates that older, more distinguished citizens ought to show respect for the younger and try to persuade them to be virtuous rather than force them to do so (729b-c). Connected to this, Plato claims that all children can be persuaded to live virtuously as long as the entire community helps participate in their education (664a-c). He also believes that the more simple people of the past are actually wiser and more virtuous than contemporary citizens (679e). While Plato makes distinctions between individuals and their respective chances of becoming virtuous, he does not claim that some individuals are innately vicious, but rather he claims that the combination of their natural temperament and upbringing is a matter of fact. As such, not all individuals will achieve the same level of virtue, so both laws and education need to be put in place to ensure a measure of virtue in society. Similarly, in the *Statesman*, the visitor claims that *every* citizen ought to be taught "to share in a disposition that is courageous and moderate, and whatever else belongs to the sphere of virtue" (308e–309a), and only those who act unjustly will be excluded from full citizenship in the city. The same goes for public offices, which have the same criteria for participation—namely, having the capacity to be governed by the proper amount of courage and moderation as the situation requires (310e–311e). The fact is that throughout his corpus Plato continually encourages an education in the virtues of courage, moderation, and justice for *all* citizens and argues that these virtues can only come by way of habit and practice. The fact that philosophers embody these virtues to a greater degree than non-philosophers does not mean that non-philosophers should not be taught the virtues, but simply that it will be harder, or take longer, for them to achieve as high a level of virtue.

Escaping the Body and Contemplating the "Realm of the Forms"

Now that we have seen that Plato thinks that habituation is necessary for the virtuous life, we still have to consider the standard view that, for Plato, philosophers are able to contemplate the Realm of the Forms and in so doing are the only people who are genuinely virtuous, because they alone have complete knowledge of virtue. This seems to be the real sticking point for the accusation that Plato is an intellectualist with respect to virtue in the middle dialogues. He is an intellectualist in the *Phaedo*—so the standard interpretation claims—because he thinks that the virtues gained by non-philosophers through habit and practice are false and only a shadow of the true virtues gained by philosophers through contemplation of the Realm of the Forms. However, tempting this interpretation is—and it is very tempting because it is so thoroughly entrenched in the lore regarding Plato's metaphysics, ethics, and epistemology—it is simply not Plato's view in the *Phaedo*. We know this because he says it in no uncertain terms.

Plato claims that it is impossible to obtain pure knowledge while we remain embodied beings, and therefore just like non-philosophers, philosophers, or philosopher-kings will never be able to escape their bodies and achieve a beatific vision of the Forms.

> It really has been shown to us that, if we are ever to have pure knowledge, we must escape from the body and observe things in themselves with the soul by itself. It seems likely that we shall, only then, when we are dead, attain that which we desire of which we claim to be lovers, namely, wisdom, as our argument shows, not while we live; for it is impossible to attain any pure knowledge with the body, then one of two things is true: either we can never attain knowledge or we can do so after death.
>
> (*Phaedo* 66e)

It is true that Plato recommends avoiding the unnecessary desires of the body to the degree that it is possible, but he does not believe that such avoidance will ever lead to a vision of pure virtue—rather, "a true philosopher [must be] firmly convinced that he will not find pure knowledge anywhere except [after death]" (*Phaedo* 68a). Why then should a person avoid the unnecessary desires of the body if it is impossible to achieve pure knowledge? According to Plato's myth, the answer is that while *pure* knowledge is impossible until after death, human beings will be more or less virtuous to the degree that they do not pursue unnecessary bodily desires.

> While we live, we shall be closest to knowledge if we refrain as much as possible from association with the body and do not join with it more than we must, if we are not infected with its nature but purify ourselves

from it. . . . In this way we shall escape contamination of the body's folly; we shall be likely to be in the company of people of the same kind.

(*Phaedo* 67a)

Importantly, this does not mean that human beings should be ascetics in an extreme sense, as this passage can seem. Rather they should engage in the proper amount of bodily pleasures, a proper amount of fear and so on. We know this because Socrates claims at the end of his life that he was one who "practiced philosophy in the right way" (*Phaedo* 69d), which meant that he had what he called "real courage and moderation and justice and, in a word, true virtue, with wisdom, whether pleasures and fears and all such things be present or absent" (*Phaedo* 69b). Socrates enjoyed the pleasures of wine, food, sex, and love, just like his fellow Athenians, and also harbored fears of all sorts, but unlike his fellow Athenians he acted moderately with respect to these pleasures and acted courageously with respect to his fears, etc. Unlike his fellow citizens, he was able "to not get swept off one's feet by one's passions" (*Phaedo* 68c). In sum, when Socrates stresses the importance of philosophers avoiding bodily desires and fears, he does not mean that human beings should not engage in them at all, but that one should do so moderately, courageously, and justly. And as we have seen, engaging in human activities moderately, courageously and justly, requires a habituation process.

The real distinction between the philosophers and non-philosophers is not the latter's ability to achieve pure and undefiled knowledge of the Form of Good—something which Socrates claims cannot happen until after death—but from their ability to gain as *full* of knowledge as possible which is obtained from practicing the virtues over and over again. Therefore the "practicing philosophy in the right way" that Socrates discusses earlier turns out to be practicing virtue in all the ways that Plato has been encouraging his interlocutors (explicitly or implicitly) through the early, middle and late dialogues. Engaging in philosophy includes discussion and dialogue, but it also includes "refraining as much as possible from association with the body," which turns out to be just another way of saying, practicing moderation, courage, and justice.

What Socrates means by the "body" are those passions which cause us to behave viciously. If we give into fear, if we have too much to drink, or if we greedily take from others, we are associating with the body in ways that pollute our souls. The only way around polluting our bodies is not to try to escape them to inhabit the Realm of the Forms but to *habitually* face our fears courageously and face our desire for drink moderately and deny our greed and behave justly towards others. Practicing the virtues in this way will not only deepen our cognitive knowledge of virtue but will also form our affections and conation, which will lead us closer to *full* knowledge of virtue. But of course, if we do not have full knowledge of the virtues in the first place, how will we know how to practice them at all? The answer is our rehabituation process must be led by people who can help us know how and what to practice. In the next chapter we discuss Plato's habituation process in more detail.

Before moving on to our discussion of habituation in the next chapter, we want to return to the *Republic* and the standard interpretation that Plato believes that the philosopher-kings are people who become fully virtuous by escaping the corruption of their bodies and achieving a beatific vision of the Form of the Good. As we discussed in the introduction (and as we will discuss further in Chapter 5 and the Appendix), there is significant reason to doubt that Plato meant for the *kallipolis* to be understood as a desirable and realistic city; and there is also significant reason to doubt that the philosopher-kings depicted in the *kallipolis* are meant to be realistic models of philosophers. In the story of the *Republic*, from the first to the last, the philosopher-kings represent the virtue of wisdom in a human being, a virtue that gives cognitive access to the other virtues but is ineffective by itself without a habituation in the other virtues. We see in the other middle dialogues that Plato does not believe the soul can attain a pure and undefiled vision of the virtues, and the fact that the philosopher-kings appear to achieve that vision suggests that either he changed his mind in this single dialogue or that he meant what he said in the *Republic*—namely, that the philosopher-kings are a metaphor for the virtue of wisdom and should not be considered, as they so often are, as a model to which philosophers should aspire.

Conclusion

In the preceding analysis we have seen that accusations of intellectualism in the middle dialogues are as unfounded as they are for the early dialogues. It is true that Plato places a premium on knowledge and thinks that it is necessary in order to obtain full virtue, but it is equally clear that that knowledge cannot be arrived at through dialogue alone or through a disembodied contemplation of the Realm of the Forms. Rather full knowledge of virtue comes through a rigorous process of habituation that includes acting virtuously over and over again and through discussions about those virtues. Habituation creates the desires to perform the virtues and the virtue of wisdom gives us understanding of what the virtues are and how they are best exercised. We also saw that Plato believes that all humans must begin the habituation process as early as possible in order to rid themselves of the "encrustations" that necessarily begin immediately after birth. Those individuals who are habituated well will have the best chance of becoming philosophers. Yet this does not mean that those who have missed this early habituation cannot begin it later in life, approaching, to the degree they can, full virtue. In the next chapter we will examine this habituation process in more detail and explore how Plato thinks it should proceed and what it produces in the soul of the person being habituated—how it creates in them a "kinship" to virtue.

Notes

1. Interestingly, while both D.S. Mackay (1928) and Holger Thesleff (1989) do place *Meno* in the category of "early dialogues" they do so, not for the typical chronological reason of the standard view but rather because their reinterpretation of the order of Plato's dialogues lends itself to an atypical division. Debra Nails (1994), building on Jacob Howland's (1991) rejection of the standard view of the chronology of the dialogues, places *Meno* in a middle cluster due to the development of ideas it contains. A. Boyce Gibson (1957) summarizes this conversation, regarding both dating Plato's dialogues and the Meno as a "systematizer's nightmare." We can see, then, that not just *Meno*'s placement in the ordering of the dialogues but also the long held view of the dialogues' order itself is coming under scrutiny from many different angles.

2. It should be mentioned that it is not at all clear that Socrates affirms the learner's paradox himself. As David Ebrey (2014, p. 5) points out, Socrates' primary goal throughout the dialogue is to convince Meno that inquiry is valuable; the Theory of Recollection lies subordinate to this purpose and therefore should be interpreted in this light.

3. Naturally, the question arises as to how souls originally come to contain knowledge. Socrates claims that it is because souls are immortal and have always existed, and because they have always existed they must have always had that knowledge or learned it at some other time (*Meno*, 86a). Of course, this is not an entirely satisfactory answer because the learner's paradox would apply even for the soul. If a soul cannot learn in a human body, then it cannot learn apart from the human body. Thus, either the soul has always existed and has always contained the knowledge, or it must have recollected it. But this leads to an infinite regress. Fortunately, this paradox will be partially reconciled in subsequent dialogues through the metaphor of the Realm of the Forms, in which souls supposedly interact with perfect Forms and gain knowledge of them through that interaction. There is much dispute about whether Plato actually believes that the Realm of the Forms exists as a separate, heaven-like realm. We follow Iris Murdoch, Julia Annas, John McDowell, and others in claiming that he does not believe in such a realm, but rather he invents it as an illustrative metaphor that is supposed to inspire readers and interlocutors to search continually for how best to live. This view is supported by Socrates, when, immediately following his claim that the soul is immortal and must have previously contained that knowledge, states,

> I do not insist that my argument is right in all other respects, but I would contend at all costs both in word and deed as far as I could that we will be better men, braver and less idle, if we believe that one must search for the things one does not know, rather than if we believe that it is not possible to find out what we do not know and that we must not look for it.
>
> (86b-c)

This is characteristic of all of the famous doctrines of the middle dialogues. After giving what seems like a convincing argument for a particular metaphysical claim, Socrates suggests that his ideas are not to be taken as true in every sense. Another example is the tripartite structure of the soul, as outlined in the *Republic*. At the end of the *Republic*, Socrates argues that in spite of his previous claims that the soul has a definite tripartite structure, he and his interlocutors have not discovered its true nature. At the very end of the book, Socrates admits that the discussion he and his interlocutors had concerning the soul failed "to discover its true nature," and that they would have to look elsewhere "to see what [the soul's] true nature is and be able to determine whether it has many parts or just one and whether or in what manner it is put together" (612a). Similarly, Plato's supposed doctrine that philosopher-kings could, with a proper education, achieve unmediated access to the Forms through contemplation is shown to be impossible in the *Phaedo.*

> It really has been shown to us that, if we are ever to have pure knowledge, we must escape from the body and observe things in themselves with the soul by itself. It seems likely that we shall, only then, when we are dead, attain that which we desire of which we claim to be lovers, namely, wisdom, as our argument shows, not while we live; for it is impossible to attain any pure knowledge with the body, then one of two things is true: either we can never attain knowledge or we can do so after death.
>
> (66e)

4. For another interpretation of *why* Socrates chooses to put forth the Theory of Recollection at this point of the dialogue, see Theodore Ebert's (1968) article "Plato's Theory of Recollection Reconsidered: An Interpretation of Meno," in which he demonstrates not only the literary irony taking place but also that Socrates uses the slave boy demonstration to show Meno that he has a misconception about knowledge itself. Namely, Meno believes knowledge to be twofold, either it is attained or not. Ebert, however, submits that Plato wants to demonstrate that knowledge has many more levels than what Meno believes.
5. It is with Socrates' introduction of the theory of recollection here that we arrive at the first of Plato's great metaphysical "doctrines" of the middle dialogues. In the earlier dialogues, Socrates used a variety of myths that were drawn from the Ancient traditions. But now Plato is offering metaphysical descriptions that seem to be literal doctrines as opposed to the figurative doctrines found in the traditional myths. It is precisely because of this that Plato does not want us to take this doctrine as it is literally presented, which becomes obvious in the second half of the *Meno* when Socrates shows that virtue cannot readily be drawn out of individuals.
6. Of course, this same ambiguity occurs throughout the Platonic corpus, whether early, middle, or late. In some places, Socrates or other interlocutors suggest that wisdom is the only virtue (*Protagoras* 360d-e, *Laches* 194d), but in other places he claims that there are other virtues (*Crito*, 47c; *Republic*, 428a; *Phaedo*, 115a).
7. George Rudebusch (2009) makes the bold conclusion in his paper "Socrates, Wisdom, and Pedagogy" that "In none of these dialogues (*Laches, Meno,* and *Euthyphro*) is there even one argument driving us towards a part/whole account of virtue" (p. 168). Unfortunately, in developing his argument, Rudebusch contradicts himself. While he correctly mentions in passing that we should not "expect Socrates to have been developing positive doctrines" (p. 165) in his dialogues because he uses the "False-lead" method to lead his interlocutors through levels of knowledge, Rudebusch's argument clearly relies on this very expectation when he outlines two "doctrines" found in *Protagoras* and the *Meno* that supposedly demonstrate that Plato believes that knowledge is sufficient for virtue (p. 156).
8. Importantly, unlike Aristotle, Plato does not make a sharp distinction between practical wisdom (Aristotle's *phronesis*) and theoretical wisdom (Aristotle's

sophia). Plato uses the terms interchangeably. Sometimes he uses *phronesis* to suggest something like practical intelligence; at other times, he uses the same word to suggest a more theoretical wisdom. It is the same with *sophia*—sometimes it connotes theoretical wisdom, and sometimes it connotes practical wisdom.

9. Daniel Devereux (1978) phrases this distinction as knowledge being "*both* teachable and possessed by nature" (p. 121). The fact that it is teachable, for Devereux, means that knowledge can come from without, and the fact that it is possessed by nature means that it is also found within a soul. In fact, in his footnote Devereux even specifies that this knowledge from without most likely comes about due to repeated practice, as indicated by Socrates' repeated questioning of the slave boy.

10. Of course, to become a professional geometer, one would need special kinds of desires, and thus rational dialogue would not be enough, but Meno's slave boy is not being convinced to be a professional geometer. He is merely being led to geometric principles by the asking of questions, and once he has learned one of the principles he can proceed rationally to understand further principles.

11. This is not to say that it is impossible for a person whose wisdom is redirected towards virtue eventually to *desire* virtue for themselves. In Chapters 4–6, we discuss Plato's belief that certain people—if they have souls that are open to it—can have *epiphanies* concerning virtue that temporarily reorient their desires. When the reorientation of desire happens they are open to the prospect of undergoing a rehabituation process in which their affections and dispositions are retrained. When this happens, they can, over time, develop the cognition, affection, and conation necessary to develop into a virtuous person.

3   Habituation and Kinship
With Virtue

Introduction

In the previous two chapters, we examined the charges of intellectualism in Plato's early and middle dialogues. From that analysis, we concluded that Plato advocates habituation as a central component in the moral education of students. In this chapter, we examine what the habituation process consists in, and why Plato believes that it is a condition for developing full knowledge of virtue—a knowledge that includes cognitive, affective, and conative dimensions. As we have seen, Plato believes that all individuals have an innate wisdom, a capacity to desire the good and see the good, insofar as the individual is looking at the good. But, importantly, while Plato shows that the virtue of wisdom never loses its power to desire the good, he does say that it can, for all intents and purposes, lose its ability to guide the soul correctly. Plato uses the metaphor of the "encrusted soul" to show how bad habits distort the soul's virtue of wisdom and make it unable to see the true good. Plato claims that the only way to free a soul from these encrustations is to hammer the encrustations off, which happens during the habituation process. The habituation process should happen as early as possible in life, because the longer bad habits continue, the thicker the encrustations become, until eventually the soul is all but irredeemable. Plato considers his contemporaries to be almost totally devoid of the proper use of wisdom and virtue because they have been raised in the vicious, Athenian society. "For there isn't now, hasn't been in the past, nor ever will be in the future anyone with a character so unusual that he has been educated to virtue in spite of the contrary education received from the mob" (*Republic*, 492e). Even though the capacity for proper wisdom is innate, the education children are given and the personal choices they make when they are older serve either to improve their capacity for this wisdom or to diminish it.

Next, we pose the question: How can individuals be freed from such cultural influences and encrustations? Or to put it in terms that Plato uses in the Allegory of the Cave, which is central to our argument in this chapter: How can individuals be turned from a world of shadows to reality? To answer this question, we turn to Plato's concept of kinship in the final section of the chapter and show how he thinks the soul of the well-brought-up child develops a kind of family relationship to virtue. This relationship harmonizes the individual's wisdom with the other virtues, ensuring that it remains pointed in the right direction. We examine the details of the upbringing Plato recommends for creating this kinship and argue that he believes all people are capable of developing it, even if not all people develop it to the same degree.

The Encrusted Soul

Our discussion of Plato's educational theory in the *Republic* begins by returning to the Allegory of the Cave. In the allegory, Socrates describes three individuals who have been chained in the back of a cave for their entire lives. They are unable to move their heads or bodies and are therefore not aware of their own physical existence or the broader world. The prisoners spend their days watching shadows on a wall in front of them, which are cast by a fire from behind. Because they have been chained since their birth, Socrates claims that, for them, the truth is nothing but shadows.

Socrates relates what will happen if one of the prisoners is freed and "compelled to stand up, turn his head, walk, and look up toward the light" (515c). He claims that the prisoner will be pained and dazzled by the bright light of the fire, unable to see anything since he will quickly shut his eyes to avoid the searing pain. As such, he will believe that what he used to see is truer than what he sees now because what he sees now is obscured. Socrates' point is that the prisoner is suffering only a temporary illusion. Eventually, the prisoner will get used to the light and come to recognize that what he is now seeing is more real than what he formerly saw.

However, before the prisoner can enjoy his new situation, he is "dragged . . . away from there by force, up the rough steep path, and . . . into the sunlight" (515e). At every turn, the prisoner is led from pain to pain and is never allowed to enjoy himself until he finally grows accustomed to the light of the sun itself, at which point the prisoner is delighted with his new situation. Unfortunately, we are told that he begins to pity his former den-mates and wishes to help them. Socrates then describes what would happen if the freed prisoner went back into the cave to rescue his former friends. He would be blinded once again because of the dimly lit cave and, even worse, because he cannot see, when his former den-mates ask him questions about which shadows will follow each other on the wall, he will be unable to give a correct answer because of his temporary blindness. Then, when he attempts to tell them about his new knowledge and how he can "see" so much better in the upper world, his former friends mock him because of his temporary blindness and refuse to listen to him. Indeed, they are offended by his claims to be enlightened and threaten to kill him or anybody else that tries to lead others to the upper world. The allegory can be read as a metaphorical account of Socrates' death at the hands of the people of Athens—but it is much more than just that.

The broader purpose of the Allegory is to describe the human condition as one in which human beings live in metaphorical caves and interact with realities that are but shadows of a true reality, which supersedes the quasi-illusions of what humans normally take to be real. It is tempting to interpret the allegory narrowly, as anticipating Plato's discussion of the Forms and the need for philosopher-kings to access them in order genuinely to "know" what virtue is, as Vasiliou does.[1] However, as we have seen, Plato does not think that it is possible for humans to access such a Realm because such access can only exist after death. The closest they can come is to be habituated in the virtues in a way that produces not only cognitive knowledge of virtue but also the desire to embody the virtues and the strength of will to follow through on those desires. To interpret the allegory as merely focusing on the ascent to the Realm of the Forms by the philosopher-kings is to miss the more general important educational ideas found therein—ideas that Socrates spells out immediately following the allegory.

Rather than moving to the education of the philosopher-kings and a description of the Forms that these philosopher-kings are meant to apprehend, Socrates instead follows the allegory by deriving some general educational principles applicable to all human beings.[2] As we saw in the last chapter, his first principle is that the

> power to learn is present in everyone's soul . . . and [education] isn't the craft of putting sight into the soul . . . but takes for granted that sight is there but that it isn't turned in the right way or looking where it ought to look.
>
> (*Republic*, 518c-d)

Socrates claims that all human beings have the ability to "know the good," which is made possible by the virtue of wisdom, but that their souls must be properly turned to discover it. This is what initially happens to Socrates' cave dweller—someone unlocks his chains and then "compels" him to turn around and walk towards the light. What is important is that Socrates claims this power to learn is present in "everyone's" soul, but that individuals must be compelled to redirect their learning. As we saw in the last chapter, to "know the good" does not mean to have unmediated access to transcendental knowledge.

Although the Allegory of the Cave is therefore an admirable and even inspiring statement of Plato's egalitarian stance on moral education, it is not a fully satisfying account of how this moral education takes place. Namely, in the allegory, the compulsion required for the prisoner to be freed from his enchainment takes only a few seconds. In reality Plato believes it will take much longer. A more realistic metaphor is the metaphor of the encrusted soul, which Plato uses twice in the *Republic*.[3]

In the very last pages of Book X of the *Republic*, Plato returns to the idea of the soul and its innate virtue of wisdom. Socrates explains that in spite of the conclusions that he and his interlocutors have drawn about the soul, they are still without knowledge of what the soul is in its nature. Socrates compares the soul to the sea god Glaucus,

> whose primary nature can't easily be made out by those who catch glimpses of him. Some of the original parts have been broken off, others have been crushed, and his whole body has been maimed by the waves and by the shells, seaweeds, and stones that have attached themselves to him, so that he looks more like a wild animal than his natural self. The soul, too, is in a similar condition when we study it, beset by many evils.
> (611c-d)

Socrates goes on to say that although the soul is "akin to the divine and immortal" it would need to have its "many stones and shells (those which have grown all over it in a wild, earthy, and stone profusion because it feasts at those happy feastings on earth) . . . hammered off it" (611e–612a). Socrates claims that all souls—because they are akin to the divine—have the capacity and the desire to know the good, but because of the "feasts" which the soul participates in on earth, it becomes encrusted and is no longer capable of desiring the good. Yet, this does not mean that the soul is ontologically ruined or corrupted—rather, it remains as pure as before and "longs to have intercourse with [wisdom]" (611e); it is just that these longings do not have the motivational impetus to lead to wisdom because the soul has become encrusted by its long pursuit of vice. Thus, even though the soul longs for the good deep down, the human being who is encrusted by the effects of vicious actions will continually pursue vice, increasing the encrustation, leading to a vicious cycle. Fortunately, Socrates claims that there is a way out of this vicious cycle—the soul must be "hammered" upon so that these encrustations can be broken off.

This usage of the hammering metaphor is the second time it appears in the *Republic*. The first time comes in the discussion immediately following the Allegory of the Cave. There Socrates describes people whose souls are "vicious but clever." He argues that it is not their inborn capacity for wisdom that is deficient in these people—for all people are capable of wisdom—but, rather, that their reason has been "pulled down" by "feasting, greed, and other such pleasures."

> However, the virtue of [phronesis] belongs above all to something more divine, which *never loses its power but is either useful and beneficial or useless and harmful, depending on the way it is turned*. Or have you never noticed this about people who are said to be vicious but clever, how keen the vision of their little souls is and how sharply it distinguishes the things it is turned towards? This shows that its sight

isn't inferior but rather forced to serve evil ends, so that the sharper it sees, the more evil it accomplishes. . . . However, if a nature of this sort had been hammered at from childhood and freed from the bonds of kinship with becoming, which had been fastened to it by feasting, greed, and other such pleasures and which, like leaden weights, pull its vision downward—if being rid of these, it turned to look at true things, then I say that the same soul of the same person would see these most sharply, just as it now does the things it is presently turned towards.

(*Republic*, 518e–519b; emphasis added)

There are two points in this passage that require analysis. The first is that while the soul is affected by bad actions, its ability to "see" is not permanently impaired; the soul is capable of "apprehending the good," no matter how corrupt it seems. The second is that even a corrupted soul can be freed of its weights if it is "hammered at from childhood." This is important because the soul that Socrates describes seems to be especially wicked insofar as it has a keenness of vision, which makes it highly effective in "the evil it accomplishes." This means that it is more effective in its pursuit of feasting, greed, and so on.

Juxtaposed with one another, these two instances of the hammering metaphor suggest two ways of interpreting its educational meaning. While the passage in Book X implies a "hammering off" of psychical encrustations so that the soul's virtue of wisdom can "see" more clearly what moral virtue demands, the passage in Book VII connotes hammering as "forging," i.e., molding and shaping. When he recommends hammering on a child to free it from becoming, he means forging and shaping in youth through an intentional pedagogy of habituation and imitation. A child has a predisposed tendency to want pleasure and will naturally pursue that pleasure immoderately and without regard to what it ought to be pursuing. Because of its young age, though, the child will not have had as much opportunity as an adult has had to participate in feasting and greed, and therefore they will not need to be "hammered on" to the same degree as the encrusted adult soul found in Book X. Nevertheless, they need forging because their desire for pleasure—which was habituated in them as infants, whose parents encouraged feasting on breastmilk and protected the child from all fears and privation—needs to be redirected so as to avoid vice. Because of its mortal frame, the child will necessarily focus its *phronesis* in the wrong direction and will not "apprehend the good," being content to focus its attention on earthly goods.

Thus Plato is not offering two separate doctrines of moral education, one for children and one for adults. Rather, he believes that hammering in both senses is required by both parties. Against this backdrop, we will now examine how and why Plato advocates habituation and imitation as the best way to overcome the misguided wisdom of a child who sees bodily pleasures as the best route to happiness.

Hammering at the Soul Through Habituation and Imitation

In order to develop the proper desire for virtue and to eliminate the misguided desire for bodily pleasures that characterizes young children, new desires must be implanted in the soul. To begin this process, Plato turns to stories, myths, poetry, and music. These interrelated arts work together to shape the souls of students.[4]

Plato begins by focusing on the content of stories. He claims that stories told to young children help mold their reason and emotions. These stories are meant to form the soul of the child so that it not only believes certain things are true but also enjoys them.

> You know, don't you, that the beginning of any process is most important, especially for anything young and tender? It's at that time that it is most malleable and takes on any pattern one wishes to impress on it. . . . Then shall we carelessly allow the children to hear any old stories, told by just anyone, and to take beliefs into their souls that are for the most part opposite to the ones we think they should hold when they are grown up? . . . We'll select their stories whenever they are fine and beautiful and reject them when they aren't. . . . And we'll persuade nurses and mothers to tell their children the ones we have selected, since they will shape their children's souls with stories more than they shape their bodies by handling them.
>
> (*Republic*, 377a-c)

There are two important ideas in this passage that need to be discussed. The first is Plato's belief that human beings' souls are shaped by what they hear and are taught. This is a common refrain in Plato. Plato believes ideas have more than a cognitive effect on the individuals who entertain them; they actually alter the ontological shape of the individuals' souls. When we take in ideas, *we* are shaped by them, he claims; we become the types of beings who believe and feel things in light of those ideas. The second is that our souls are malleable, and given enough time, even the most recalcitrant can become a different person through education.

It is not only stories and their content that can have a significant impact on the formation of reason and the emotions; tragedies, poems, and music also play an important role. Socrates first highlights how tragedies and the role of dramatically acting out the tragedies effects habituation in reason and emotion (*Republic*, 394e–398a). When students attempt to give a realistic rendering of a part of a tragedy or a poem, Plato considers this to be imitation. Individuals who imitate virtuous people will come to see virtue to be what the people they are imitating do and will begin to enjoy imitating their virtues in speech, and they will therefore be more likely to enjoy similar things when they are not intentionally imitating.

On the other hand, imitating vicious people leads to seeing vicious acts as beneficial and leads to the enjoyment of doing vicious acts. Consequently, Plato believes that a proper education in the virtues requires extensive imitation of characters found in a variety of written forms. However, their common characteristic must be their singular focus on virtue and the *eudaimonia* it leads to. As uncomfortable as this may make us, this seems to be Plato's position.

After outlining the ways the *content* of stories and poetry can lead to the cultivation of the virtues, Socrates goes on to discuss the effects that tones, rhythms, and harmonies can have on the formation of the soul. Reflecting on the education prescribed in Books II and III, Socrates argues that "music and poetry. . . . educated the guardians through habits. Its harmonies gave them a certain harmoniousness, not knowledge; its rhythms gave them a certain rhythmical quality" (522a). On the face of it, these habits seem distinct from the virtues themselves. But when we look at the education Socrates prescribes, we see that harmoniousness and rhythmicity are important in the development of the virtues. Socrates argues that he and his interlocutors must find musical modes that inculcate the virtues.

> I don't know all the musical modes. Just leave me the mode that would suitably imitate the tone and rhythm of a courageous person who is . . . fighting off his fate steadily with self-control. Leave me also another mode, that of someone engaged in a peaceful, unforced, voluntary action, persuading someone or asking for a favor of a god in prayer or of a human being through teaching and exhortation, or on the other hand, of someone submitting to the supplications of another who is teaching him and trying to get him to change his mind, and who, in all these circumstances, is acting with moderation and self-control, not with arrogance but with understanding, and content with the outcome. Leave me, then, these two modes which will best imitate the violent or voluntary tones of voice of those who are moderate and courageous, whether in good fortune or bad.
>
> (*Republic*, 399a-c)

The reason that these musical modes must be found is that Plato believes that music has a unique ability to habituate the soul such that a person who is habitually trained in music will develop a kind of ethical intuition about what is virtuous or vicious. Music provides, as it were, a subconscious recognition of what virtue is and what it isn't, even if the individual does not have propositional knowledge *per se*.

> Aren't these the reasons, Glaucon, that education in music and poetry is the most important? First, because rhythm and harmony permeate the inner part of the soul more than anything else, affecting it most strongly and bringing it grace, so that if someone is properly educated

in music and poetry will sense it acutely when something has been omitted from a thing and when it hasn't been finely crafted or finely made by nature. And since he has the right distastes, he'll praise the fine things, be pleased by them, receive them into his soul, and being nurtured by them become fine and good. He'll rightly object to what is shameful, hating it while he's still young and unable to grasp the reason, but, having been educated in this way, he will welcome the reason when it comes and recognize it easily because of its kinship with himself.

(Republic, 401d–402a)

The recognition of the virtues that is found through harmoniousness and rhythmicity is not cognitive knowledge but is a kind of intuition by which one can *feel* the rightness and wrongness of some action; people who have this intuition have been given the right tastes and distastes. The virtue of wisdom provides cognitive knowledge, whereas habituation in rhythm and music forms the affective and conative dimensions of understanding. The previous habituation process leads to a change in tastes and desires. The child who undergoes the previous habituation process *wants* to be virtuous, even if they cannot explain in clearly why they want it.

Habituation Through Physical Education and Childhood Games

After outlining the training in virtue accomplished by stories, tragedies, music, and poetry, Plato outlines the role physical training plays in the cultivation of right desires. Socrates claims that a proper education in music and poetry gives the soul a certain harmony and that a proper education in physical training gives the body the same harmony.

I believe that we'd be right to compare this diet and this entire life-style to the kinds of lyric odes and songs that are composed in all sorts of modes and rhythms. . . . Just as embellishment in the one gives rise to licentiousness, doesn't it give rise to illness in the other? But simplicity in music and poetry makes for moderation in the soul, and in physical training it makes for bodily health?

(Republic, 404d-e)

The diet and exercises that students are supposed to be given also reflect the virtues found in the modes and rhythms of music and poetry. In other words, a proper diet and a regimen of physical exercise trains the body to be in harmony with the virtues in the same way that music and poetry trains the soul to be in harmony with the virtues.

At first glance, it would seem that Plato is making a sharp distinction between the activities of the soul and the activities of the body, but a few pages later Socrates claims that a sick body "makes any kind of learning, thought, or private meditation difficult" (*Republic*, 407b), and then goes on to state explicitly that the care of the soul through music and poetry and the care of the body through physical training and moderation with respect to luxuries and delicacies are both meant, ultimately, for the cultivation of the *soul*.

> Then, Glaucon, did those who established education in music and poetry and in physical training do so with the aim that people attribute to them, which is to take care of the body with the latter and the soul with the former, or with some other aim? . . . It looks as though they are established both chiefly for the soul. . . . It seems, then, that a god has given music and physical training to human beings not, except incidentally, for the body and the soul but for the spirited and wisdom-loving parts of the soul itself, in order that these might be in harmony with each other.
>
> (*Republic*, 410b–411e)

A proper diet and exercise regimen—while seemingly focused on the body—are actually meant to cultivate the virtues in the soul, in this instance: moderation and courage. Concerning the former, the appetitive part of the soul is tamed through the required restrictions on the quality and quantity of food that is appropriate. As Wilberding correctly argues:

> If so, then Plato is suggesting that the appetitive education will consist in eliminating unnecessary appetites and 'domesticating' necessary appetites. . . . Any superfluous appetite, no matter how harmless its direct consequences are, takes away from the intensity of our other desires, including our rational desires. Hence, superfluous desires should be eliminated.
>
> (Wilberding, 2012, p. 137)

Concerning the latter, the physical regimen is prescribed "in order to arouse the spirited part (courage) of his nature" (*Republic*, 410a), which helps to make him courageous. Unfortunately, if the spirited part is aroused to excess the individual will become "like a wild animal" who "bulls his way through every situation by force and savagery" (411d). To prevent this, the guardians must be prevented from working too "hard at physical training . . . and do[ing] nothing else" (411c-d). Even though physical training is good for the soul, in excess it becomes dangerous. Thus, not only are unnecessary appetites bad for the soul, any appetite can become bad if it is indulged in without moderation.

It is not only physical education that trains students in virtue, but it is also law-abiding games that help the virtues seep into the students like dye into wool. "But when children play the right games from the beginning and absorb lawfulness from music and poetry, it follows them in everything and fosters their growth, correcting anything in the city that may have gone wrong before" (425a).

Ultimately, music, poetry, physical education, and law-abiding games fundamentally change the soul of the individual who participates in them. If habituated in these things correctly, the students will have a character that cannot easily be turned from virtue:

> Their beliefs about what they should fear and all the rest would become so fast that even such extremely effective detergents as pleasure, pain, fear, and desire wouldn't wash it out. . . . And this power to preserve through everything the correct and law-inculcated belief about what is to be feared and what isn't is what I call courage.
>
> (*Republic*, 430b-c)

Summarizing the Education Program of Books II and III: The Cultivation of the Four Cardinal Virtues

From what we have seen so far, the early educational program laid out in Books II and III is supposed to cultivate three of the four cardinal virtues: moderation, courage, and wisdom. Moderation and courage are directly supplied through a process of habituation that includes an intellectual education in music and poetry and a partially intellectual and partially physical education in diet, physical exercise, and play through childhood games. The innate capacity for wisdom on the other hand, while not being *directly* supplied by the education, is implicitly turned in the right direction by the habituation of the soul and body. Because students are *not* allowed to feast or act greedily in the habituation process, the virtue of wisdom is protected from becoming encrusted; moreover, because the content of the poetry and music is "fine and good" the educated student, "since he has the right distastes," will "praise fine things, be pleased by them, receive them into his soul, and, being nurtured by them, will become fine and good" (*Republic*, 401e). This student has an intuitive sense of what is virtuous, even if he is "unable to grasp the reason" (402a) why it is virtuous—but most importantly he will *desire* to do virtuous acts.

Now that we have come to see the importance of habituation for the cultivation of the virtues in the soul, it will be helpful to examine in a bit more detail just how these habits and practices create the desires in the soul to perform them continually and voluntarily. To understand how this process works we will examine Plato's notion of "kinship" (*oikeion*) in his educational and ethical thought.

On Kinship Between the Virtues and the Soul

Plato introduces the metaphor of kinship in a passage we have already noted.

> because rhythm and harmony permeate the inner part of the soul more than anything else, affecting it most strongly and bringing it grace, so

that if someone is properly educated in music and poetry, it makes him graceful, but if not, then the opposite. Second, because anyone who has been properly educated in music and poetry will sense it acutely when something has been omitted from a thing and when it hasn't been finely crafted or finely made by nature. And since he has the right tastes, he'll praise fine things, be pleased by them, receive them into his soul, and, being nurtured by them, become fine and good. He'll rightly object to what is shameful, hating it while he's still young and unable to grasp the reason, but, having been educated in this way, he will welcome the reason when it comes and recognize it easily because of its kinship with himself.

(*Republic*, 401d–402a)

Plato uses the word "kinship" to reflect the ineradicable connection that is created between one's soul and the beautiful thing which it is participating in. Kinship implies blood relation. When we are the kin of another, we will always be connected to them in ways that cannot be undone. Even if we are miles apart, or even if we never see our kin again, we cannot erase the connection in our body. For Plato it is the same when we are habituated into kinship. Our souls have become fused, as it were, to the beautiful and harmonious things.

This fusion does not mean, however, that we necessarily understand the mechanics of the connection or why the virtue in question is beautiful, fine or noble; indeed, just like children that are kin to each other, they do not understand the genetic connection and how those genes create similar phenotypes, but when they interact with each other, or look at each other, they *see* the similarities. Plato thinks that the *understanding* of the kinship only comes later, when reason is cultivated through philosophical reflection, but the soul is ready for reason if and when it comes.

Plato reinforces this idea in the *Laws* when he says:

I call 'education' the initial acquisition of virtue by the child, when the feelings of pleasure and affection, pain and hatred, that well up in his soul are channeled in the right courses before he can understand the reason why. Then we he does understand, his reason and his emotions agree in telling him that he has been properly trained by inculcation of appropriate habits. Virtue is this general concord of reason and emotion. But there is one element you could isolate in any account you give, and this is the correct formation of our feelings of pleasure and pain, which make us hate what we ought to hate from first to last, and love what we ought to love.

(*Laws*, 653b-c)

According to Plato habituation to establish a kinship between one's psyche (one's internal motivational structure) and virtuous objects, making it possible for the student to sense which objects are beautiful or noble. Notice that "grasping the rational account" is *not* included in habituation: it is what comes *afterwards*. One cannot fully appreciate the value of the habituation one has been given until one has been habituated. Once one has learned to take pleasure in the right things and be pained by immoral and ugly things, one can then affirm that one has been habituated well. This is an experience that musicians experience as an adult; they look back on those many hours of practice and find themselves grateful for the habituation and grateful for the pleasure they take in playing piano. Habituation—learning to take pleasure in those things and actions that are virtuous—is the foundation of education and is a condition for understanding the goodness of the flourishing life. Plato is keen to show that moral education is about habituation, so keen that he contrasts someone who has been habituated with someone who has not been habituated but who nevertheless has correct cognitive knowledge:

> Now then, take a man whose opinion about what is good is correct (it really *is* good), and likewise in the case of the bad (it really *is* bad), and follows this judgment in practice. He may be able to represent, by word and gesture, and with invariable success, his intellectual conception of what is good, even though he gets no pleasure from it and feels no hatred for what is bad. Another man may not be very good at keeping on the right lines when he uses his body and his voice to represent the good, or at trying to form some intellectual conception of it; but he may be very much on the right lines in his feelings of pleasure and pain, because he welcomes what is good and loathes what is bad.
>
> (*Laws*, 654c-d)

The question is, which one of them is better educated in the relevant sense? Plato answers it is the second: "As far as education is concerned . . . the second is infinitely superior" (*Laws*, 654d).

By Plato's lights, an understanding of why one takes pleasure in virtuous and fine things and why one hates shameful actions and ugly things comes *after* habituation. It is not the task of moral education to train, directly, one's capacity to understand the attractions of the virtuous life, but rather, first, to make one capable of being attracted to the life of virtue through habituation. Moral education for Plato is shaping one's propensities to find this or that pleasurable and this or that painful, only after which the understanding will be in a position to grasp, be persuaded by, and even argue for the good of virtue and the fineness of fine things.

Plato shows that a thoughtful habituation or a haphazard habituation has far reaching consequences. If we are habituated in the wrong kind of way, we will develop a kinship—an intimate bond—with actions and objects that will neither inspire virtue nor lead to a flourishing life but rather a dysfunctional life.[5] Habituation is, in a better or worse form, always going on. Plato shows that moral education cannot get by on a diet of dialogue and intellectual exploration alone, for dialogue alone cannot habituate, that is, it cannot psychologically shape our propensities for pleasure and pain.

Conclusion

In this chapter, we have argued that, for Plato, individuals require a rigorous habituation process in order to attain moral virtue. This habituation process consists in the development of a kinship with virtue. This means students who have been properly habituated will intuitively know which actions are virtuous and which are not, and only desire to perform those actions that are virtuous. Plato's habituation process includes music, poetry, imitation, physical training, playing childhood games, and obeying laws. At the beginning these activities develop the affective and conative dimensions of the human person—they create a desire in students to want to perform virtuous acts, and they create a strength of character necessary to follow through on those desires. Simultaneously, the stories and laws in particular help create cognitive knowledge. As we saw, for children the cognitive dimension of virtue usually comes later than the affective and conative (*Republic*, 401e–402a; *Laws* 653a-c). It is when all three of these are in harmony that a person has full knowledge of virtue; but before full knowledge comes, anyone who, later in life, willingly restarts or returns to the habituation process can grow in all three dimensions found in the development of virtue. In the next chapter, we explore the ways Plato believes adults can restart the rehabituation process and how his theory of dialogue plays a role in that process.

Notes

1. According to Vasiliou, Socrates cannot explain what virtue is because he is not himself a philosopher-king, who is the only type of person capable of truly knowing the virtues. Philosopher-kings are the only individuals capable of knowing the virtues because they are the only individuals capable of accessing the Realm of the Forms. From our point of view, while Vasiliou is correct in his assessment that the educational plan in the *Republic* is incomplete as a systematic plan, he misunderstands why it is incomplete. It is incomplete not because Plato thinks that philosopher-kings must establish true virtue; it is incomplete because he cannot explain the virtues in words, except in metaphor.
2. For an in-depth and instructive treatment of the ways that the educational plan in the *Republic* is meant to educate all three parts of the soul, see Wilberding (2012).
3. For a variety of perspectives on the various ways Plato describes the soul, see Ferrari (2007, Chapter 7 in Ferrari Ed.); Woolf (2012, Chapter 7 in Barney Ed); Brown (2012, Chapter 3 in Barney); Bobonich (2002, pp. 216–292).
4. A central task of musical education is crafting the moral aesthetic of the youths who undergo such an education. Their sense of what is fine and shameful and what is beautiful and ugly is shaped by what they are exposed to. As a result of this education, they have a finely tuned moral aesthetic and react appropriately,

welcoming the good and rejecting the bad. They are able to do this, at least in part, because they come to resemble the very things that surround them. The stories of brave men will make them into brave individuals (*Republic*, 395c3–5). Good rhythm makes them graceful (400c7–9). Even the beautiful buildings, embroidery, and furniture that surround them in the city are meant to ensure that they are led "from childhood on, to resemblance, friendship, and harmony with the beautiful reason (tô kalô logô)" (401d1–3). It is this kinship, both in terms of resemblance and in terms of friendship, which makes the musical education so beneficial (Jenkins, 2015).

5. Jonathan Lear suggests (1992) that "in the parlance of contemporary psycho-analysis . . . Plato has a theory of 'object-relations'" (p. 185).

4 Dialogue as a Method for Cultivating the Virtues

Introduction

As we saw in the previous chapter, Plato argues that if one has been given an improper upbringing in one's youth, she will have the wrong conception of virtue and the wrong tastes; and therefore, without intervention, will be forever corrupted. "For no man under heaven who has cultivated such practices (vices) from his youth could possibly grow up to be wise—so miraculous a temper is against nature—or become temperate, or indeed acquire any other part of virtue" (*Seventh Letter*, 326c). Plato argues that for people to develop full virtue, they must have been properly habituated from their youth. Such individuals not only know how to identify virtuous acts, they also want to perform them—they have developed a taste for them and seek out opportunities to act accordingly (*Republic*, 395c-d, 518d; *Laws*, 635b, 792d-e).

This leads to a problem, however. According to this view of moral education, the only possibility of creating virtuous citizens is to shape their desires and attitudes from the earliest stages. If they are properly habituated, Plato thinks that they will consistently act virtuously for the rest of their lives. But what about those individuals who were not raised virtuously from their earliest youth. Indeed, Aristotle says, "Hence we ought to have been brought up in a particular way from our very youth, as Plato says, so as both to delight in and to be pained by the things that we ought; for this is the right education" (*Nicomachean Ethics*, 1104b). Is there any hope for those who have been miseducated morally? The answer would seem to be an unqualified "no."

Plato, like Aristotle after him, argues that adults who have not had a proper upbringing in the virtues have no chance to become virtuous. Aristotle claims:

> What argument would remold such people? It is hard, if not impossible, to remove by argument the traits that have long since been incorporated in the character. . . . For he who lives as passion directs will not hear argument that dissuades him, nor understand it if he does; and

how can we persuade in such a state to change his ways? And in general
passion seems to yield not to argument but to force.

(*Nicomachean Ethics*, 1179b1–15)[1]

Plato's theory of moral development is similar to Aristotle's in his seeming
pessimism regarding the potential of individuals with bad upbringings to
ever achieve full virtue. Plato argues that if one has been given an *improper*
habituation in one's youth, she will have the wrong conception of virtue
and the wrong tastes and therefore will be forever corrupted. But, unlike
Aristotle, hope is not entirely lost. A close examination of Plato's ideas
concerning dialogue reveals a theory of transformation for individuals who
have a bad upbringing. But it is *not* the theory that is so often attributed
to Plato—namely, the Kohlberg, L. (1970) "Platonic"-inspired theory that
dialogue allows individuals to *recollect true knowledge of the good*, which
will ensure that they act on the good. As we have seen in the previous
chapters, this view of Plato cannot be maintained.

Plato's theory of dialogue is much more modest. He believes that the
role of dialogue is to temporarily open the eyes of individuals so as to
inspire a *desire for rehabituation*. Plato suggests that while no poorly
raised individual can ever come to full virtue through teaching alone,
she can be so impacted by a well-crafted dialogue that she can start the
long process towards developing a different set of habits, habits that can
eventually serve as a foundation for deeper philosophical reflection on
the virtues, which can then, in turn, inspire further virtuous activity. Plato
does not believe that dialogue alone can achieve complete moral transformation—at most it can "only half realize [the individuals] potentiali-
ties for virtue" (*Laws*, 647d)—but believes that it can *start a process* of
moral transformation that has the potential to create lasting change, so
long as the individual develops new habits. In this chapter we look at
Plato's theory of dialogue in detail and explain the ways it can lead to
the temporary transformation of students' desires by creating epiphanic
visions of virtue.

In order to understand Plato's ideas concerning the moral transformation of adults, we must first explore his theory of dialogue. In the last thirty
years, there have been a number of articles and book chapters written on
the so-called "Socratic Method" of dialogue. Broadly speaking these articles fall into three categories. The first category is composed of articles and
book chapters that primarily trace the history of the use of the Socratic
Method in educational contexts (Rud, 1997; Mintz, 2006; Schneider,
2013); the second category is composed of texts that attempt to explain
the Socratic Method through a broad swath of Platonic texts, analyzing
general characteristics of Socrates' project (Haroutunian-Gordon, 1987;
Reich, 1998; Boghossian, 2012; Brickhouse & Smith, 2009; Pekarsky,
1994); the third category is composed of articles that primarily analyze
one particular text and draw general conclusions from it (Hansen, 1988;

Haroutunian-Gordon, 1986, 1987, 1988, 1990; Jonas, 2015). Combined, these articles are very helpful in providing a well-rounded picture of the variety of ways Socrates conducts himself in his dialogues.[2] What we explore in the first half of this chapter is a different issue, though, concerning Plato's explicit theory of dialogue rather than Socrates' conduct. In a sense, we are interested not so much in Socrates "Method" but Plato's "Method." The Socratic Method is the one Socrates uses as a character in the dialogues, whereas we will examine Plato's method of dialogue as the writer of the dialogues. Specifically, using the *Seventh Letter*, we will outline the reasons Plato believes dialogue is the only adequate way of doing philosophy and examine what Plato hopes to achieve through dialogue. After examining Plato's theory of dialogue in the *Seventh Letter*, we will turn to examples of that theory found in the *Lysis*, the *Alcibiades*, and the *Symposium*, and show the ways Socrates uses dialogue to create epiphanies in his interlocutors.

Dialogue in the *Seventh Letter*

Of the previous articles, not one examines Plato's discussion of dialogue in the *Seventh Letter*.[3] There are potential explanations for this. The first is that the authenticity of the *Seventh Letter* has been debated. While there is significant stylometric, philosophical and historical evidence supporting its authenticity, several scholars have challenged its authenticity.[4] The second is that, even if authentic, the *Seventh Letter* reflects Plato's thoughts on dialogue but does not mention Socrates or the elenctic method that Socrates employed. Thus, while Socrates' dialogical method has fascinated readers, the fact that Plato does not mention it in the *Seventh Letter* makes it seem, correctly or incorrectly, that perhaps the dialogue in the *Seventh Letter* is different from Socrates' dialogical method. Connected to the second, the third is that the letter is not a dialogue and therefore the figure of Socrates is not on display. Considering that the previous articles are concerned about Socrates and the Socratic Method, it makes sense that the letter would not be referenced. However, as we are trying to establish Plato's "Method" (as opposed to Socrates') the *Seventh Letter* is indispensable, as it explicitly lays out Plato's theory of dialogue.

Plato does not think that simply lecturing students or presenting them with treatises on appropriate moral behavior will produce moral transformation. A specific mode of dialogue, though, can produce flashes of insights in students with respect to the virtues. These epiphanic flashes have the potential to create temporary desires in the interlocutors to live virtuously.

In the *Seventh Letter*, Plato describes the power of dialogue to transform individuals when he recounts the epiphany of Dion, the advisor to the tyrant Dionysius II of Syracuse. Plato claims that through conversation Dion had come to understand virtue and to desire the virtuous life. Plato relates that Dion "recalled our conversations together and how effectively they had aroused in him the desire for a life of nobility and virtue" (327d). Plato then confirms Dion's radical change stating that he

> listened with a zeal and attentiveness I had never encountered in any young man, and he resolved to spend the rest of his life differently from most Italians and Sicilians, since he had come to love virtue more than pleasure and luxury.
>
> (327b-c)

Dion had a glimpse of virtue and an epiphany of why it is preferable to live a virtuous life rather than a life of luxury and pleasure. How did his love of virtue develop? According to Plato's educational philosophy, these kinds of desires are usually present only in those individuals who were given a proper education in their youth—a habituation in virtue.

> I call 'education' the initial acquisition of virtue by the child, when the feelings of pleasure and affection, pain and hatred, that well up in his soul are channeled in the right courses before he can understand the reason why. Then when he does understand, his reason and his emotions agree in telling him that he has been properly trained by inculcation of appropriate habits. Virtue is the general accord of reason and emotion.
>
> (*Laws*, 635b).

But Plato makes it clear that Dion was raised in the lifestyle of the Syracusans, which involved:

> men gorging themselves twice a day and never sleeping alone at night, and following all the other customs that go along with this way of living . . . and spending their all on excesses, and being easy going about everything except the feasts and the drinking bouts and the pleasures of love that they pursue with professional zeal.
>
> (*Seventh Letter*, 326b-d)

Despite this poor habituation, Dion's desires were transformed. How did this come about? According to Plato, Dion's desires were, we might say, "temporarily" transformed through dialogue, in which Plato and Dion discussed "what was best for men." Through their dialogues, Plato "urged [Dion] to put [the virtues] into practice" and Dion "resolved to spend the rest of his life differently from most Italians and Sicilians" (327a-b). The reversal of Dion's goals and desires is remarkable because Dion freely admitted that it was not until after his discussions with Plato that he conceived of the worth of virtue (327b), even though Plato seems to claim that the reformation of individuals raised to prefer vice is more or less impossible elsewhere in his corpus (*Republic*, 492e; *Seventh Letter*, 326c). So how exactly did Plato manage this transformation in Dion?

Like Aristotle, Plato claims that if someone is to develop a radically different understanding of virtue's desirability, they cannot be simply lectured on the topic, like what might happen if they were just being taught straightforward information.

> For this knowledge is not something that can be put into words like other sciences; but after long-continued intercourse between teacher and pupil, in joint pursuit of the subject, suddenly, like light flashing forth when a fire is kindled, it is born in the soul and straightaway nourishes itself.
>
> (*Seventh Letter*, 341c)

Plato explains that this kind of knowledge isn't able to be placed in "books and lectures," even if he happens to be the author of them. This epiphanic flash of knowledge in a person's soul is an *outcome of dialogue*.

> Only when all of these other things—names, definitions, and visual and other perceptions—have been rubbed against one another and tested, pupil and teacher asking and answering questions in good will and without envy—only then, when reason and knowledge are at the very extremity of human effort, can they illuminate the nature of any object.
>
> (*Seventh Letter*, 344b)

Apparently, then, in a particular kind of dialogue, someone who does not already possess knowledge of virtue is able to achieve an epiphany of virtue—a vision that can lead to a desire to live a life of virtue, like it did in Dion. For Plato's purposes, an epiphany happens when two distinct events occur. The first is a vision of virtue in which the "encrustations" of vice are "separated" briefly, and our wisdom can see past the stones and shells that prevent it from seeing what is truly good. At that moment, the soul cognitively apprehends something about virtue—even if what it apprehends is only dimly discernible. The second is that this vision of virtue is only effective if there is an accompanying desire to pursue the image of virtue that is glimpsed in between the stones and shells. As we saw, the stones and shells not only drag our *vision* down so that our wisdom cannot not see and *cognize* what is truly virtuous, but they also drag our emotions towards vice so that we will not have the right *affections* regarding what is truly virtuous. For an epiphany to be a true epiphany, both of these components must be present.[5] If a person is able to catch a glimpse of virtue and recognizes that certain actions are virtuous, but does not desire to act in a way consistent with that glimpse then he has not had a true epiphany. This is, for example, what happens to Thrasymachus in the *Republic*, who begrudgingly acknowledges that perhaps

Socrates has a point when he shows that might does not make right, and yet because of his emotional commitment to vice, Thrasymachus has not had an epiphany in the relevant sense. His wisdom was pointed in the right direction, but his emotional desires were not engaged. On the other hand, if a sophist leads a person to "see" that a certain vicious activity is, contrary to the actual truth, virtuous and that person has a strong desire to pursue that vicious activity, then he has not had an epiphany in the relevant sense. This is the case with Meno, who claims he was led to the knowledge of virtue by the sophist Gorgias, and who seems genuinely interested in living a life of virtue, and yet because Gorgias led him to have false knowledge about virtue, Meno has also not had an epiphany in the relevant sense.

Of course, this leads to the question of why it is that some people have a glimpse of true virtue but *do not* desire to follow it (like Thrasymachus), while other people have a glimpse of true virtue and *do* desire to follow it (like Dion). Plato never tells us exactly what the difference is beyond that some people are just more open and have a predisposition (either innate or learned) to want virtue. But as we shall see in this chapter and the next, he makes it clear that a person who wants to induce epiphanies in interlocutors must evaluate the psychological conditions of her interlocutors and use pedagogical techniques that will achieve the epiphany—but only in those who are ready for the epiphany. For those who are not ready, the goal of the dialogue should merely reveal their poor reasoning in the hopes that the shame or embarrassment of being a poor reasoner might lead to a place of humility that could, although unlikely, eventually lead to the openness to epiphanies. Most of Socrates' interlocutors in the dialogues are in this latter camp, but, as we shall see, there are several who are open to epiphanies and end up experiencing them.

With this outline of the two essential characteristics of epiphanies found in Plato, we are now in a position to see how epiphanies signifies a brief, potent, but, as we shall see, an inevitably incomplete glimpse of virtue. Plato later explains that we know this glimpse is both brief and incomplete because he states that until people have been rigorously rehabituated in virtue they "will never fully attain knowledge of [virtue]" (*Seventh Letter*, 342e). Therefore, while the epiphanic flash that Dion had did indeed "nourish itself," and in that sense his desire for virtue continued to grow, Dion would need to make changes in his lifestyle in order for the epiphany to grow into full knowledge of virtue. In order for full knowledge to come into being, Dion understood that he would need to be rehabituated, which is the reason why he "resolved to spend the rest of his life differently . . . since he had come to love virtue more than pleasure and luxury" (327b). This was his own voluntary plan to start a process of rehabituation. Like Plato, Dion understood that his epiphany had only started him on the road to virtue and that years of habituation would be required before he actually achieved it.

Within the *Seventh Letter*, Plato also relates a story about his *unsuccessful* attempts to convert Dionysius II from a life of intemperance and unjust hedonism to the life of a moderate and virtuous philosopher. He was successful with Dion, but not Dionysius. Within this story, Plato provides a second aspect of his theory of dialogue in a brief "excursus," on the relationship between dialogue and knowledge. Plato's stated reason for writing this excursus is to repudiate Dionysius II's claims that he understood Plato's teaching on epistemology and dialogue and had elaborated those ideas in writing. Plato emphatically rejects Dionysius' claim, arguing that if Dionysius had really understood Plato's ideas, he would never have written the ideas down, for the most important ideas cannot be explained in writing. True knowledge cannot be captured by words but can only be apprehended through dialogue. Plato argues that "there is no writing of mine about these matters, nor will there ever be one. For this knowledge is not something that can be put into words like other sciences" (341c). These words not only recall what occurred for Dion but also reveal much about the Platonic dialogues and why Plato *only* wrote dialogues: Plato did not believe that he could communicate directly in discursive treatises the truths that he wanted his readers to know. This is why he invites his readers to become vicarious interlocutors in dialogues in which he hoped they would, "through long-continued intercourse," come to a recognition of the truth, the truth that would "flash forth" in the process of dialogue.

After arguing for the connection between dialogue and knowledge, Plato outlines in very general terms what constitutes the highest form of knowledge—which we have been calling "full virtue." He claims that there are five levels of understanding or "knowledge," but only the fifth level constitutes ultimate knowledge. The first level is merely the name of the knowledge, e.g., "courage." The second level is the definition of the knowledge. The third is a representation of the knowledge. In the case of courage this would be a description of a courageous deed. The fourth is the ability to correctly identify—either by knowledge (*episteme*), reason (*nous*), or correct opinion (*alexthes doxa*)—virtuous actions when one sees them. The fourth level constitutes the level of understanding available to most human beings without the aid of dialogue—the fourth can come through habituation alone. None of these, however, constitute the "flash" of true insight. Levels one through four constitute some level of knowledge but not the highest and most important (*Seventh Letter*, 342a-e). While Plato does not explicitly claim that the first four levels of understanding are sequential stages, where one has to master each of the ones coming before it, he does claim that "whoever does not somehow grasp the four things mentioned will never fully attain knowledge of the fifth" (342e). However, even though people will never be able to fully attain the knowledge of the fifth level without mastering the previous four, they can, as we saw in Dion's epiphany, and will see again later in this chapter, attain a *partial glimpse* of the fifth which can initiate a transformation of the individual's desires, which can lead back to a rehabituation process which allows people to develop the fourth level of knowledge and provides the foundation for full knowledge.

The correctness of this thesis is made even clearer when we consider that Plato never actually explains what the fifth level is, apart from the fact that it is a sort of perception that flashes across one's mind. For not only are the masses unable to understand the ideas, but it is impossible to explain the fifth level of knowledge without distorting that knowledge.[6] He argues that because of the weakness of language, one can never express the actual "being" of a thing but only its "particular properties." Thus, Plato claims that no sensible person would ever try to explain the true being of a thing. "On this account no sensible man will venture to express his deepest thoughts (which is where true knowledge lies) in words, especially in a form that is unchangeable, as is true of written outlines" (*Seventh Letter*, 343a). When Plato says this, he does not mean that people cannot use words to describe their experiences in approximate or metaphorical ways—like when a cobbler "explains" to his novice that she must stretch shoe leather "just enough but not too much"—but they must not believe they can explain the essence of a thing in a way that actually captures the essence. The fifth level of knowledge that a craftsperson has about shoes, or shipbuilding, or virtue, etc., can only be expressed in approximate and metaphorical ways.

Kahn (1996) worries that Plato's skepticism regarding the ability of humans to express their deepest knowledge in words may lead (as it has) to the charge of mysticism. The charge of mysticism in this case is based on the assumption that if ideas cannot be expressed in words, then they are by definition non-rational, and if they are non-rational then they must be of mystical origins. Kahn (1996) argues against the thesis that Plato is a mystic by challenging the view that just because knowledge is incommunicable does not mean that it is "non-rational or trans-rational, beyond the reach of intellectual understanding" (p. 390). Kahn is right on this point for at least two reasons.

The first reason is that, as we saw in Chapter 1, Socrates compares knowledge of virtue to craft-knowledge which by its very nature cannot be fully articulated in words. Craftspersons can, of course, offer *approximations* of the knowledge they have, but they cannot cash out the entirety of their knowledge in words. There is an aesthetic perception in a craftsperson about her craft that is developed over years of practice and habit that defies exact representation. At some point, language comes up short and only those who have experienced the craft-knowledge themselves can understand the hints and gestures of the craftsperson. Thus, when Plato explicitly claims that he has never written his most important ideas down, and that such ideas are impossible to articulate through the medium of language, he is merely echoing what he implicitly claimed in the early dialogues and his use of the craft-analogy.

The second reason to think that Kahn is correct in his rejection of mysticism is that nowhere in the *Seventh Letter* does Plato claim that virtue is beyond the reach of cognitive understanding. On the contrary, he explicitly claims it is within the reach of cognitive understanding.

> it is barely possible for knowledge to be engendered of an object naturally good, in a man naturally good; but if his nature is defective, as is that of most men, for the acquisition of knowledge and the so-called virtues, and if the qualities he has have been corrupted, then not even Lynceus could make such a man see. In short, neither quickness of learning nor even a good memory can make a man see when his nature is not akin to the object, for this knowledge never takes root in an alien nature; so that no man who is not naturally inclined and akin to justice and all other forms of excellence, even though he may be quick at learning and remembering this and that and other things, nor any man who, though akin to justice, is slow at learning and forgetful, will ever attain the truth that is attainable about virtue.
>
> (343e–344a)

The last line makes it clear that Plato believes that knowledge of virtue is capable of being attained by cognitive understanding. However, this knowledge is not easily arrived at; it takes a combination of the right moral nature and the right intellectual nature, which could lend support, in a way, to the view that this knowledge may be mystical, insofar as it can only be attained by the few. If only a few people can achieve this vision, and they have to have special "natures" to do so—perhaps these people are quasi-divine. However, if we understand what Plato means by "nature," and what it means to be "akin" to an object of knowledge, then we see that moral knowledge can be gained by typical human beings. As we saw in the last chapter, kinship between humans and virtues happens not by innate predisposition, but through the habituation process. It is habits and practice—like the kinds found in craftspeople—that leads to kinship with virtue.

There is a sense in which Plato believes that people have a certain nature to become virtuous. In the *Republic*, for example, he claims that the Auxiliaries must have a natural tendency towards spiritedness in their nature (*Republic*, 429c–430b). Spiritedness is the raw desire to fight when put in a dangerous situation. Without that raw desire he thinks that people cannot become courageous. Yet, we also saw in Chapters 1, 2, and 3 that the raw desire to act courageously can be slowly developed if individuals are habituated properly. Doing courageous activities over and over again leads to a change in the students' "nature," as they develop "kinship" with virtue. Of course, developing kinship takes a long time, which is why Socrates insists that the Auxiliaries must have the natural tendency towards spiritedness from the beginning. This will allow them to develop courage more quickly. But given enough time, all people can develop kinship if they are habituated correctly. When they do this, they develop a second nature, as it were. He claims that when people have the right natures (either because they were born with them or developed them through habituation) and have the right beliefs, they become permanently virtuous. He claims they are like wool that has been permanently dyed the color purple. No amount of washing can make the fabric lose its color. Similarly, people who have the raw desire and the wisdom about how to direct the raw desire will be permanently virtuous. (*Republic*, 429e–430a).

But this leads us back to the example of Dion. How is it that he achieved an epiphany of virtue, when he was given an upbringing that was opposed to virtue. As we saw before, Socrates claims that "no man under heaven who has cultivated such practices (vices) from his youth could possibly grow up to be wise—so miraculous a temper is against nature—or become temperate, or indeed acquire any other part of virtue" (*Seventh Letter*, 326c). Yet, Dion seems to have become convinced that he should be virtuous. How did this happen? The answer lies in Plato's belief that certain individuals who have an innate or learned openness to virtue can, through dialogue, achieve a temporary glimpse of virtue that calls to that innate longing for a virtuous life. These individuals may at the outset of the conversation appear to have no interest in virtue, and yet if the teacher leads the dialogue correctly, something "miraculous" can happen, and the eyes of their soul partially can see through the encrustations of vice. There is just enough beauty in these visions that their souls are reminded of what every soul longs for deep down. Plato claims that every soul, because it is divine, has an innate "love of wisdom. . . . [which] it grasps and longs to have intercourse with, because it is divine and immortal" (*Republic*, 611e). The problem is that Plato believes that most people in his time were so encrusted with vice that they simply cannot see through the encrustations even though their souls long to. It is different for some reason with Dion, who Plato claims was the person most able to see with his soul that Plato had ever met (*Seventh Letter*, 327b-c).

But Dion is not alone. Plato gives us several examples in the Platonic dialogues of interlocutors who are similarly able to experience an epiphany. Of course, most of the time, the dialogues depict people who are far too encrusted with vice to experience an epiphany. This is especially the case for sophists and other people in positions of power like politicians, rhetoricians, lawyers, etc. In the next chapter we will look in detail at what it is about these individuals that make them unsusceptible to epiphanies. But there are interlocutors who do achieve a vision of the good, and it is to a couple of examples that we will turn to in the rest of this chapter. In what remains in this chapter we will turn to two examples, that of Lysis and Alcibiades, and in the next chapter we will examine the case of Glaucon. All three of these individuals had epiphanies that demonstrated their ability to catch a glimpse of virtue, even if they do not fully reform themselves in the way that Dion did.

The Case of Lysis

The *Lysis* is the first dialogue we will look to in which an epiphany can be witnessed. While a great deal has been written on Plato's *Lysis* in philosophy and philology journals over the last thirty years,[7] nothing has been published on *Lysis* in the major Anglo-American philosophy of education journals during that time. This is not altogether surprising considering that *Lysis* is not regarded as one of Plato's most important or well-written dialogues; nor does it directly address education like *Republic, Meno*, or *Apology* does; nor does it have the cultural and literary capital associated with it like *Symposium* or *Phaedrus*. Nevertheless, it is important for our purposes because it dramatically depicts an epiphany in the main character. Socrates uses moments of *aporia* as well as direct instruction in a carefully guided process he believes will lead to an epiphanic experience that brings clarity to the question at hand, even if that clarity cannot be expressed in words.

The context for the dialogue is that Hippothales, a contemporary of Socrates who is smitten with the young and beautiful Lysis, sings the praises of Lysis to Socrates who claims that talking in the manner of Hippothales will surely lead Lysis to having an inflated image of himself and will tease Hippothales mercilessly unless Hippothales takes a different tack in wooing Lysis. Socrates claims that he can show how to cut beautiful young men down to size and by humbling them make them more likely to become one's lover. Socrates then asks Hippothales to watch Socrates as he demonstrates his tactics.

Socrates begins his clinic by inviting Lysis into a conversation about friendship. Of course, this topic is chosen explicitly for the context because Socrates believes that Lysis is morally obligated to be a friend of Hippothales, even if he does not become his lover. Socrates begins his attempt to lead Lysis to an epiphany by first generating an *aporia* in Lysis.

After explaining his dialogical intentions to his interlocutors, Socrates attracts the attention of Lysis and wastes no time moving him towards an initial *aporia*. Through dialogue, Socrates reveals to Lysis that people love him only to the degree that Lysis has knowledge. In those areas where Lysis is deficient, people cannot love or respect him and will try to limit his freedom. This means that his parents do not love him or respect him, the very thing Lysis originally thought (*Lysis*, 207a–210d). As commentators have long pointed out, the cogency of Socrates' arguments in *Lysis* is highly suspect (Gadamer, 1980, p. 2; Rider, 2011, pp. 40–41). For example, Socrates gets Lysis to agree that his parents "trust a hired hand . . . to do whatever he likes with the[ir] horses" (208a). This is obviously not the case. They hire a charioteer not to do whatever he likes with the horses, but to take care of them, so that the horses can be of use to Lysis' parents. In encouraging Lysis to see the matter this way, he convinces Lysis that his parents must care about their hired hands more than him. Much of the conversation with Lysis runs this way. This fact is important as it suggests that Socrates' goal in *Lysis* is *not* to teach students how to employ the rules of logic or how to make cogent arguments. Neither is it merely to use sophistry to cause *aporia*. His goal is to help Lysis catch a glimpse of what true friendship is and what he must do to enact it. Socrates is therefore, at crucial moments, willing to use specious arguments because he believes that they will better achieve his goal of helping his students come to the epiphany he seeks for them. As we shall see, sometimes epiphanies can be better attained by avoiding logically consistent arguments. Thus, Socrates will use a variety of means necessary—some justified, some questionable—to help a student come to knowledge. His dialogical form is merely expedient. In fact, he drops it when he thinks a speech will work better;[8] or, at times he only nominally uses it, not really caring whether or not the interlocutor responds, like he does with Thrasymachus in the closing pages of Book I of the *Republic*. The point is that in *Lysis* we see him using a very large number of specious arguments, which, while logically untenable, help place Lysis in *aporia* more quickly than he would be able to without them. The goal is not primarily an intellectually honest, dialogical relationship with Lysis but a transformative epiphany and, as we shall see, subsequent action.[9]

It is important to note that Socrates leads Lysis in the first half of the dialogue to something like an *aporia* inasmuch as Lysis contradicts what he stated earlier. And yet Lysis does not seem to be touched by it. His response is a seemingly jovial, "You've got me there, Socrates!" (*Lysis*, 210d). He even follows by whispering "with a good deal of boyish friendliness" (211a) into Socrates' ear, that Socrates should make the same arguments with Menexenus. Interestingly, Socrates claims that he almost blurts out to Hippothales that he has shown him how to cut boyfriends down to size rather than swelling them up (210e). The fact that Socrates continues after this humbling of Lysis further suggests that his goal is not merely to show how to humble students but how to lead them to knowledge and just action. Lysis' response also reveals that *aporia* alone does not lead to transformation; there must be an attending epiphany of the implications.

Socrates refuses to make the same arguments with Menexenus and instead starts a new line of dialogue on friendship with both Lysis and Menexenus. Once again, we see Socrates using numerous specious arguments to reveal the poverty of his interlocutor's understanding.[10] Through these arguments Socrates forces his interlocutors to contradict themselves time and time again. In his characteristic fashion, he starts over once he has arrived at one contradiction. Moreover, we find another example of Socrates using some methods of dialogue that are antithetical to the notion that he is trying to build an open-ended dialogical relationship with his students: From the beginning of conversation to the end, Lysis and Menexenus never once utter a substantive remark or question. Socrates never asks a truly open-ended question. Most of his questions are actually just statements that require assent or dissent. It is hard to dismiss the conclusion that if Socrates is concerned about the well-being of the students his concern cannot be to teach them *through* dialectic but *by* dialectic. Put differently, the intended transformative result is not found in the give and take of the dialogue, as some educationists assume, but in the leading of the students to the effect of *aporia*. Having illustrated some of the salient features of Socrates' *method* of argumentation in *Lysis*, I will turn to its *effects*.

As Pierre Hadot correctly points out, Socrates' ultimate goal is to produce students who *live* just lives rather than be able to communicate their knowledge of justice. We have seen this across Plato's corpus, which is why Hadot and Davidson (1995) argues that

> [Socrates] sought to demonstrate the limits of language. . . . Justice, like every authentic reality, is indefinable, and this is what Socrates sought to make his interlocutor understand in order to 'live' justice. The questioning of discourse leads to the questioning of the individual, who must decide whether or not he will resolve to live according to his conscience and to reason.
>
> (p. 15)

Running throughout the *Lysis* and other dialogues is an undercurrent of activity. Socrates and his interlocutors almost always pursue questions that have "live" implications. The *Lysis* is a case in point. The themes are love and friendship, ideas that entail a relationship between one person and another. The relationships imply activity. Love and friendship without activity are not love and friendship.

At the end of the dialogue, Socrates has reduced both Lysis and Menexenus to *aporia* by leading them from contradiction to contradiction regarding the nature of friendship. The *aporia* sets the stage for the epiphany Socrates hopes for Lysis to experience. As Socrates claimed earlier in the dialogue (*Lysis*, 216c), the interlocutors have been through a dizzying array of arguments which all come out to be deficient. By the end, they have come around to the beginning on more than one occasion. But all of a sudden, to consummate the *aporia*, Socrates literally "screams" out "Oh, no! . . . Lysis and Menexenus our wealth has all been a dream. . . . I am afraid we've fallen in with arguments about friendship that are no better than con artists" (*Lysis*, 218c-d). Shortly after declaring so, he turns the argument in a brand new, hitherto unexplored direction—the direction that will lead to an epiphany. It must be unexplored because Socrates only wants to reveal the truth when Lysis is ready for it. He must wait, in other words, for the peak of *aporia* before he helps to reveal knowledge.

It is at this point that we see the transition from *aporia* to epiphany. Having repeatedly reduced them to confusion by forcing them into circular arguments, the reader begins to sense Lysis and Menexnus' inability to assimilate information. Lysis and Menexenus seem, like Meno described himself, to be stunned by the torpedo fish, which he likens to Socrates (*Meno*, 83a-b). At the peak of their *aporia*, Socrates changes directions. In their confused state of no longer "knowing" which way is up, their ability to analyze arguments, to subject them to rigorous dialectical argument, is spent. This seeming inability to *think*, becomes for Socrates the moment when an epiphany can be achieved. As Socrates leads the conversation to this place of knowledge, we witness, albeit indirectly, the recognition of truth, first in Lysis and then Menexenus.

To make visible the moment of epiphany in Lysis and Menexenus, it will be helpful to have the relevant text before us. Socrates has just recently changed direction in the dialogue when he comments:

"Then it is what belongs to oneself, it seems, that passionate love and
    friendship and desire are directed towards, Menexenus and Lysis."
They both agreed.
"And if you two are friends with each other, then in some way you
    naturally belong to each other."
"Absolutely," they said together.
"And if one person desires another, my boys, or loves him passionately,
    he would not desire him or love him passionately or as a friend
    unless he somehow belonged to his beloved either in his soul or in
    some characteristic habit, or aspect of his soul."
"Certainly," said Menexenus, but Lysis was silent.
"All right," I said, "what belongs to us by nature has shown itself to us
    as something we must love."
"It looks like it," [Menexenus] said."
"Then the genuine and not the pretended lover must be befriended by
    his boy."
Lysis and Menexenus just managed a nod of assent, but Hippothales
    [Lysis' suitor] beamed every color in the rainbow in his delight.

Lysis, who throughout the dialogue has been an eager participant, falls silent at the exact moment when Socrates has made his new, altogether unexplored assertion of what friendship is. "'Certainly', said Menexenus, but Lysis was silent" (*Lysis*, 222a). Lysis' silence is telling, precisely because Plato contrasts it with Menexenus' "certainly."[11] Up until this point, the two have been univocal in their agreement or disagreement. But here their contrasting responses highlight an internal change. Lysis has recognized something that Menexenus has not. The reader almost feels the epiphany happening.[12] Lysis, who until this point had been almost over eager to blurt out his answers (*Lysis*, 213d), but who never fully understood the implications of the conversation, all of a sudden realizes that Socrates' new assertion about friendship holds implications for him, while Menexenus does not yet understand (he will shortly, however). Socrates guides Lysis to this epiphany by conditioning his mind to receive the epiphany. Ironically, his conditioning for this epiphanic insight includes the use of *aporias*—which on a propositional/linguistic level cause disorientation and doubt, but through the disorientation make possible the epiphanic insight. For Socrates, what a friend is, and how a friend should behave to others, cannot fully be captured in propositional categories. As Tindale (1984) argues:

> To describe in words alone what friendship is would be to falsify it in some way, to prevent the necessary moment of encounter in the discovery of the idea. . . . What have been seen as defective arguments within a perplexing context emphasizes the inadequacy of definition without an underlying experience.
>
> (p. 107)

As such, in order for any person to genuinely understand what a friend is, they must cease relying on a primarily linguistic, rationalist conceptualization of friendship. They must simply *see* what a friend is—and this requires a kind of epiphany.

While it is tempting to see Socrates as being exclusively interested in defining friendship using logical and propositional statements, he uses these statements to lead his interlocutors towards an insight that is beyond the statements. The logical and propositional form of the argument is important to reduce Lysis to *aporia*, but the *aporia* is merely one step in "redirecting his attention." The confusion caused by the *aporia* is not accidental or incidental—it is an essential precursor to epiphany because, as studies have shown, epiphanies are often the result of internal conflict. Epiphanies are characterized by a "sudden, discontinuous change, leading to profound positive, and enduring transformation through the reconfiguration of an individual's most deeply held beliefs about the self and world. . . . [and are] preceded by a period of internal conflict" (Jarvis, 1996, p. vi). Because of *aporia*, Lysis has been reduced to a condition in which he is able to understand what true friendship with a beloved is.

This knowledge is confirmed in Lysis (and is shared by Menexenus) a few lines later when Socrates draws an inference that necessarily follows from his previous statement that Lysis silently acknowledges. Socrates claims: "then the genuine [Hippothales] and not the pretended [Menexenus] lover must be befriended by his boy [Lysis]." To which Lysis and Menexenus sheepishly nod their assent while "Hippothales beamed every color of the rainbow" (*Lysis*, 223b). All three of the main interlocutors (Lysis, Menexenus, and Hippothales) recognize the truth of Socrates' point. Lysis has been a false friend to Hippothales by playing his little games with Menexenus, who, although a friend, is not his true lover.[13]

But Socrates, as I have already indicated, is not interested in merely revealing knowledge of a just friendship; he wants Lysis to act in response to that knowledge. We see this in the moments immediately following Lysis' initial recognition. Socrates states what *must* be done, what must be enacted. First Socrates says, "what belongs to us by nature has shown itself to us as something we must love" (*Lysis*, 222a). There are two things to be noticed in this statement. The first is that Socrates uses the words "shown itself to us." In saying this, Socrates illustrates the primacy of epiphany. The knowledge of what true friendship is has been revealed; it is an epiphany that confronts the boys. The second point to notice in this first statement is that it is partially ambiguous what we must do. Socrates says we "must love." But what does love mean? If we feel love, is that enough? Does it actually imply that there is any other necessary action? Socrates however is not through with his practical injunctions. Although the command for love could be idealized, his next statement cannot. He says that "the genuine and not the pretended lover must be befriended by his boy" (*Lysis*, 222b). Socrates' statement is, obviously, made in the abstract and is not directly addressed to Lysis. Nevertheless, it is clear that Socrates, knowing from Lysis' silence and comportment, that Lysis has had the epiphany Socrates intended for him, intends the statement to apply to Lysis. And what is more, he knows that Lysis will know it applies to him. Lysis' epiphany carries with it a call to action, which Socrates seeks to reinforce. The operative words are 'must be befriended.' Socrates is making the point that loving from a distance is not enough. Lysis' epiphany beckons him to live in the light of the truth that has been revealed. It must be embodied—otherwise it would not be knowledge. For Plato, an epiphany is both a cognitive realization of what virtue requires and a desire to act on that realization. Lysis must befriend his true lover, Hippothales, and must quit pretending with his false lover, Menexenus.

By arguing thus, we are not suggesting that Socrates thinks that Lysis should immediately become the sexual lover (*eromenos*) of Hippothales—whether Hippothales would be a suitable lover (*erastes*) could be determined only after a friendship with him was initiated—but that he should quit acting the tease with Menexenus, which was driving Hippothales to distraction. Socrates is thus calling Lysis to a place of growing maturity, wisdom, and virtue. Having shown himself ready for wisdom and maturity by virtue of having the ability to have the epiphany he does, Lysis is now in a place to begin the pursuit of a virtuous life. Socrates' ultimate goal is to cultivate the moral development in Lysis, not to persuade him to become the sexual lover of Hippothales.

Importantly, Socrates does not end here. Instead of insisting on the epiphany he has just helped Lysis to attain, he renews his questioning as to its validity and ultimately claims to be unable to satisfactorily answer the question. In ending the dialogue this way he leaves his interlocutors with nothing else but the injunction that "they should think over everything that has been said" (*Lysis*, 222e). This does not mean that Socrates intends Lysis to start doubting afresh the epiphany he has received. Rather, he intends his statement of *aporia* to compel him to make his epiphany his own. He does not want to give him the opportunity to pin his understanding of friendship on *Socrates'* verbal formulation of it.

In a very skillful, if sophistical, manner Socrates has led Lysis first to *aporia*, then to an epiphany, then to the injunction to live justly, all the while protecting Lysis' agency. Without each of these steps Lysis would never be in a position to act with justice in his relationships with Hippothales and Menexenus; he is simply too immature and obsessed with maintaining the affections of two lovers to think through the implication of his actions. To overcome Lysis' immaturity, Socrates has to compel Lysis to quit *thinking* and begin *seeing*, as it were. Once Lysis' *rational* comprehension is overwhelmed, his *moral* comprehension is open through epiphany to understand what it means to be a true friend. In this way he is able to see what justice is, and what actions are required to fulfill that justice.

The epiphany of the *Lysis* is very clear insofar as we saw a physical manifestation of some sort of realization happening in Lysis, but it is only Socrates who claims that Lysis must take rehabituative action. Lysis, on the other hand, never explicitly claims he will take action. It is clear that he is thinking about his actions, but we do not know what his future intentions are. As such, Plato does not make it explicitly clear that Lysis has had a complete epiphany. To recall, an epiphany includes a reorientation of one's cognitive vision but also a reorientation of affective desire. It is clear that Lysis has had the former, and it is clear that Socrates hopes Lysis has had the former, but the slave boy called Lysis away and we are never told that Lysis' desires were temporarily reoriented. As we saw, it was different with Dion, who clearly desires the virtue he now sees and acknowledges his need for rehabituation in order to fulfill his desire to embody the virtues. In the next example of an epiphanic experience, Alcibiades not only has the cognitive component of the epiphany Lysis had, but, like Dion, he makes it clear that the cognitive insight requires that he live differently, and he explicitly claims that he wants to live differently by proceeding with a rehabituation program that he hopes will be guided by Socrates.

The Case of Alcibiades

The *Alcibiades I* is considered by some to be of doubtful authenticity. The main argument against its authenticity is that it is a little too neat and tidy of a dialogue, with the conversion of Alcibiades at the climax. It is argued that Socrates is more explicit concerning virtue, and since in many other dialogues he is not as explicit, then *Alcibiades I* might be written by later, more dogmatic, Neoplatonists who were more concerned with promoting their own doctrines than faithfully representing Plato's. Of course it is impossible to say with any certainty whether Plato wrote it or not, but the stylometric evidence suggests that he did. There is very little in the way of stylometric discrepancies between *Alcibiades I* and other undisputed Platonic texts. But, in any event, even if it is spurious it is clear that Plato believed that the character of Alcibiades did experience several epiphanic visions in his dealings with Socrates. We know this because Plato paints a vivid picture of the results of these epiphanies in the *Symposium*—which was indisputably written by Plato—when Alcibiades bursts into the party where Socrates and others are describing love to one another. Alcibiades descriptions of the epiphanies he experienced in discussion with Socrates are clear, dramatic, and reflect the epiphany Alcibiades achieves in *Alcibiades I*. Take for example Alcibiades description of the following:

> If I were to describe for you what an extraordinary effect his words have always had on me (I can feel it this moment even as I'm speaking), you might actually suspect that I'm drunk! Still, I swear to you, the moment he starts to speak, I am beside myself: my heart starts leaping in my chest, the tears come streaming down my face, even the frenzied Corybantes seem sane compared to me—and, let me tell you, I am not alone. I have heard Pericles and many other great orators, and I have admired their speeches. But nothing like this ever happened to me: they never upset me so deeply that my very own soul started protesting that my life—*my* life!—was no better than the most miserable slave's. And yet that is exactly how this Marsyas here at my side makes me feel all the time: he makes it seem that my life isn't worth living!
>
> (*Symposium* 215b-c)

The language of his "heart leaping" in his chest and his eyes streaming with tears reflects the affective transformation of Alcibiades emotions and desires. Like Dion earlier, he has not merely come to an intellectual recognition that his current life is inferior to the life of virtue that he has been led to see, but his desires have been transformed.

It is important to note, however, that Socrates brings these things about not by way of logical entailment. It is tempting to assume that Alcibiades desires are transformed because of a chain of *logical* reasoning that leads indubitably to a particular conclusion. There is indeed a chain of reasoning, but like we saw in the *Lysis*, the arguments are not necessarily cogent arguments. Socrates makes *bad* arguments in the *Alcibiades*, just like he does in the *Lysis*. But his bad arguments are no accident, and Alcibiades recognizes this. He tells the interlocutors in the *Symposium* that what matters is not the logical cogency of Socrates' arguments but what lies behind the arguments. It is not what the propositions precisely say, but what they open the soul up to.

> If you are foolish, or simply unfamiliar with him, you'd find it impossible not to laugh at his arguments. But if you see them when they open up like the statues, if you go behind their surface, you'll realize that

no other arguments make any sense. They're truly worthy of a god, bursting with figures of virtue inside. They're of great—no, of the greatest—importance for anyone who wants to become a truly good man.

(*Symposium*, 221e–222a)

It is interesting that because of the epiphanies Alcibiades has received, he not only realizes that the ridiculousness of Socrates arguments does not take away from their power, but the ridiculousness of the arguments *is* the power of them. It is possible that if Socrates used *only* cogent arguments, he might have been *less* effective than he would otherwise be. Good arguments often remain at the level of rational cognition and when they do, they sometimes do not have the same penetrative power. This is of course characteristic of human beings: logical arguments often do not touch us in the way that irony, myth, stories, humor, shame, and so on, do.

That Plato thinks epiphanies are essential to the moral development of young people is reflected in Alcibiades' claim that the figures of virtue that he sees behind Socrates' arguments are of the "greatest" importance to the moral life. According to Plato, if an adult is to become a truly good person, she must be able to see these figures bursting forth. Their importance lies in their tendency to touch the *emotions* and *desires* in the person who sees them. The desire is so strong that Alcibiades wants to undergo the habituation process that he knows living a virtuous life would require. This is seen both in the *Symposium* and also in the *Alcibiades I*. In the *Symposium*, Alcibiades says:

But I once caught him when he was open like Silenus' statues, and I had a glimpse of the figures he keeps hidden within: they were so godlike—so bright and beautiful, so utterly amazing—that I no longer had a choice—I just had to do whatever he told me.

(216e–217a)

In the *Alcibiades I*, he says something similar:

We're probably going to change roles, Socrates, I'll be playing yours and you'll be playing mine, for from this day forward I will never fail to attend on you, and you will always have me as your attendant. . . . Yes, that is right. I'll start to cultivate justice in myself right now.

(*Alcibiades*, 135d–e)

The fact that Alcibiades claims that he will "start" the cultivation of justice is important. Alcibiades has come to see his former desires and his former way of life as incompatible with virtue and the happiness it will bring, but he also recognizes that this knowledge alone does not make him virtuous; it prepares him for virtue but does not fully accomplish the fact. This is the nature of epiphanies. He must start the process of cultivating a virtue which does not yet exist in him. Plato makes this abundantly clear through the lines that preceded the previous quotation. After Alcibiades' epiphany, Socrates asks Alcibiades to recognize that he is currently in a condition which is inferior and conducive to unhappiness.

SOCRATES: Can you see the condition you're now in? Is it appropriate for a free man or not?
ALCIBIADES: I think I see only too clearly.
SOCRATES: Then do you know how to escape from your present state? . . .
ALCIBIADES: I do
SOCRATES: How?

(*Alcibiades* 135c-d)

The answer Alcibiades gives harkens back to a slightly earlier point in the dialogue when Alcibiades agrees with Socrates that in order to "acquire virtue" one must "be ruled by somebody superior" (*Alcibiades*, 135b), which is why Alcibiades wants to change rolls with Socrates and let Socrates rule him, as we saw expressed in the *Symposium*. Alcibiades wants to be rehabituated by someone superior to him.

In both the *Symposium* and the *Alcibiades I*, it is clear that Alcibiades, like Dion earlier, has had an epiphany regarding the desirability of living a virtuous life, and he also recognizes, again like Dion, that the only way to achieve that life is to submit himself to a rehabituation process under the guidance of a virtuous mentor, who Alcibiades believes should be Socrates. Unfortunately, both the *Symposium* and the *Alcibiades* suggest that Alcibiades does not make good on his commitment to follow Socrates' guidance concerning how to become a virtuous person. In the *Alcibiades I*, Socrates prophetically hints at the problems Alcibiades will have in changing his way of life when he says: "I should like to believe you that you'll persevere, but I am afraid—not because I distrust your nature, but because I know how powerful the city is—I'm afraid it might get the better of both me and you" (*Alcibiades*, 135c-d). This passage suggests the dangers to the poorly brought-up individual who has had an epiphany about virtue. Alcibiades *knows* that he is not living the way he should be living; he also *wants* to stop living that way. But Socrates indicates that merely having the knowledge and the desire to live virtuously does not guarantee that one will do so. Alcibiades has some cognitive knowledge, and his affective attitude has been changed, but there is still the problem of changing the conative dimension of Alcibiades' soul. Socrates claims that Alcibiades must "escape" from his present state. Yet, Alcibiades has already had his epiphany. Clearly then having the knowledge and desire found in the epiphany does not free a person. Escaping the habits created by years of living his former lifestyle is still an issue—and a daunting issue at that.

We know that it is daunting because Socrates expresses his doubt that Alcibiades will actually be able to escape. Socrates does not doubt the epiphany that Alcibiades has received nor his genuine desire to escape his vicious condition, but he knows full well that the power of a vicious culture can make changing one's vicious habits difficult. Socrates' last comments foreshadow Alcibiades' moral demise in Athens and Socrates' physical demise. In the case of Alcibiades, Athens' vicious culture was partially responsible for Alcibiades' bad upbringing and thus Socrates knew that it would not support Alcibiades in the changing of his habits, but rather it would bring him back to his bad habits again and again. Plato points out, in a general form, the power a vicious culture has when it attempts to keep people enslaved to vice. In the *Republic* Socrates says:

> And even if a young man of that sort somehow sees the point and is guided and drawn to philosophy because of his noble nature and his kinship with reason, what do you think those people will do, if they believe that they're losing their use of him and his companionship? Is there anything they won't do or say to him to prevent him from being persuaded? Or anything they won't do or say about his persuader— whether plotting against him in private or publicly bringing him into court—to prevent him from such persuasion?
>
> (*Republic*, 494d-e)

In this passage, Plato articulates the way a vicious society will do everything they can to draw a person like Alcibiades back to his former way of life. This is the case even if the person has a "nature" that is drawn to virtue, as Socrates claims that Alcibiades' is. At the innate level of his soul, Alcibiades' nature is pure, just like everyone else's is, but he is a beautiful and wealthy Athenian youth who has men falling at his feet offering themselves to him. Having that much success and power is dangerous to Alcibiades, who did not have the right upbringing, even if Alcibiades had a genuine epiphany, which is clearly that he has had. The habits he developed in his youth are very powerful, especially when coupled with his "friends" who are strategically trying to prevent him from changing his habits.

However it is not just the Athenians who want to sabotage Alcibiades' desire to live a virtuous life. Even though he has a nature that is innately drawn to virtue, which is what helped him to have the epiphany in the first place, he is also subject to his previous habituation, which encourages him to avoid real attempts to becoming virtuous. The vision of the virtuous life that caused him to weep and make his heart leap will easily be drowned out in a short time, if he does not immediately find new friends and subject himself to a rehabituation process under the guidance of a mentor. In the *Symposium*, Alcibiades admits his tendency to return to his bad habits, and the conflict that exists in his soul regarding the life that, because of his epiphanies, he knows is the best life, and the life that he had previously led, the inferior life of vice.

> Yet, the moment I leave his side, I go back to my old ways: I cave in to my desire to please the crowd. My whole life has become one constant effort to escape from him and keep away, but when I see him, I feel deeply ashamed, because I'm doing nothing about my way of life, though I have already agreed with him that I should. Sometimes, believe me, I think I would be happier if he were dead. And yet I know that if he dies I'll be even more miserable. I can't live with him, and I can't live without him!
>
> (*Symposium*, 216b-c)

We see in this passage the powerful psychological forces that govern Alcibiades' character. He is double-minded in a high degree, which is what we would expect from a spoiled young man who was allowed to indulge in every form of pleasure and vice. With these bad habits, is it any wonder that he would find it difficult to follow the epiphany, even if it was so powerful that it reduced him to tears? Nevertheless, there is some hope, as we saw in the case of Dion, that, with help from a supportive community and a committed mentor, a person could overcome the vicious citizens around them and could overcome their own habituated desires to pursue vice and start a process of pursuing virtue. If this process could take off, it could gather steam, and a complete turnaround of the person's life could be effected.

Conclusion

From the following examination, we have seen the way Plato believes that dialogues have the potential to create "glimpses" of virtues that, in the right people, can produce a powerful, if temporary, desire to become virtuous themselves. These glimpses do not produce the full knowledge that includes the cognitive, affective and conative dimensions of virtue, but they do redirect the sight of a person having them enough to produce the potential for lasting change. However, Plato believes that these glimpses have to be accompanied by a desire to embody the virtue, which occurs only in certain individuals. People who are not psychologically open to epiphanies (either because of their innate make-up or their upbringing) simply will not have genuine epiphanies. We examined a few examples of people who had epiphanies and showed the effects that it had on them. In the case of Alcibiades, the epiphany did not produce the full knowledge of virtue found in craft-knowledge, but it has the potential to lead to craft-knowledge if the epiphany is followed by a rigorous rehabituation process, like it did for Dion.

Having examined the role dialogue can play in creating epiphanies in people in creating a desire to pursue a virtuous life, in the next chapter we

will turn to a systematic examination of how Socrates goes about inducing epiphanies in his interlocutors. In particular, we examine the method
Socrates employs to induce and epiphany in Glaucon in the *Republic*.
Using a complex strategy of dialogue that includes philosophical, psychological, and pedagogical dimensions, Socrates is able to temporarily
redirect Glaucon's vision, such that Glaucon cognitively understands what
justice demands, and desires to become just himself in the space of the dialogue. Glaucon goes from immoderately desiring the luxuries and bodily
pleasures at the beginning of the dialogue to desiring self-control, justice,
and the rest of the virtues by the end of the dialogue. Following that
chapter, we move onto the second part of the book in which we examine
some of the ways contemporary educators can induce epiphanies in their
students and begin the rehabituation process.

In Chapter 6, we turn away from the one-on-one epiphanic experience
in the Platonic dialogues and turn to the ways epiphanies can be generated
in several students at the same time in a modern classroom. We examine
some of the contemporary discussions of the roles epiphanies can play
in the classroom, and we analyze several different modes of producing
epiphanies, including inducing them by *showing*, *telling*, and *doing*. In
Chapter 7, we discuss the ways teachers might help guide their students in
the initial phases of rehabituation, focusing especially on ways classroom
communities can be sites of rehabituation and the role friendships can
extend rehabituation outside the classroom. We examine several examples
of the ways these things can be achieved.

Notes

1. There is one, obscure passage in Aristotle's *corpus* that offers more hope:

    The bad man, if he is being brought into a better way of life and thought,
    may make some advance, however slight, and if he should once improve,
    even ever so little, it is plain that he might change completely, or at any
    rate make very great progress; for a man becomes more and more easily
    moved to virtue, however small the improvement was at first. It is, therefore,
    natural to suppose that he will make yet greater progress than he has made
    in the past, and as this progress goes on, it will change him completely and
    establish him in the contrary state, provided he is not hindered by lack of
    time.

    Categories, 13a22–33

2. Beyond articles and book chapters explicitly committed to education, countless
    books, book chapters, and scholarly articles have been written on the Socratic
    Method by philosophers, classicists, philologists, and philosophers of herme-
    neutics. A few examples include: Burnyeat (1990), Seeskin (1987), Gadamer
    (1980), Brickhouse and Smith (1994, 2000), Benson (2000), and Clay (2000).
3. That is not to say nothing has been written on Plato's theory of dialogue in the
    Seventh Letter (cf. Kahn, 1996; McDonough, 2013); but compared to discus-
    sions concerning Plato's theory of dialogue drawn from the dialogues them-
    selves, the number is miniscule.

4. Challengers of the *Seventh Letter*'s authenticity must rely on the philosophical content because the style of the letter has already been shown to be consistent with Plato's other texts written around the same time (Morrow, 1929, pp. 44–45; Deane, 1973; Ledger, 1989; Burnyeat & Frede, 2015). Myles Burnyeat argues that the content of the *Seventh Letter* is philosophically incompetent; since Plato was not philosophically incompetent, Burnyeat claims Plato cannot be the author of the *Seventh Letter* (Burnyeat & Frede, 2015, pp. 122–135) This begs the question of whether philosophically competent people always, and every-where express themselves in a philosophically competent way. Michael Frede claims that the *Seventh Letter*, "as often noted, has somewhat the character of an open letter. In any case it certainly is not addressed to philosophers, but to a wider public" (Burnyeat & Frede, 2015, p. 41; see, also, Morrow, 1929, pp. 45–46). Since, according to Frede, the letter is not written to philosophers, it would be natural to expect it to lack just the precision and rigor that it is lacking. Additionally, Burnyeat applies modern notions of analytic rigor to the *Seventh Letter* without acknowledging that over and over again Plato commits errors of analysis throughout his corpus. Of course, most commentators assume that Plato knows that he is making invalid, unsound or not cogent arguments, but has rhetorical purposes for why he makes them. The same could be said for the *Seventh Letter*—even if it were true that the writer made an invalid argument, there is no reason to assume he did so because he is philosophical incompetent.

5. These same two components are necessary for virtue to be present in human beings who are raised correctly. To return to a passage from the *Laws*.

> He may be able to represent, by word and gesture, and with invariable success, his intellectual conception of what is good, even though he gets no pleasure from it and feels no hatred for what is bad. Another man may not be very good at keeping on the right lines when he uses his body and his voice to represent the good, or at trying to form some intellectual concep-tion of it; but he may be very much on the right lines in his feelings of plea-sure and pain, because he welcomes what is good and loathes what is bad.
> (654c-d)

6. Surprisingly, Plato claims that having the fifth level of knowledge does not guar-antee that it cannot be refuted. On the contrary, the minute a person attempts to explain the fifth level of knowledge in words, those words can easily be turned around and twisted so as to undermine the truth that was apprehended (343d). This is why no sensible person would ever try to express their true knowledge in a discursive manner—rather, if she wants to communicate her ideas in writing, it is necessary to write dialogues. Knowledge at levels one through four may be communicated through discursive text, but ultimate knowledge cannot.

7. A small sampling of article length treatments of *Lysis* include: Benjamin A. Rider (2011, pp. 40–41), Tessitore (1990, pp. 115–132), Gonzalez (1995, pp. 69–90), Wolfsdorf (2007, pp. 327–356), Versenyi (1975, pp. 185–198), Tindale (1984, 102–109), Gadamer, (1980, pp. 1–20), Haden (1983, pp. 327–356), and Nich-ols (2009, pp. 152–194). In addition to these and many other article length treatments, there are two contemporary book length interpretations, including Bolotin (1979) and Penner and Rowe (2005).

8. See, for example, *Republic* (614a–621d), *Menexenus* (236d–249c), and *Gor-gias* (523a–527e), where Socrates drops his questioning and lapses into long speeches.

9. This is not only the case for *Lysis* but for many of Plato's dialogues. While it is true that Socrates does also want some type of relationship, it seems through-out the dialogues that it is secondary to knowledge and action. The fact is

that Socrates utilizes a wide variety of pedagogical tools, many of which are manipulative, embarrassing, and absurd. As a consequence, to read him as primarily interested in cultivating a sense of dialogical community (in any morally legitimate sense) is problematic and requires significant explanation.

10. For example, Socrates suggests at 214c that it is "impossible for those who do an injustice and those who suffer it to be friends." This is, of course, untrue. I, for one, have done injustices to my friends, and they have suffered the injustices, without it diminishing our friendship at all. In fact, it has often deepened it.

11. Numerous commentators have highlighted the centrality of Lysis' silence in the passage and in the interpretation of the dialogue as a whole (Gonzalez, 1995, p. 84; Gadamer, 1980, p. 19; Tindale, 1984, pp. 106–107; Bolotin, 1979, pp. 186–187). They all agree that his silence is an indication of some sort of understanding, but just what the understanding amounts to is debated. Gonzalez (1995, p. 84) argues that it is the recognition of the fact that Menexenus (and Hippothales) are false friends, and only Socrates is the true friend. Tindale (1984, p. 106) argues that Lysis' silence is his recognition that true friendship exists when one friend is willing to humble and embarrass another friend—just as Socrates has done to Lysis—so as to help him mature. According to Tindale, Lysis recognizes what Menexenus does not recognize, namely that being humbled by Socrates is an instance of Socrates friendship because it teaches the pursuit of philosophy. As we shall see, our view, however, is the more straightforward reading offered by Gadamer (1980, p. 19) and Bolotin (1979, p. 186), who argue that Lysis' silence represents the recognition that he must befriend his true lover, Hippothales.

12. Up until this point, the two have been univocal in their agreement or disagreement. But here their contrasting responses highlight an internal change. Lysis has recognized something that Menexenus has not. The reader almost feels the epiphany happening.

13. As we have seen, this conclusion is debated among scholars. While Gadamer (1980) and Bolotin (1979) agree that the epiphany is related to the befriending of Hippothales, others disagree. As we will argue shortly, Socrates ultimate hope is not so much that Lysis will become Hippothales sexual lover but that he will begin a pursuit of wisdom and virtue, which begins by developing mature friendships with others and refusing to play the tease with Menexenus.

5 The Socratic Method of Inducing Epiphanies

Introduction

According to Plato it is impossible for any person to become virtuous unless they undergo a thoroughgoing habituation process in which the desires to perform virtuous actions are lined up with an understanding of what constitutes virtue. This understanding cannot come through cognitive means alone. No matter how much rational discussion a person engages in with a student, no matter how much cognitive assent is arrived at, and no matter how much vicious behavior is shown to be inconsistent with happiness, no person will *fully* know what virtue is without this habituation; and therefore such a person cannot be counted on to act virtuously consistently or without failure. The only way to ensure that full knowledge of virtue is achieved is to habituate the person over a long period of time, while simultaneously discussing virtue with them. Only then will the person's desires, dispositions, and cognitive assent be sufficiently aligned to guarantee virtuous behavior.

Aristotle agrees with Plato that habituation is the key to virtue and any person who was not properly habituated would never achieve virtue. Aristotle famously argues for this in the *Nicomachean Ethics*, where he explains how habits form both dispositions and knowledge. But Aristotle stops there. He does not seem to offer the individual any hope if the habituation process is not properly carried out in youth. He claims that if children are not properly habituated in their youth, there is not much to be done for them beyond giving them laws to protect them from living totally depraved lives (*Nicomachean Ethics*, 1103b, 1150b, 1165b).

This view of moral life causes a serious problem. If habituation is required for full virtue to be present, then it would seem that only those individuals who have been properly habituated from their youth have the potential to be virtuous. And yet Plato shows us that there are experiences, which we have called epiphanies, that can call people to virtue. These experiences do not create immediate reformations of the person, such that they necessarily become virtuous—Plato does not think this is possible— rather, they are glimpses of the value of virtue that impel individuals to desire to *rehabituate* themselves. In other words, Plato believes that there is more hope than Aristotle would admit. He believes certain kinds of dialogues can produce a temporary reorientation of individuals' desires such that even if their characters are formed in the wrong direction, their soul's eyes, as it were, can be temporarily opened to such a degree that they can see the inferiority of their current *telos*, and simultaneously see that a better *telos* is possible for them. They can have *epiphanies* regarding the good life and can actively seek to be rehabituated in light of those epiphanies.

The importance and depth of this Platonic solution is clearly seen when taken alongside his cultural critique. Plato believes that Athenian society is so corrupt that there is almost no one that can provide a model of virtuous moral behavior. He claims, "For there isn't now, hasn't been in the past, nor ever will be in the future anyone with a character so unusual that he has been educated to virtue in spite of the contrary education received from the mob" (492e). Plato claims that there have been only a few exceptions to this rule in recent times; people like Socrates and Theages, who for a variety of reasons were protected from the influence of the viciousness of Athenian culture (496a-d). The problem is that, according to Plato, the average Athenian parent does not realize that the only way to produce genuine virtue in his child is to refuse to let the child engage in the aristocratic culture that had traditionally been seen as part and parcel with the child's education in virtue. As their children spend more time engaging in this popular aristocratic culture—in order to develop qualities such as rhetorical ability and political savvy, for example—they become progressively corrupted and vicious. This happens over and over again among the youth of his time, and Plato dramatically depicts the consequences in his dialogues. Sending their children to tutors or sophists only makes matters worse. These teachers lack virtue themselves and thus pass on a taste for vice, even if it is supposedly clothed in the language of virtue.[1]

It may be that it is precisely for this reason that Plato uses the dialogues to provide a way out of this dilemma. He shows us that even if we encounter young adults who were not protected adequately from the influence of Athenian culture, certain kinds of dialogue can reach them when they are older and are, in a sense, more capable of recognizing the dangers of Athenian culture and may voluntarily want to avoid it. Plato seems to be saying that it is better to place our stock in moral epiphanies than moral exemplarism as a means of rehabituation.

In addition to the examples of epiphanies of Dion, Lysis, and Alcibiades discussed in the previous chapters, one central example of such an epiphany in the Platonic corpus is found in the *Republic*, where Glaucon's conception of justice and its relationship to his *telos* is transformed in the space of the dialogue. At the beginning of the dialogue, Glaucon shows himself to be a person philosophically interested in justice, but one who is ultimately committed to a lifestyle of luxury and convenience, even if it means forsaking justice. Yet, by the end of the dialogue, Glaucon is transformed into a person who desires justice and moderation and is willing to spend the rest of his life in pursuit of it. What is noteworthy is that at the end of the dialogue he recognizes that justice requires the strict moderation of his desires, and he gladly accepts that he will have to spend his whole life working to moderate them, even though at the beginning of the dialogue he is totally opposed to the notion that he or anybody should have to moderate any except their most vicious desires.

This impressive turn-around in Glaucon's soul is no accident; Socrates brings this transformation about through the dialogue. Interestingly, the transformation of Glaucon is rarely discussed in the philosophical literature on the *Republic*.[2] Yet as we demonstrate in this chapter, Glaucon's epiphany gives us a powerful paradigm to which educators can look if they are interested in the moral transformation of their students. By examining the way Socrates creates an epiphany in Glaucon, we can draw general educational principles that could help contemporary educators create moral epiphanies in their own students. As we shall see, Socrates uses philosophical, psychological, and pedagogical modes of engagement with Glaucon. First, Socrates has *philosophical* knowledge about the virtue he wants to impart to Glaucon. Second, through the dialogue Socrates gains *psychological* knowledge of the conscious and subconscious barriers that serve to obstruct Glaucon's moral progress. Third, Socrates has a clear and nuanced sense of which *pedagogical* principles will best overcome the psychological barriers that exist in Glaucon. In this chapter, we examine Glaucon's epiphanic experience in the *Republic* and outline Socrates' use of philosophical, psychological, and pedagogical insights to induce an epiphany in Glaucon. We then conclude with some implications for contemporary educators.

The Philosophical Dimension of Inducing Epiphanies

We begin our examination of the transformation of Glaucon's desires by outlining the philosophical dimension of Socrates' engagement with him. As we indicated, the philosophical dimension of inducing an epiphany is based on the teacher's knowledge of the virtue she wants to impart and a recognition that her student lacks the virtue. Epiphanies can happen spontaneously as well, but if a teacher wants to impart a specific virtue, it is best to have philosophical knowledge of what the virtue is and what it would look like for her students to embody it.

We see such knowledge at work in Socrates in the *Republic*. In Book II and following books, Socrates indicates that he knows what the virtue of justice is and believes he can lead Glaucon to knowledge of it. Importantly, not only is Socrates going to help Glaucon discover what justice is at the cognitive level, but Plato tells us through the mouth of Glaucon himself that Socrates is going to help Glaucon see what "power" it has "when it's by itself in the soul" (358b). Glaucon further says:

> Don't, then, give us only a theoretical argument that justice is stronger than injustice, but show what effect each has because of itself on the person who has it—the one for good and the other for bad—whether it remains hidden from gods and human beings or not.

> (367e)

This is exactly what Socrates does, but for this "showing" to be effective it cannot be mere rational argument leading to cognitive assent—it must be a showing that *reveals* the effects of justice on the soul. It must be, in other words, an epiphany if Glaucon is to truly understand justice and its power in the soul. Only then will he get a genuine taste of the existential benefits of justice that remain hidden from most human beings.

It might be argued that we are too quick to claim that Socrates has knowledge of justice in the *Republic*, since he disavows such knowledge in Book I in his discussion with Thrasymachus (337e). Yet the difference between his claim of ignorance in Book I and the knowledge he claims to have in Book II and following should not be overlooked. It is assumed by many that in the early dialogues Socrates is in complete doubt about the virtues he discusses in them, just as he says he is in Book I of the *Republic*. Because of this, many interpreters include Book I in the set of early dialogues. These commentators assume that perhaps Plato wrote Book I as a stand-alone dialogue early in Plato's career and only later appended it to the rest of the *Republic*. While there is no way to determine for sure, it is more plausible that Plato has a clear sense of the virtues in all of the dialogues but for pedagogical reasons chose to allow the early dialogues to end in doubt (Jonas, 2018).

Naturally, how we interpret the doubt expressed in the early dialogues and in Book I of the *Republic*, impacts how we perceive the apparent differences between the dialogues. "Literalist" interpreters who argue that the changes in the dialogues reflect changes in Plato's philosophical outlook have to break the *Republic* into the early (Book I) and late (Book II-X) periods, in order to maintain the literalism they favor. "Pedagogical" interpreters who argue that argumentative changes in the dialogues reflect Plato's pedagogical goals do not need to break the *Republic* into early and middle periods, because they can simply posit that Socrates was employing different pedagogical strategies based on his changing main interlocutors.

The intuitive plausibility of the pedagogical interpretation in the case of the *Republic* is based on the fact that Socrates' dialogue partners change substantially between Books I and II. In Book I, Socrates' claim to ignorance concerning justice is directed at Thrasymachus, who is a well-known sophist, and, in the *Republic* at least, a famously belligerent one. In all of the dialogues with sophists (*Gorgias*, *Protagoras*, *Euthydemus*), Socrates similarly claims ignorance and seems merely interested in undermining the credibility of the sophists' beliefs rather than imparting knowledge of virtue to them. It stands to reason that he takes this tack because he knows that, being sophists, they are not open to persuasion; on the contrary, they have made up their mind about virtue and have made a career out of persuading people that their views are correct. Therefore, Socrates, knowing that he has little hope of persuading the sophists, merely attempts to show that their views of virtue are untenable. It is different, however, with Glaucon. Unlike the sophists, Socrates claims that he trusts Glaucon's soul and believes that Glaucon desires virtue at some level, even though he does not know what it is (367e–368b). The earnestness of Glaucon's search for justice, unlike the sophists, gives Socrates hope that he can induce an epiphany in Glaucon, and so he uses a different pedagogical strategy, one that includes attempting to lead Glaucon to an epiphanic vision of justice.

This leads to the question of whether Socrates has *full* knowledge of virtue, and by extension, whether any teacher wishing to create epiphanies also needs to have full knowledge. The answer is that even though Socrates does not have full knowledge of virtue—which includes the cognitive, affective, and conative—he is still able to induce epiphanies; and it is the same for contemporary educators. It is clear from within the *Republic* and across the dialogues that Socrates does not have full knowledge of virtue. Within the *Republic* itself, Socrates explicitly claims that he does not have full knowledge, which would be knowledge of the source of all virtue (506b, 533a). But, at the same time, he acknowledges that he knows something about the virtues, insofar as they are the offspring of the source of all virtue.[3] And he also believes that, though limited, he knows enough to lead Glaucon to desire the virtues for himself, which is achieved by the end of the dialogue.

In the same way that Socrates does not have full knowledge of virtue, neither must teachers. No person that we have ever met who seemed wise claimed to have full knowledge. They all claim to be on a path towards increasing virtue, and in that sense know some of the differences between virtue and vice, which is what Socrates claims to know throughout all of the dialogues. Teachers who want to create epiphanies regarding virtue in the classroom need to know enough to identify virtue in some forms and vice in some forms, but they do not have to have full knowledge of virtue. However they must have *some* cognitive knowledge of the virtues, *some* affective desire to pursue the virtues, and *some* strength of character to follow through on that pursuit.

The Psychological Dimension of Inducing Epiphanies

Now that Socrates has decided on what virtue he wants to encourage in Glaucon, he now has to assess the barriers to inducing a moral progress.

This is an important next step. Socrates also assessed the psychological barriers that might have impeded his attempt to create an epiphany in Thrasymachus, and decided, like he had with Protagoras, Gorgias, and countless others, that the barriers were so substantial that he ought not to make the attempt. As we mentioned earlier, in these cases, he seems content merely to show these interlocutors that their current way of thinking about the virtues is rationally bankrupt (even though most of them are unwilling to admit this). But Socrates has more hope for Glaucon.

Of course, his hope is tempered by the fact that Glaucon, along with the help of Adeimantus, uses an augmented myth of the ring of Gyges to make a compelling case for the benefits of injustice and the problems with justice. Glaucon's and Adeimantus' use of the myth and the augmentation of it suggests that they are more interested in pursuing their own pleasures and passions even if the rights of others are sacrificed for them to secure their pleasures and passions. However, they are quick to admit that they are not necessarily convinced by these stories and want Socrates to help prove the stories wrong. Glaucon says:

> It isn't, Socrates, that I believe any of that myself. I am perplexed, indeed, and my ears are deafened listening to Thrasymachus and countless others. But I've yet to hear anyone defend justice in the way I want, proving that it is better than injustice. I want to hear justice praised *by itself*, and I think that I am most likely to hear this from you. Therefore, I am going to speak at length praising the unjust life, and in doing so I'll show you the way I want to hear you praising justice and denouncing injustice.
>
> (358c-d)

The fact that Glaucon admits he is not convinced of these arguments suggests that there is an openness in Glaucon, but this does not necessarily mean that he is psychologically ready to accept the demands of virtue. As Howland (2005) observes, Socrates must still gather more information about Glaucon's psychological preparedness for an epiphany.

> Socrates observes that the arguments of Glaucon and Adeimantus, taken by themselves, would suggest that they are partisans of injustice. But he infers otherwise, because he is already familiar with the *tropos*, the "way" of the brothers or the turn of their souls. . . . Yet while Socrates has imaginatively "entered into" their characters and claims to "see through" them, he has no direct acquaintance with their inner natures.
>
> (p. 217)

Therefore, if Socrates is to accomplish his task, he must find a way to assess the deeper state of Glaucon's soul. He claims that he is convinced that at the theoretical and philosophical level Glaucon is a truth seeker who wants to know and do the right thing, but there is still the question of the degree to which subconscious forces are operating in Glaucon—forces which might undermine his ability to have an epiphany. The question is once confronted with the need to sacrifice some of his pleasures for justice, would Glaucon be willing to follow his philosophical convictions, once understood? Socrates gathers this information by drawing Glaucon's attention away from the kind of discussions regarding justice that the myth of the Ring of Gyges presents—which is about dramatic harms and benefits that come by way of personal choices of individuals—and instead focuses on justice in a city.

Famously, Socrates claims that he is shifting his focus because "a city is bigger than a soul," and therefore it will be easier to see justice in it. It has always been head-scratching why Socrates makes this specious argument about size, because the actual size of the object under consideration does not have any bearing on the question, any more than saying that the injustice of an imaginary, full-sized adult stealing an S.U.V. is easier to see than a small person stealing a Mini-Cooper. The question of injustice is not the size of the subject or object, but the action in question and its relationship to the virtue of justice. Because of the weakness of the plausibility of the city-soul analogy, it has been assumed by some that he was merely using it as an excuse to get to what he was ultimately interested in—but it is at least as likely (and even more likely as we will show shortly) that he was doing it for pedagogical reasons. What seems to be going on is that the metaphor of the city will help Socrates establish the condition of Glaucon's soul. When claiming that the city is easier to see than the soul, he is speaking more about his own seeing of Glaucon's soul than the idea that he actually thinks the size of a city makes it easier to see the inner workings of the soul. Under the literalist view, when Socrates claims that justice in a city will be easier to see because of its size, he actually thinks that the size of the object matters. While there is no way to prove that Socrates does not hold this untenable view, it seems far more consistent with Socrates' intelligence and argumentative sophistication to think that there may be a pedagogical reason for making the claim. Glaucon's vision is directed towards the city—and whether he would want to live in this city. This is pedagogically clever of Socrates because it allows Glaucon to talk honestly about the city without realizing (until it is too late) that what is actually being talked about is his own soul.

What comes then of Socrates' psychological inquiry into the state of Glaucon's soul? Socrates learns that while Glaucon is philosophically interested in living a just life, he is not *affectively* invested in living a just life; Glaucon is, in fact, so caught up with the luxuries and bodily pleasures he has come to enjoy in Athenian culture that he is instinctively unwilling to forgo those, even if doing so leads to a more just life.

How does Socrates come to this knowledge? He does so through the invention of a simple city in which inhabitants each perform their own job and trade their resources with others. Early in Book II of the *Republic* (370c–372d), Socrates briefly depicts a city where each inhabitant contributes to the welfare of all by carrying out the role for which each is naturally suited. Citizens of the city are happy and content, having all their basic needs met and enjoying simple pleasures in peace and safety. Socrates calls this city the "true city" and the "healthy one." But, crucially, Glaucon objects, calling this city a "city for pigs." He does so because it lacks the luxuries and conveniences to which he has grown accustomed. Socrates responds by claiming that it is not a "healthy" city that Glaucon desires, but instead a "feverish" and "luxurious" one. The reason Glaucon rejects the first city is because

> It seems that you make your people feast without any delicacies, Glaucon interrupted. . . . If you were founding a city for pigs, Socrates, he replied, wouldn't you fatten them on the same diet?" "Then how should I feed these people, Glaucon?" I asked. "In the conventional way. If they aren't to suffer hardship, they should recline on proper couches, dine at a table, and have the delicacies and desserts that people have nowadays."
>
> (372d)

The city that Glaucon and Socrates settle on is one that includes prostitutes, acquisitive war, lawsuits between citizens, gluttonous eating habits, the endless acquisition of money, and so on; all of these things Socrates claims are characteristic of a city with a "fever." Moreover, he clearly indicates that having them will create immoderation in citizens, the deterioration of their physical health, and the increase of war with neighboring cities. Socrates summarizes the effects of all these vices by claiming that together they stem "from those same desires that are most of all responsible for the bad things that happen to cities and the individuals in them" (372e–373e). Rather than flinch at these ill results, or even express hesitation, Glaucon unreservedly accepts them. Socrates, registers surprise at first (372d), but seeing that Glaucon believes that these pleasures are essential to human life, Socrates proceeds to describe the feverish city, which eventually becomes the *kallipolis*.

Importantly for our thesis, in acquiescing to Glaucon's desires for the luxurious city, Socrates claims that creating such a city "may not be a bad idea, for by examining it, we might very well see how justice and injustice grow up in cities" (372e). Socrates' hope is that by juxtaposing justice and injustice, Glaucon will be able to better see justice in the soul. On the pedagogical interpretation, Socrates realizes that in spite of Glaucon's cognitive openness to justice, he is psychologically unable to give up a desire for luxury and bodily pleasure even when faced with the injustices that will issue from it.

Socrates therefore recognizes that a new tack must be taken if he is to help Glaucon see the desirability of justice. And this leads us to the pedagogical dimension of inducing epiphanies in students. Socrates has, through questioning, ascertained the psychological barriers that will impede Glaucon's epiphany—namely, that Glaucon is obsessed with luxuries, bodily pleasures, and conveniences—and now it is up to Socrates to find a pedagogical way to overcome these barriers. The way he comes up with is to create the *kallipolis*, the city at the center of the *Republic* that has been so often misinterpreted as the ultimate statement of Plato's political theory.[4]

The Pedagogical Dimension of Inducing Epiphanies

In order for Socrates' strategy to work with Glaucon, he must find a way to lead Glaucon to an epiphany without going directly at Glaucon's immoderate desires. Socrates claims that when people have obstinate opinions that are not based in truth, they sometimes get angry and need to be soothed to learn the truth.

> What if the person who has opinion but not knowledge is angry with us and disputes the truth of what we are saying? Is there some way to console him and persuade him gently, while hiding from him that he isn't in his right mind?
>
> (476d-e)

Ironically, when Socrates asks this question, Glaucon does not realize that this is precisely what is happening to him; having been angry about the lack of luxuries in the city of pigs, Socrates is consoling him and gently persuading him. And, further, Socrates describes what happens when someone tries to teach virtue to an otherwise noble young man (which is what Glaucon is) who has no understanding of virtue. Even if this hypothetical young man is "drawn to philosophy because of his noble nature," Socrates claims he will initially be unconvinced.

> And if someone approaches a young man in that condition and gently tells the truth, namely, that there's no understanding in him, that he needs it, and that it can't be acquired unless he works like a slave to attain it, do you think it will be easy for him to listen when he's in the midst of so many evils?
>
> (494d)

Again, Glaucon agrees, not realizing that this fact about human beings is a fact about him.

Taking his own advice, Socrates is willing to try to help Glaucon see his lack of understanding by "persuading" Glaucon "gently" by using the image and metaphor of justice in a city, which begins with the shape of injustice in a luxurious city, and the effects of that injustice on the citizens of that city.

To begin, Socrates describes the need for prostitutes, jewelry, beauticians, and chefs to cook and bake delicacies. All of this does not sound immoral (except, perhaps, for the prostitutes), but Socrates immediately claims that while not immoral in themselves, these desires have an impact on the health of the citizens. He says, "And if we live like that, we'll have a far greater need for doctors than we did before," to which Glaucon agrees. Then Socrates asserts that they will need more land, because their small city will not be large enough to create these luxuries.

> Then we'll have to seize some of our neighbors' land if we're to have enough pasture and ploughland. And won't our neighbors want to seize part of ours as well, if they too have surrendered themselves to the endless acquisition of money and have overstepped the limits of their necessities.
>
> (373b-e)

Glaucon replies that "That's completely inevitable, Socrates" (373b-e).

Here we see confirmation of Glaucon's own immoderate desires. The fact that he can easily and enthusiastically justify an "endless acquisition of money" even if it means killing people for it through war suggests that Socrates is right that Glaucon will need time to come to see that there is something wrong with his soul. This becomes even more obvious when a few lines later Socrates says that the desires which lead to war are also "responsible for the bad things that happen to cities and the individuals in them." From here Socrates creates a warrior-class who will eventually become the guardians, both the auxiliaries and the philosopher-kings.

At this point, Glaucon's psychological unwillingness to moderate his desires is clear. But as Socrates starts to fill out the details of the *kallipolis* he begins the process of overcoming the psychological barriers in Glaucon. At a critical moment in Book IV, Socrates introduces the political danger of immoderation with respect to luxury and bodily desires. Socrates claims that the city they are creating must not be either rich or poor, for both will lead to corruption. This should afront Glaucon's desires because, as we saw, he insisted on a rich and luxurious city. Adeimantus immediately protests by reminding Socrates that a rich city was what he and Glaucon desire. Socrates responds by appealing to a passion in both Glaucon and Adeimantus that he thinks is stronger than their desire for pleasure: the desire for honor through strength and courage. Socrates claims that in the *kallipolis* that those bred for war "will easily be able to fight twice or three times their own numbers in a war" (322d). As many commentators have pointed out, Glaucon and Adeimantus are known for their love of manly honor, and by appealing to honor, Socrates is able to subtly undermine their insistence on luxuries and bodily pleasures being the ultimate necessity in a city. Socrates argues that the *kallipolis* must not be rich because wealth makes citizens hedonistic and self-centered; money and luxury make them soft. This is anathema to Glaucon and Adeimantus. Socrates claims that if the city is not rich but has enough of what it needs, it will be the strongest and most powerful city.

> And as long as your own city is moderately governed in the way that we have just arranged, it will, even if it has only a thousand men to fight for it, be the greatest. Not in reputation; I don't mean that, but the greatest in fact. Indeed, you won't find a city as great as this one among either the Greeks or the barbarians, although many that are many times its size may seem to be as great.
>
> (423a)

In his willingness to accept this point, Glaucon has gone from the view that luxury and bodily pleasure are the highest good; instead, strength and manly courage becomes the highest pleasure, which the *kallipolis* has in abundance.

The next move that Socrates makes is to take the lesson Glaucon learned through the *kallipolis* and expand it to other city-states. This is an important next move because it, again, allows Glaucon to come to see the desirability of justice in a city without directly contradicting his own personal desires for those pleasures that make justice in a city impossible. In Socrates' description of the *kallipolis*, he makes it clear that the central virtue of the city is that "moderation spreads throughout the whole" (431e). Unfortunately, the moderation of the producers is much less moderate than the guardians—they are allowed to indulge their appetitive desires—but as a whole the city avoids the wealth or poverty that would lead to the internal and external destruction of the city. Socrates emphasizes this moderation over and over again, and Glaucon continually agrees with him. This mantra-like refrain works like a kind of habituation principle in the dialogue and begins to impact Glaucon's outlook. This verbal habituation pays dividends in Book VIII when Socrates turns Glaucon's attention to cities that do not have moderation at their core. Socrates outlines these cities and shows their devolution, with the first climax coming with democracy, in which the city becomes a multicolored and seemingly beautiful paradise where every person gets to choose their own way of life (560d–562a). But unfortunately, what ends up developing in such a city is chaos, with every person being absorbed in pleasure and caprice. But democracy gives way to something even worse: tyranny—a person who has given themselves and the city over to extreme desire for luxury and bodily pleasures and makes citizens of the city suffer.

> What is the beginning of the transformation from leader of the people to tyrant? Isn't it clear that it happens when the leader begins to behave

like the man in the story told about the temple of the Lycean Zeus in Arcadia?. . . . Then doesn't the same happen with a leader of the people who dominates a docile mob and doesn't restrain himself from spilling kindred blood: He brings someone to trial on false charges and murders him (as tyrants so often do), and, by thus blotting out a human life, his impious tongue and lips taste kindred citizen blood. He banishes some, kills others. . . . And because of these things, isn't a man like that inevitably fated either to be killed by his enemies or to be transformed from a man to a wolf by becoming a tyrant?

(565e–566a)

Socrates description is vivid, and it has a significant impact on Glaucon: his disgust at the tyrannical figure is strong, even though the figure is a magnification of Glaucon's own tyrannical desire for luxury and pleasure that he expressed at the beginning of the dialogue. The mythical image is bringing Glaucon to an epiphany that cannot be ignored. Glaucon's repulsion has become visual and visceral. He has discovered, just like he prophetically hoped he would discover, the "power" injustice has "when it's by itself in the soul" (358b). With the power of injustice revealed, and Glaucon's repulsion to it, Socrates now only has to show that this is what happens to a soul that lacks moderation. At first the person is just a democratic soul who seeks to satisfy seemingly innocuous desires for delicacies, prostitutes, couches and the like, but he will slowly become a tyrannical man.

It remains, I said, to consider the tyrannical man himself, how he evolves from a democrat, what he is like when he comes into being, and whether he is wretched or blessedly happy. . . . Some of our unnecessary pleasures and desires seem to me to be lawless. They are probably present in everyone, but they are held in check by the laws and the better desires in alliance with reason. . . . [But when the desires are no longer restrained by reason] then the beastly and savage part, full of food and drink, casts off sleep and seeks to find a way to gratify itself. . . . And when the other desires—filled with incense, myrrh, wreaths, wine and the other pleasures found in their company—buzz around the drone, nurturing it and making it grow as large as possible, they plant the sting of longing in it. Then this leader of the soul adopts madness as its bodyguard and becomes frenzied. If it finds any beliefs or desires in the man that are thought to be good or that still have some shame, it destroys them and throws them out, until it's purged him of moderation and filled him with imported madness.

(571a–573b)

The madness to which Socrates is referring directly harkens back to the first city and its emphasis on moderation. In the first "healthy" city, Socrates uses the exact same pleasures—myrrh, wreaths and wine—to claim that they are appropriate and good. And indeed they are. But in the image of the tyranni-cal man even these pleasures become corrupted and will lead him into even further madness. The only way that simple pleasures can be good is if they are found in a soul that values and promotes moderation as an indispensable virtue. Socrates' reference back to the first city is the closest he has come in a couple hundred pages to directly confront Glaucon's earlier immoderation. But he takes the risk because he senses that an epiphany is happening in Glaucon and it is time for Glaucon to want moderation for himself.

The climax of the epiphany is all that is left, and that will come about as Socrates finally produces his positive vision of justice in the soul and is able to speak directly to Glaucon about the necessity for him to adopt the vision. He wants to create a desire in Glaucon to "internalize the ideal of virtue as a 'city of himself (592a7—that is he should internalize in his soul the structure pictured in the ideal city" (Annas, 1999, p. 81). To do this he starts by asking Glaucon whether the tyrannical city and the tyrannical man are unfree and unhappy. Socrates asks the question: "First, speaking of the city, would you say that a tyrannical city is free or enslaved?" To which Glaucon does not just give a "yes or no" answer; rather, he exclaims in no uncertain terms: "It is enslaved as could possibly be." This answer is strong and definitive and provides evidence that the insight is his own and not that he is merely agreeing with Socrates. This leads to Socrates' next question in which he explicitly compares the city and the soul:

> Then, if a man and a city are alike, mustn't the same structure be in him too? And mustn't his soul be full of slavery and unfreedom, with the most decent parts enslaved and with a small part, the maddest and most vicious, as their master?

Glaucon replies that "It must." To drive the point home, Socrates then poses the final question: "What will you say about such a soul then? Is it free or slave?" Glaucon again definitively responds by saying "Slave, of course" (577d-c).

The fact that Socrates does not merely ask "yes or no" questions, here, but rather he demands that Glaucon take a stand is important as it gives Socrates information about how deeply Glaucon understands the epiph-any. Later on, Glaucon uses definite language when asked similar ques-tions. He responds with statements like: "That's exactly what he's like, Socrates, and what you say is absolutely true" (579d); and "That's easy. I rank them in virtue and vice, in happiness and its opposite in the order of their appearance, as I must judge courses" (580b).

Glaucon's complete turn-around in his views about the need of luxury and bodily pleasures for himself and other citizens is further seen a little later in the dialogue:

> Therefore those who have no experience of reason or virtue, but are always occupied with feasts and the like, are brought down and then

back up to the middle, as it seems, and wander in this way throughout their lives, never reaching beyond this to what is truly higher up at it or being brought up to it, and so they aren't filled with that which really is and never taste any stable or pure pleasure. Instead, they always look down at the ground like cattle, and, with their heads bent over the dinner table, the feed, fatten, and fornicate. . . . [Glaucon replies] Socrates, you've exactly described the life of the majority of people, just like an oracle.

(586a-b)

Glaucon's final statement is poetically ironic in two ways: the first is that Socrates' description of people without moderation and virtue is almost identical to Glaucon's reasons why the city of pigs should be rejected because the people in that city, Glaucon claims, shouldn't have to "suffer hardship . . . [and] should recline on proper couches, dine at a table, and have the delicacies and desserts that people have nowadays" (372d). Socrates likens these people to cattle which is reminiscent of Glaucon's reference to pigs. What is ironic is that Glaucon had earlier objected to the first city because he believed it depicted a way of life that only animals would be satisfied with, but now he believes that a way of life that includes luxuries and an absorption of bodily pleasures is a life fit only for animals. This complete about face is striking. The second poetic irony is that in calling Socrates an oracle, Glaucon has aptly described Socrates' quasi-divine ability to bring about an epiphany without Glaucon being aware that it is happening. Glaucon's turnaround is now complete and it does seem almost miraculous that the change is so complete.

Through the construction of the *kallipolis*, Glaucon comes to understand justice, and affirms it as something that should be authoritative in his life. He is purged of his fever, at least temporarily. This is seen towards the end of the dialogue when Socrates summarizes what he and his interlocutors have learned from the *kallipolis* (618c–619a). Instead of an encomium on the beauty, virtue, and justice found in the *kallipolis* (which is what we might expect after constructing a just city), Socrates backs away from any talk of the *kallipolis* whatsoever. Instead he ends with an exhortation to take what they have learned from the dialogue and apply it to their lives. Socrates claims that they must

learn those [subjects] that will enable him to distinguish the good life from the bad and always to make the best choice possible in every situation. He should think over all the things we have mentioned and how they jointly and severally determine what the virtuous life is like. That way he will know what the good and bad effects of beauty are when it is mixed with wealth, poverty, and a particular state of the soul. . . . And from all this he will be able, by considering the nature of the soul, to reason out which life is better and which life is worse and to choose accordingly.

(618c–619a)

The change in Glaucon has not been significantly appreciated in the secondary literature. The *Republic* begins with Socrates insisting that pleasure does not lead to ultimate happiness and that living a life of justice does, and then he ends the dialogue with the same discussion—the only difference being that at the beginning of the dialogue, Glaucon is opposed to this view, but by the end of the dialogue he is in complete agreement. What has happened in between? The *kallipolis* has been constructed, and in the construction Glaucon's perspective changes. Ironically, this is exactly what we *should* expect, considering that Socrates explicitly claims that the fundamental point of creating the *kallipolis* was to reveal justice in the soul. The fact that Glaucon now understands (at the cognitive and affective level) that justice in the soul is a function of moderation, we should not be surprised that Socrates drops all discussion of the *kallipolis* from the later chapters. The *kallipolis* has fulfilled its purpose and since Socrates never once suggested that it was meant to fulfill any other purpose, there is no reason to continue to discuss it. The fact that this later silence regarding the *kallipolis* is almost universally ignored in the philosophical literature speaks to the intractability of the standard view that the *Republic* is primarily a political document in which Plato seeks to express his totalitarian views about the need for the absolute political authority of philosophers and for the deferential obedience of the average human being. In light of the transformation of Glaucon's cognitive and affective understanding of justice, and in light of the fact that Glaucon explicitly asked Socrates to help him come to that understanding (358c-d), it seems bizarre, at the very least, that these facts are so often ignored and that the *raison d'etre* of the *kallipolis* is still so often assumed to be Plato's intention to construct an ideal political philosophy.

The question now becomes whether Glaucon is permanently transformed by the epiphany he has received. The answer is a decisive "no." As Howland (2014) has argued, Plato picked the character of Glaucon specifically to communicate that Glaucon's transformation is *not* permanent. Glaucon has without doubt had a dramatic epiphany and it has led to a transformation of his desires, but, sadly, Glaucon famously went on to commit unjust acts against Athens. Just like the epiphany and seeming transformation of Alcibiades in *Alcibiades I*, Glaucon is only temporarily transformed. This is exactly what we should expect since Plato believes the only way individuals can become truly virtuous is for them to undergo a long habituation process whereby virtue becomes part of the fabric of individuals' souls. For Glaucon (or Alcibiades, or anybody else) to be permanently transformed, he would need to undergo a rehabituation process. Both Glaucon and Alcibiades claim that they are willing to be rehabituated after having their epiphanies, but in real life, neither of these individuals remained committed to the rehabituation process, and therefore the epiphany grew dimmer and dimmer until they fell headlong into a vicious lifestyle.

Conclusion

As we indicated at the beginning of this chapter, Plato believes a person's conception of what is worth striving for can be dramatically altered through a pedagogical encounter. While Aristotle and Plato are correct that a permanent change in a person's moral development can only occur through a habituation process, Plato has shown us that people can experience epiphanies, which can, at the very least, temporarily change their conception of what constitutes the good life and can inspire them to seek out habituation in the right direction. Glaucon's epiphany in the *Republic* serves as an example to contemporary educators if they want to produce these potentially life-altering epiphanies. First, it seems important that the teacher has a clear sense of which virtue they want to inculcate in their students. This means that, ideally, the teacher would already be virtue-seeking and already have substantial (although incomplete) knowledge of virtue. It also seems like it would be helpful for the teacher to have a passion, like Socrates does, to see her students become virtuous themselves. Second, a teacher's ability to uncover the psychological obstacles that stand in the way of her students' epiphany will greatly assist the teacher in generating epiphanies. This is especially difficult in contemporary teaching contexts where the teacher may instruct up to 150 students a day. Nevertheless, it seems possible (although difficult) that a teacher could, through probing questions, informal discussion, formal Socratic dialogues, and so on, begin to sense what those barriers are. Third, once a teacher understands the barriers, it seems important to be able to devise indirect means of overcoming those barriers to produce an epiphany. This is, of course, easier said than done; but it can be done, as Socrates has shown us. We have also seen it done by teachers on numerous occasions. Watching other teachers who excel in this is a great way to learn. Even imaginary depictions of teachers who produce epiphanies can be helpful. In any event, it seems clear that the more the philosophical, psychologically, and pedagogically astute the teacher is, the more likely she is to produce epiphanies in her students. She will likely need to be able to make split-second decisions on how to adjust tactics and move discussions in the right way. Finally, once the epiphany is achieved, Plato reminds us that the student's transformation has only just begun, and for it to continue, she will need to find a community in which she can start a rehabituation process. While difficult, teachers can help in this process by getting to know their students, and ascertaining the significance of the epiphany, and, in dialogue with the students, help them decide for themselves how to find or develop such a community. Students want to flourish; they just do not know what it looks like because many aspects of popular culture are intent on leading them towards inferior kinds of flourishing. The use of epiphanies can help students start on a different path of flourishing, the kind that ends in *eudaimonia*.

In the second part of this book, we take the ideas gleaned from Plato regarding the role that habituation and epiphanic experiences play in the moral development of human beings and move on to an analysis of how his ideas could be applied in contemporary democratic classrooms. In Chapter 6, we explore the ways teachers can produce epiphanies in their students, and in Chapter 7, we explore the ways teachers can help encourage students in a rehabituation process.

Notes

1. Of course, it could be, and has been argued, that Plato provides a method for dealing with the corrupting influences of Athenian society—namely, the creation of the ideal state found in the *kallipolis* in which all the genuinely gifted students are separated from popular culture and habituated in the virtues. The education of these leaders lasts a lifetime and is, under the strictures of the educational regime set up in the *kallipolis*, protected from the corrupting influences of the rabble. However, not only is this education not possible because the ideal political arrangement he proposes is not realistic, it is not actually the political arrangement he has any intention of trying to realize. The story of the *kallipolis* is meant to demonstrate the educational principles that must form the foundation of a habituation process if it is ever to succeed, but not to provide a systematic plan of action for realizing a perfect educational system.

   As we have argued throughout this book, Plato chooses to make his case using dramatic dialogues, which has caused a great deal of confusion (especially in the last century or so) about how to interpret his thought. In particular, for the last 100 years or so, it has been assumed that the dramatic dialogues that Plato wrote are best understood as his idiosyncratic way of laying out a line by line systematic political, ethical, or educational theory. Put differently, the fact that they are dramatic should largely be ignored and interpreters should assume that the interpreters job is to determine which of the interlocutors statements which literally represented Plato's actual thought and then build a system connecting those statements with a other statements by the same interlocutor, which must also, necessarily, and literally, represent Plato's actual beliefs.

   This anachronistic reading causes the sorts of problems we outlined in the introduction, and, in any event, it ignores the far more straightforward reading of Plato; that Plato is using the drama of the dialogue to cause the reader to have certain experiences. And it is these experiences that we believe are central to how Plato is applicable to the contemporary classroom. The dialogues themselves allow us to see the method by which we can jump start the (re)habituation process.

2. Two noteworthy exceptions to this are Gallagher (2004) and Howland (2018, 2014). Both of these interpreters recognize that the transformation of Glaucon is the most significant aspect of the *Republic*, and they both acknowledge that the effect of the dialogue on Glaucon is usually overlooked. Importantly, Howland's exegetical perspective shifts over time. In his early work he was more optimistic that an enduring change had occurred in Glaucon, but in his later work he argues that Plato intentionally uses the figure of Glaucon—who famously became a tyrant and failed to live a just life—to show that the apparent transformation of

Glaucon was *not* enduring. We think that Howland is right on both accounts. As we shall show in this chapter, Glaucon does receive a profound epiphany that temporarily reorients his conception of justice and the role it plays in his life. But, because of Plato's belief that only rehabituation can make the epiphanies permanent, he uses the figure of Glaucon as an example of what happens if we only induce epiphanies in our students without helping them to find a community in which they can undergo a rehabituation process.

3. It is the same with all of the so-called "early dialogues." In those dialogues Socrates makes many knowledge claims regarding virtue and attempts to persuade many of his interlocutors to follow his example. See, for example, *Crito* (47b-d), *Gorgias* (526d–527e), *Apology* (30b), *Laches* (200c–201a). These are only a few of the countless virtue claims he makes. The inconsistency in Socrates' claims about being completely ignorant of virtue and also that he has knowledge of virtue has bothered commentators, and as a consequence many have tried to reconcile Socrates' claims by appealing to different kinds of knowledge. Vlastos (1985, pp. 11–18), for example, makes the distinction between "elenctic knowledge" and "certain knowledge"; Reeve (1989, pp. 37–53) and Woodruff (1992, pp. 90–91) make the distinction between "non-expert knowledge" and "expert knowledge"; McPherran (1992, pp. 230–231) makes the distinction between "fallible human knowledge" and "infallible divine knowledge"; and Brickhouse and Smith (1994, pp. 38–45; 2000, pp. 108–109) make the distinction between "knowing that" and "knowing why"—a distinction that they rightly claim is elaborated in Aristotle. Brickhouse and Smith argue that Socrates believes that it is possible to know *that* something is true, without knowing *why* or *how* it is true.

> We have already explained why we do not believe that Socrates' profession of ignorance disclaims merely knowing that some statement about right and wrong is true. In this case, Socrates is saying that he does not know *how it is* that the claim for which he has such good arguments is true; he does not have the sort of knowledge by which he could *explain* the proposition's truth and by which he would qualify as an expert concerning such issues. He only has good reason to think *that* his conviction is true.
>
> (Brickhouse & Smith, 1994, p. 39)

And

> Without a suitable understanding of the nature of justice, then, Socrates is not in a position to explain *why* it is that it is better, for example, to suffer than to do injustice. But *that* it is better may be demonstrated by repeated (and adamantine) elenctic arguments. So Socrates may know that suffering is better than doing evil without knowing *how it is* that this is true.
>
> (Brickhouse & Smith, 1994, p. 40)

On their view, the knowledge that Socrates has is a genuine form of knowledge—a kind that he can confidently assert—but it is not the *full* knowledge that would be required to offer a robust explanation of the knowledge. Brickhouse and Smith (1994, p. 38) further argue that the distinction that Socrates employs was one that was likely present in Ancient Greek culture, which is why none of Socrates' interlocutors called him to task for his seeming inconsistency; because they all understood the distinction, they did not find it odd that Socrates used it.

However we construe Socrates' inconsistencies, what is clear is that he does not have either full knowledge of virtue, nor does he lack knowledge of virtue altogether. Thus, the pedagogical strategy he uses with Thrasymachus of claiming he lacks knowledge of justice is true, while the pedagogical strategy he uses with Glaucon of claiming that he has knowledge of justice is also true.

4. That is not to say that Plato does not offer some politically relevant views in the *Republic*. In fact, it could be argued that he does articulate his preferred political arrangement in the *Republic*, but that preferred arrangement is not the *kallipolis*—the city that dominates much of the dialogue—but the first, simple city outlined in Book II, which Socrates calls the "true" and "healthy" city. Socrates never offers such praise for the *kallipolis*. He never praises the *kallipolis* because it contains injustices that the first city does not. The *kallipolis* is founded on the principles of acquisitive war, the giving in to appetitive desires, the need for potential lawsuits, and the promotion of unhealthy eating habits (373b–374a); all of these are the hallmarks of a city whose citizens lack moderation and justice.

Of course, it might be claimed that though the city was founded on these principles, Plato eventually purges the city of injustice and it becomes a fully just city. This is true insofar as the city eventually meets the formal requirement of justice—that each part does its own job—but the injustice that is done away with is not the injustice found in acquisitive war, appetitive desires, potential lawsuits, and poor eating habits. Although there are limits that protect them from going to extremes, the auxiliaries still go to war to protect and acquire wealth (537a), the class of producers are still encouraged to give in to their appetitive desires (465b–466c), are given provisions to sue one another in court (464d-e; 405a-b), and still eat unhealthy meals (404e–405b), to name just a few behaviors that Plato believes are vicious and conducive of unhappiness. Moreover, these individuals are never given an education that would help them develop the virtues to overcome these vices. They are given laws that prevent them from indulging in these vices to extreme degrees (465b), but they are given opportunities and even encouraged to live lives rooted in the satisfaction of unnecessary desires.

It is different in the first city, in which citizens eat healthy, live peacefully and moderately, and have no need to sue one another or increase their material wealth or acquire more land. This is why Socrates calls it the true and healthy city, and why it makes sense to think that it is Plato's preferred political arrangement.

6 Inducing Epiphanies in Contemporary Classrooms

Introduction

In this chapter, we will take the insights gained from examining Plato's theory of moral education and apply them to contemporary classrooms in pluralistic democracies. As we discussed in our introduction, on the standard interpretation, Plato's views on moral education would seem to be poor candidates for Western pluralistic classrooms. He is usually assumed to have and implausible *intellectualist* epistemology, an extravagant *dualist* metaphysics, and an elitist *totalitarian* political philosophy. Because of these views, it seems unrealistic at best, and dangerous at worst, to use him as a guide for moral education. However, as we have seen in the last five chapters, these interpretations of Plato's philosophy are largely false or greatly exaggerated. Nevertheless, even if our interpretation is correct, there is still the problem of how applicable his views are in contemporary classrooms which have twenty to forty students in them and are made up of students from an increasingly diverse set of backgrounds. Plato's views on the cultivation of virtue in human beings are rich, provocative and suggestive—especially for how teachers might jumpstart a desire for virtue in otherwise disinterested and poorly habituated students, and how, after jumpstarting them in this way, teachers can lead students on a path of rehabituation. Unfortunately, all of the examples Plato offers us are informal conversations between Socrates or Plato and one or two aristocratic Greek young men. Is the transformation of students into virtue-seeking young people that Plato recommends possible in contemporary school settings? Can epiphanies be generated and rehabituation fostered in contemporary times between one teacher and a class full of students? We believe the answer to both questions is yes.

To show how teachers can do this we first explore the nature and characteristics of epiphanies in greater depth. The kinds of epiphanies we are interested in are life-altering or trajectory-reorienting moral experiences in which students actively want to live differently after having them. We distinguish these from more ordinary aha moments. While aha moments are often educationally significant, we are interested in the more profound, and therefore rarer, moral experiences found in epiphanies of the kinds Socrates interlocutors have.

After exploring the nature and characteristics of epiphanies in more detail, we focus on the fundamental ineffability of epiphanies. As Kahn (1996) drew our attention to, Plato has sometimes been accused of mysticism because he claims that knowledge of virtue is in some respect ineffable. We have argued that though epiphanies are fundamentally ineffable, they are not mystical because they are still capable of being understood without positing a transcendent being or realm. It is quite common for people to experience moments of epiphanies—perhaps regarding something of beauty, or a moment of awe, or an uplifting experience—that they find it difficult to explain after it is over. They cannot quite explain why the thing was beautiful, or awesome, or uplifting. Of course, they can give a rough approximation of the experience, or use metaphors that gesture to what the experience was like, but ultimately language bottoms out and they cannot fully explain what they experienced. Later, we examine this fundamental incommunicability in greater detail. There are things a teacher can say that can help bring epiphanies about in students, but she cannot fully lay out the epiphany for the students using words, arguments, reasoning, metaphors and so on.

After exploring the nature and characteristics of epiphanies and the limits of language to help create them, we examine three general methods teachers can use in inducing them. The first method is where the teacher induces epiphanies by having students *perform* certain actions inside or outside the classroom—actions that reveal the virtues the teacher hopes to help her students see. This method implicitly acknowledges the ineffability of epiphanies and largely avoids explaining them. The next method also avoids attempting to explain the epiphanies, but in this instance the teacher attempts to *show* the students the value of the virtues in question. She shows the students the values by exemplifying the virtues in her actions in the classroom. This does not mean that the teacher does a single virtuous action which is performed merely to show the students what the virtue looks like. Rather, the teacher continually embodies the virtues in the classroom on a daily basis. The emphasis in this method is not on the verbal explanations of the virtue that the teacher gives to the students, but on how she conducts herself. Naturally, she will not be completely silent about what she is doing in the class, but her explanations will usually not be directly about the virtues. The third method of inducing epiphanies when the teacher attempts to *tell* the students what the epiphany is she is hoping to induce in them. At first glance, it might appear to undermine our claim about the ineffability of epiphanies, but, as we will see, the teacher uses words to draw attention to certain features of the experience—features with words associated with them that are only verbal *approximations* of the experience she hopes his students will have. A teacher can say that acting justly is beautiful, and she can even give reasons why she believes it to be beautiful, but to the student who does not see justice as beautiful her words will have no effect. Only an epiphany of the beauty of justice will do—an epiphany that can be partially mediated by words, but not fully.

The Nature and Characteristics of Epiphanies

Before discussing the ways contemporary teachers might induce epiphanies in formal educational settings, it will be helpful if we first discuss epiphanies in a little more detail. For our purposes, the word "epiphany" is used to mark a realization of profound significance, so profound that at the time it is happening, the person may think of the experience as a life-altering or trajectory-reorienting event.[1] This is in contrast to the more mundane "aha moments," as when a person realizes that she has been pronouncing a word incorrectly her whole lives, or that the reason a person has views about parenting different from her spouse is because of a particular experience she had when he was a child, or the realization that rain is actually produced by small particles of dust in clouds that water vapor condenses around. There is little doubt that aha moments can and do routinely happen in contemporary classrooms and that they are important. But what we want to consider is the possibility of epiphanies (in the more profound sense) happening in the classroom, especially moral epiphanies.

By and large, the concept of epiphany has remained outside the purview of educational theorists throughout most of the twentieth century.[2] From Kohlberg through the present time, there has been very little systematic research done on the significance of moral epiphanies in the classroom. There has been a smattering of articles written on "epiphanies," but usually these discussions are limited to aha moments (Hernandez-Santamaria, 2006; McCormack, 2015). Previously, the morally profound epiphanies that Plato suggests are possible—and the ones we are concerned about in this book—have received less attention. Recently, however, there has been a trickle of interest in these trajectory-reorienting epiphanies in particular, there have been in-depth articles and book chapters on morally significant epiphanies in the work of Taylor (1989), Aldridge (2013), Jonas (2015, 2018), Kristjánsson (2016, 2020), Yacek and Ijaz (2019), Yacek (2020), Yacek and Gary (2020), and Gary and Chambers (forthcoming). Each of these investigations yield slightly different insights about the educational significance of epiphanies, but they all take seriously the fact that the phenomenon can be life-altering. Of them, the most helpful for our purposes, is Kristjánsson's (2020) most recent work found in his book *Flourishing as the Aim of Education: A Neo-Aristotelian view*.

Kristjánsson's views are relevant to our discussion in two ways. The first relates to the neo-Aristotelian outlook that Kristjánsson's work embodies. Kristjánsson has arguably done more than any single author in the twenty-first century in bringing a neo-Aristotelian educational framework to bear

on contemporary educational discourse. He has been at the forefront of
the neo-Aristotelian revival of moral and character education. From our
point of view, this movement has made a central contribution to understanding how to cultivate virtue in contemporary schools. However—and
this brings us to the relevance of Kristjánsson's new book to our book—
Kristjánsson admits that his interest in epiphanies stems from their potential to provides a means of moral growth in those who have not received
a proper, i.e., virtue-inducing upbringing. (Kristjánsson, 2020, p. 116). As
we indicated earlier, Aristotle is utterly pessimistic about the possibility of
morally reforming badly habituated people.[3] To his credit, Kristjánsson
finds this to be an oversight of Aristotle's and spends an entire chapter of
his book defending the anti- or extra-Aristotelian concept of epiphany.
This means that while Kristjánsson champions Aristotle for the contemporary age, he has to augment his proposals for moral education to make
him more useful for educators of students who are largely past the age
of habituation. This is the chief advantage of offering a Platonic theory
of moral education, we believe. At least the role of epiphanies in moral
education, Plato seems to offer a more complete picture than Aristotle.[4]

The second way Kristjánsson's views are relevant to our discussion is
that he offers a systematic analysis of the fundamental characteristics of
epiphanies. Up until this point we have relied on the basic definition of an
epiphany as a spontaneous moment of insight or realization regarding a
moral issue that has significance for how we should live our lives. These
epiphanies are experienced dramatically and are felt to be life-altering or
trajectory-reorienting. When we experience an epiphany, we believe that
a watershed moment in our lives might just have happened. This general
definition is a good starting point, but to understand the full pedagogical
potential of epiphanies, we need to understand what they are at a more
substantial level. Kristjánsson provides six characteristics of what constitutes a morally significant epiphany, which he often calls "moral conversions."[5] For both Kristjánsson and us, the epiphanies we are interested in
are those that have a morally life-altering dimension to them. Or, to be
more accurate, these are epiphanies that, at the time they are occurring,
the person having them *believes* them to be potentially life-altering. So
what characterizes these morally significant epiphanies for Kristjánsson?

The *first* characteristic is that morally significant epiphanies "constitute
abrupt, swift or even catastrophic turning points." This distinguishes them
from a more gradual psychological development that is characterized by
a series of smaller realizations or moments of novel learning that may
be slightly epiphanic at the time but do not register as significant life
events. As we indicated earlier, we think the distinction between the more
gradual psychological or cognitive growth to be an important one, but
like Kristjánsson we want to focus on the more significant epiphanies.
Kristjánsson offers one important caveat regarding the less significant
epiphanies: There are times when a series of small moral epiphanies that

all lead in the same direction can, upon retrospection, be seen as a gradual opening to a dramatic realization and the crossing of a threshold that dramatically changes one's outlook. When this happens, the person may not be able to identify which of the small epiphanies was really the big epiphany, but she will believe that she had a life-altering experience that will forever change who she is (Kristjánsson, 2020, p. 117). As we will see later in this chapter, one of the examples of classroom epiphanies happens by way of a series of small epiphanies that made possible a more significant one.

The *second* characteristic of epiphanies for Kristjánsson is his claim that for an epiphany to be morally significant it must be dramatic and include "radical reconfigurations of mental structures." The radical reconfiguration of mental structures will mean, according to Kristjánsson, that the changes are hard to define and may actually be ineffable in important respects. We highlighted this quality in our analysis of the *Lysis*. Nevertheless, even when they are technically ineffable—insofar as it is impossible to explain them rationally through the use of terms that *fully* capture the overall experience—epiphanies can be understood as an intuition of something inexpressibly beautiful that creates a desire to change our lifestyles or life-directions. Even if we cannot exactly express what our epiphany was about in a way that would satisfy, say, an analytic philosopher, we can still *understand* the epiphany at a level that has real phenomenological content (Kristjánsson, 2020, p. 117). In the next section we will return to the fundamental ineffability of epiphanies and why they cannot be produced rationally through verbal formulations.

The *third* characteristic, according to Kristjánsson, is that epiphanies are "normally . . . unplanned and fortuitous." On the face of it, this suggests that epiphanies cannot be induced by the agent themselves or someone external to the agent. However, Kristjánsson qualifies this by saying that on occasions agents or others can help to create an epiphany; but he also claims, correctly, that there will always be an element of "uncertainty and fortuitousness, because epiphanies rely on spontaneous reactions, and spontaneity can, by definition, never be fully pre-planned" (Kristjánsson, 2020, 117). We are in full agreement with Kristjánsson's claim. However, there is a tendency of some theorists who have recently written on epiphany to suggest that epiphanies are fully and irreducibly spontaneous, meaning there is almost nothing a teacher can or should do to try to induce them. We think this is misguided. It is true that, as Kristjánsson points out, it is impossible to guarantee that every student in a classroom, or even in a one-on-one discussion, will have an epiphany, but we argue that it is possible to create *conditions* for epiphanies that can significantly increase their likelihood. One of the major hopes of this book is to inspire teachers to think carefully and thoroughly about their classroom practice and how they might modify that practice to increase the likelihood that epiphanies will be experienced by their students. It will never be a science that can be systematized, replicated and reproducible, but there are certain things teachers can do to increase the possibility of epiphanies happening.

The *fourth* characteristic has been implicitly mentioned throughout our analysis of Plato but is important to acknowledge explicitly at this juncture. Kristjánsson (2020) argues that "epiphanic moral conversions are strongly emotionally laden. This can mean either that they are triggered by intense emotions, such as awe or elevation, or that they elicit fierce emotional responses during and after the conversion or both" (p. 117). Kristjánsson is correct to state that there is a strong emotional dimension in an experience of an epiphany; however, his list of what might trigger the epiphany should go beyond only awe or elevation. To name just a few others: compassion, hope, joy, and love; but epiphanies can also be laden with unpleasant emotions like shame, insecurity, or even fear. Yet in spite of what would be their unpleasantness by themselves, if they occur in a context of respect, trust, and care, they can become empowering for the individual. In addition, and crucially, they simultaneously help them see what their rational mind could not. As we shall see in the example that follows from *Dead Poets Society*, the emotional quality of the catalysts are different for different students depending on the psychological barriers they bring with them.

Kristjánsson's *fifth* characteristic of morally significant epiphanies is perhaps the most problematic from our point of view. Kristjánsson (2020) claims that the epiphanies he is interested in are "conversions [that] involve radical self-change" (p. 117). On the one hand, Kristjánsson's claim is completely to the point, so long as what he means is that when agents experience epiphanies they *believe* that what they have experienced has the *potential* to lead to radical self-change, and that they *desire* for that change to happen. What Kristjánsson does not explicitly acknowledge is that genuine morally significant epiphanies can happen in students, and yet because of the bad habits developed in the years prior to the epiphany, students may not be able to achieve radical self-change. What has radically changed in the epiphanies are their desires; and at the moment they are having them, those desires may feel like they will be permanent. But what Plato's dialogues show us is the sad fact that epiphanies do not change the fundamental condition of the psyche or eradicate the engrained habitual behaviors that reinforce that fundamental condition. What has to happen for radical self-change to be achieved is the agent must undergo a rehabituation process under the guidance of a mentor or community so that the radical self-change can come to fruition. How this rehabituation process comes about will be the subject of the next chapter.

The *sixth* and final characteristic of moral epiphanies for Kristjánsson is his belief that they must be objectively moral, inasmuch as they lead the agent to desire an objectively moral life of flourishing as an individual and as part of the human community. Realizations that make people less virtuous and more prone to personal or social vice are not epiphanies in the relevant sense. (Kristjánsson, 2020, p. 118)

With the characteristics in mind and before we explore how teachers can attempt to induce epiphanies in the classroom, we need to return to the issue of the ineffability of the content of epiphanies. It is critical to examine this claim in more detail because the reader may still be wondering if epiphanies are really necessary for moral education. Why not produce knowledge of virtue in our students by rationally arguing for it—i.e., using the proper definitions, premises and conclusions that are necessary for students to understand the virtue. If we, the objection continues, could lay hold of such a rational procedure for teaching students the value of the virtues, they could then adopt that value by assenting to it explicitly, and therefore the desire to act virtuously would arise from students' autonomous consent. While we too are concerned to preserve student agency in the process of moral development, we argue later that such a straightforward rational approach is not possible. Thus, we must find alternate ways of helping students *see* the value of virtues for themselves, even if they are never fully able to express that value to another person who has not had a similar epiphany.

The Ineffability of Epiphanies

When we say that the glimpse of virtue found in an epiphany is ineffable, we do not mean that there is nothing that can be, and should be, said about it. We might say about an epiphany concerning the virtue of justice that it was "beautiful," or "inspiring," or "humbling"; we might even use more concrete terms like "I now see what fairness demands," or "I should now appreciate the perspectives of others in a more conscientious way." But what do these utterances really mean? If someone were to say to us, "Well, that sounds really nice, but what exactly do you mean by fairness or conscientiousness?," how might we respond? For the first set of statements about the humbling or inspiring quality of the epiphany, it is not at all clear that we could say anything that would satisfy the question except to use similar value-laden terms, such as to say that the experience was "eye-opening" or "empowering." But then the reply might go: "But what do you mean by *those* words?" After trying and trying again to provide an explanation that is as clear and rational as possible, we may ultimately, have to give up and say something like: "I don't know how to answer you, but if you saw what I saw, you would know what I mean." It is similar for the other slightly more concrete descriptions of the epiphany with respect to justice. While "fairness" and "conscientious appreciation of others' perspectives" give us a little more to work with, our interrogator might still want to know what constitutes the new conception of fairness or conscientiousness that has arisen. We might attempt a fuller explanation, but at some point we may stammer and stutter in trying to get more specific. Many of us have probably had similar "stuttering experiences," as when someone asks us how we "liked" a concert or film that has deeply moved us. How can we describe what we felt, what we saw, and what we now feel and see? We know that we could never be specific enough to actually make ourselves understood. The reason we feel this way is precisely that we have caught just a glimpse of virtue, to return to the epiphany example—a glimpse that strongly motivates us to change our way of life and resolve to be more fair, or appreciate others, or even to write poetry about justice. It is just at this point that the process of rehabituation must begin. As we saw in the early chapters, it is this process that produces a much fuller understanding of the relevant virtue than the initial glimpse that came through the epiphany.

The question then becomes: could a person explain the content of the epiphany once they underwent a thorough habituation process and came to fuller knowledge of the virtue? The answer is, as we saw in Chapter 1, surprisingly, no. A person who is virtuous is a person who has what Plato calls "craft-knowledge" and that knowledge contains elements that simply cannot be fully explained in words. However, it does not mean that absolutely *no* explanation is possible. Indeed, craftspeople can say more true things about their craft than any other person—and things that even novices can understand, such as when a cobbler says, "You should space the holes for the laces exactly one inch apart." Such instructions are crucial during the habituation process because they serve as needed guidelines for the novice when she encounters uncertain situations or for honing various skills that are fundamental to the practice. But the more a novice tries to develop a fuller understanding of the craftsperson's knowledge, the less explicit instruction is possible. This Platonic insight, which was famously further developed by Wittgenstein, Heidegger, and their followers means that, in a sense, the virtuous person *can* and should offer *some* reasons and explanations regarding what virtuous actions are like and *why* they are virtuous, and at the same time the virtuous person *cannot* and should not attempt to offer *comprehensive* reasons and explanations for these things. The articulation of reasons and explanations can be helpful in inducing epiphanies and supporting rehabituation in students, but it is never sufficient for either.

This somewhat paradoxical relationship between language and craft knowledge has led to significant disagreements among virtue ethicists, especially those who take, broadly speaking, a neo-Aristotelian perspective. John McDowell (1996), Howard Curzer (2002), and Iakovos Vasiliou (1996) seem to hold that the fundamental incommunicability of general rules about what constitutes virtue is so decisive that there is no point in offering explanations at all to novices. In contrast, Julia Annas (2011), Nancy Sherman (1999), and Kristján Kristjánsson (2006b) claim that it is essential to offer reasons and explanations to students so that they come to a *proper* understanding of virtue and do not mistake vice for virtue, and *vice versa*. It may be that the former group of theorists are more faithful in their interpretation of the *Nicomachean Ethics*—both Sherman and Kristjánsson admit the previously interpreters may be—but we think that the latter group's point of view is more helpful for the formation of virtue in young people. Because it seems like explicit articulations can and do play a role in gaining and epiphany or in developing craft knowledge, we think these latter theorists have it right. That said, it should remain clear that it is never possible to offer a comprehensive system of reasons and explanations that can lead the individual through a rational process to such knowledge. The epiphanic illuminations of its final state and the habituation process needed to get there are, in an important sense, ineffable. A person with craft-knowledge simply cannot give a fully rational explanation of everything they do in every given instance, because every given instance is unique and requires a context-dependent action. And much of the context is itself based on a "feel" that the craftsperson has, and not on a fully rationally articulable set of reasons. So while a good craftsperson would give verbal instructions of what her apprentice should do in making a quality pair of shoes, her instructions will always be incomplete. She may say, "a good cobbler never cuts too much leather off the top of a shoe," but when the apprentice asks, "how much is 'too much?'" what will the cobbler reply? It is not possible to explain every situation ahead of time, and so all she could do is *show* her apprentice where to cut on every pair of shoes until the apprentice starts to get a "feel" for it on her own.

It is the same with a teacher who wants to induce epiphanies in her students. She can do her best to explain what she wants them to experience, but ultimately what she wants them to experience is only understandable to someone who has experienced it. She can use some words to explain why, for example, she thinks justice is beautiful and that justice will make students' lives more fulfilling, but ultimately the students will never be convinced until they have seen the beauty and goodness of justice for themselves.

Having explored the limits of language to induce epiphanies, we are now in a position to examine some of the ways teachers might go about inducing them. Later we outline three general strategies. The first strategy to inducing epiphanies is to illuminate the moral value of an idea or action by having the students *perform* some action which reveals the desirability of virtue to them. The second is to illuminate the moral value of an idea or action by *showing* students the beauty or significance of the virtue through demonstrations by either the teacher or someone else who is being observed. The third is to illuminate the moral value of an idea or action by *telling* students about the beauty or significance of the virtue. Here the teacher offers verbal approximations of the relevant value, which characteristically hint at or suggest the virtue's beauty or significance without attempting to exhaust its meaning. However, these categories are not mutually exclusive. In nearly all epiphanies, each of these strategies come into play to some degree, but often one of them is the main focus of the teachers' activities. In the next three sections we will focus on the *doing*, the *showing*, and the *telling*, by offering examples of teachers who generated epiphanies in students primarily by using one of these modes of epiphany generation.

One last comment needs to be made about these three strategies of generating epiphanies in students. The fact is that these are not only methods of generating epiphanies in students, they are also modes of rehabituating students to act in light of the epiphanies they receive. In this second part of the book, we have somewhat artificially divided the process of virtue development into two separate steps for mature learners. For young children, the habituation process seems to suffice because they are sufficiently young enough to (1) be willing to undergo a substantial habituation process without significant complaint because they have not developed a complete sense of agency and/or a strong sense of independence. Therefore they do not resist being compelled to perform certain actions over and over again. But (2) they also have had as much time to be habituated into other (bad) habits that would work against a (good) habituation process. Thus, for the most part, young children can, in the right circumstances, be habituated without the need for epiphanies.

It is different with older students who (1) have developed a stronger sense of agency and are far more reluctant, and even can become defiant, when compelled to do things they do not want to do. This defiance can create significant psychological barriers that make them resistant to growing in the habituation process, even if they are forced to undergo it through the use of draconian measures. But (2) they also have been alive a long time and, for most of them, have developed non-virtuous habits that work against a rehabituation process. This is why epiphanies can be extremely helpful because they undermine the resistance found in 1 and 2. They motivate students to desire to be rehabituated, and the desire mitigates the effects of 1 and 2.

But ultimately the distinction between the method of leading young children and older children to virtue is arbitrary. The three methods for creating epiphanies we outline are not just for epiphanies—they are also the methods teachers can use in the rehabituation process. Indeed, in an important sense, an epiphany a person receives that makes them want to be rehabituated is itself just the first step of rehabituation; and similarly the first steps of a rehabituation process can help jumpstart the epiphanic process, if done correctly. In the former there is a life-altering and trajectory-reorienting event that catalyzes a desire for rehabituation; in the latter there is a rehabituation process that once begins catalyzes an epiphany. In both cases, the epiphanies and rehabituation work together to produce further epiphanies and further rehabituation.

In the following three methods, our first example comes from a teacher who induces epiphanies by having students *perform* certain actions.

In this example the teacher is clearly creating an epiphany that occurs before the rehabituation process has really begun. In the second example, the teacher begins a habituation process first, which eventually leads to epiphanies that the students have in her class. The third example begins with an epiphany, but it is connected almost immediately to the rehabituation process. In sum, in this chapter on inducing epiphanies we want to acknowledge that the connection between epiphanies and rehabituation is very complex and highly context dependent.

Finally, not all of the epiphanies we include are *moral* epiphanies *per se*. Some are aesthetic or metaphysical, but even in these, they have a moral cast that shapes the moral characters of the individual students and causes them to reflect on the meaning of life and how best to live in the world. When they reflect on these questions, they recognize that the aesthetic, metaphysical, and ethical components of life are not isolated and separable but ramify into one another.

Epiphanies in Action: "Doing" as a Way of Inducing Epiphanies

The first way of producing epiphanies that we will see put into practice is having the students *perform* activities in the class that reveal something important about their place in the world and a desire to alter how they relate to the world. The example we will use is found in the movie *Freedom Writers* (Lagravenese, 2006), where Erin Gruwell (the teacher) has her own epiphany in the middle of the movie about the moral dimension of teaching that she had not previously considered, especially her biases and prejudices about her students.[6] She is a first-year teacher and does *not* initially attempt to create epiphanies, *aporias*, or anything other than what students might expect to see in a "typical" English class. She is well-meaning but does not have a philosophical vision of the virtues she wants to impart in her students, nor does she seemingly have any awareness of the intense psychological barriers that would prevent her "troubled" students from having epiphanies, even if she did want to induce them. For her, teaching English seems to be about little more than getting her students to learn grammar and figures of speech. She genuinely wants to help her students learn these things so that they can graduate from high school and be "successful" in life, but she does not have a plan for anything beyond that. As a consequence, her pedagogical strategies do very little to inspire the students to grow as learners or as people. As we learn, she was raised in a wealthy family and does not seem to recognize the need to understand the students in her class that have not been raised with the same privilege. Because she has been given "troubled" students and because she understands neither what motivates the students nor the concerns and difficulties they face on a daily basis, she succeeds only in alienating her students at the outset of her experience with them.

For the first half of the semester, her lack of philosophical, psychological, or pedagogical understanding has a disastrous effect not only on her teaching and her students ability to learn English but also on her belief in her students. Fortunately, at some point during the middle of the semester, something happens in her class where one student draws a racist, offensive caricature of another student, which all of the other students find hilarious. This racist behavior activates for the first time Ms. Gruwell's passions and she becomes angry. Her anger causes her to set aside all of the "best practices" she learned in her teacher-training program. Telling her students to "shut their workbooks!" she begins to passionately tell a story about how forms of racism similar to the one depicted in the picture helped to perpetrate the "holocaust." Her anger and the subsequent passionate lecture causes the students to respond with their own anger and defensiveness. They yell at her that "you don't understand nothing about our lives," and "why don't you just keep going along with your babysitting," and "I'm not going to give you my respect just because you're a teacher. How do I know you're not a bad person standing up there? How do I know you are not a liar?" This then provokes disbelief and anger in her. In the end, she and her students come to an impasse. But it is clear that, for the very first time, Gruwell realizes that her students are human beings who have feelings, fears, doubts, angers, and so on; and it is the first time they realize the same about her. Neither of them care for or respect each other yet, but something like an *aporia* (for her and her students) has happened.

But what comes next changes everything for her and her students' lives. After this back and forth of anger and accusation for fifteen minutes, an exhausted silence ensues. During that silence, the boy that drew the racist picture raises his hand. In disbelief, Ms. Gruwell says "Ha, you're raising your hand?" (something he has never done before in class). He then asks one very simple question: "That thing you said earlier about the Holocaust—what is it"? She then says: "You have never heard of the Holocaust?" Then she looks around and asks the rest of the students if they know what it is. The only student who raises his hand is the lone White student in the class. Silence ensues again as she looks around with deep emotion and recognition. She has just had a moral epiphany. She has made so many assumptions about these students and she realizes they have mostly been wrong.

This realization was Ms. Gruwell's own epiphany about her own lack of empathy and the stereotypes she has been operating under, but now she has seen the need for her students to have a similar moral epiphany. She now knows that she wants to cultivate the virtue of empathy in her students and the courage for them to go beyond stereotypes. At this point, she recognizes the need to have a purpose for her class. She realizes this because she has experienced the need for empathy in herself.

But now she needs to find a way to induce the same epiphany in her students. The problem is that she knows from experience that trying to "tell" her students what they should think or believe will be unsuccessful because of the strong psychological barriers to her teaching—namely, they do not trust her and definitely do not trust her when she lectures them about who they are or what they should value. Recognizing the need to overcome these barriers, she very wisely employs a method of creating an epiphany about the value of empathy in her class without having to "tell" the students they should experience it.

Her method is to create, on the following day, what she calls the "Line Game," in which she places a piece of red tape in the middle of the floor along the length of the classroom. She has half the students stand on one side of the line and the other half stand on the other side of the line. It is important to note that this class is highly racialized, where groups of racial minorities have deep suspicions and even hatred for other ethnic minorities in the class. She recognizes that these racial lines are a powerful psychological barrier that will prevent her students from having an epiphany about empathy. The groups in tension with each other include Cambodian students, Black students, and Latinx students.

Ms. Gruwell had already tried explicitly lecturing the students about how they should not see one another as enemies, and how the racial categories to which they felt allegiance belied points of connection that they might have with each other. Of course, telling them this only produced justified contempt for her in the students as it was obvious to them that she had no idea what she was talking about because she was raised in a "bubble" of white privilege and is completely unaware of the complex racial tensions that exist all over the United States. Knowing that telling them again would not work, she decided to invent a game in which she simply asked yes or no questions of the students. If they answered the question in the affirmative, they were supposed to step forward up to the line. When they did so, they were face to face with other students (often who were of different ethnicities) who also answered in the affirmative. At first her questions were relatively banal and emotionally unimportant. However, because it was a game, there was something in the students that seemed less antagonistic to her and to one another than before, beyond a few cold stares at one another as they faced each other on the line. But after a few more questions, Ms. Gruwell begins to ask more serious questions about drugs, jail time, gang violence, and the loss of loved ones to violence. The effect of these questions was palpable, especially the questions about who had been in jail and who had lost loved ones to gang violence. The vast majority of students had lost someone they loved to gang violence, and when these students stood across from each other, face to face, they begin to let go of their hostility and stereotypes and, perhaps for the first time, saw their classmates as people who had also undergone serious trauma and pain because of economic inequality, racial violence, and the death of friends and family members. As they stood their looking at each other, filled with the pain of their own memories, and realizing that their fellow students of different races were filled with the pain of the same memories, the viewer sees glimmers of epiphanies beginning to happen. What Ms. Gruwell does next is ingenious; she invites every student in the class to quietly say the names of all the people the students had lost and to pay their respects. This is a moving moment in the film, but it is moving because it helps the viewer see what the students are seeing. Rather than enemies who have nothing in common, the students realize that they have a great deal in common in their pains and fears.

The epiphany is evident on the students' faces, but Ms. Gruwell is not finished and attempts to use the vulnerability of the moment to direct students towards a lasting and, ultimately life-changing, endeavor. She goes up to the front of the room to her desk and tells the students that she has bought them each a journal in which they are to write daily about their individual stories—about their individual pains, fears, hardships, and hopes. She is asking them to share the very things they just admitted to one another in the Line Game so that she can understand them better. She recognizes the need for the students to have a venue to safely express the difficult aspects of their lives, and she also wants to continue to understand them better so that she can be a more empathetic human and a more effective teacher. She senses that they could continue to be open to further epiphanies in the right context, and she wants to partner with them in helping herself and them to practice empathy and compassion. She asks them to walk up in front of the class and pick up their journals and tells them that if they want her to read the journals they should leave them in a locked cupboard every day. But she gives them the choice; she says she will read them only if they give her permission by putting them in the cupboard. At first, none of the students walk forward. It is a vulnerable moment for her, because if they do not come forward it means that the epiphany they had did not go deep enough to create a longing for a different way of interacting with other people. The viewer can see their struggle; we can see that they want to move forward but they know doing so will be an action that, because it would constitute a tacit rejection of their previous ways of regarding people of different backgrounds as threats, may irrevocably change them and their trajectory in life. Eventually, one student quietly walks forward as the others gaze on her with a look of strange mixture of admiration and amazement, until finally they all come forward, even the most formerly hostile of them. It is a moving moment as they begin to embody the epiphanies they have experienced.

At the beginning of the film Ms. Gruwell assumed that what her students needed was a "good education" that she would provide for them, and then they would "line up at the door" to take her class. She assumed that they had little to offer her or each other. Her plan was to help them be more successful, like she believed she was. In operating in this mindset, she was blind to the ways she could learn from them, and blind to the ways their backgrounds and experiences could contribute meaningfully to the

growth of everyone in the classroom, including her. Using Freirean termi-
nology, previously she thought she needed to "make deposits" in her students, and that, if they followed her instructions, they could graduate from
high school and even go to college. Of course, at that point she wanted
to be a relevant teacher so that her "banking" would be more effective,
so she tried to use examples that she thought her students would enjoy,
like rap songs for Tupac Shakur. This backfired because the students see
this for what it is—a teacher who thinks she knows what they need, and
a teacher who thinks they do not have anything to offer in the classroom.
The students rebuff her attempts, not because she incorrectly surmised
that they were listeners of Tupac, but because they saw her methods of
instruction as patronizing—"White girl gonna teach us about rap?" says
one of her students. But the epiphany that she experienced changes her
perspective on who the students were and what they could bring to the
classroom. While the Line Game sparked a moment of understanding
between the students and Ms. Gruwell, what truly led to lasting results
(and became the benchmark for the real-life Ms. Gruwell's methods) was
introducing students to their journals. In making students' voices an inte-
gral part of the classroom, Ms. Gruwell was demonstrating her (new)
belief in both her students' *right* to forge their own education as well as
their *ability* to do so. The students (1) write, (2) if they wish, (3) about
what they want, and (4) determine themselves if they wish for anyone else
to read their writing. In the end, the best thing Ms. Gruwell did for her
students was step back and recognize the value, expertise, and meaning
of her students and their words. Ms. Gruwell did not have to fade away
as their teacher but instead had to somehow find a balance between coming alongside her students and also stepping behind them as they paved
their own paths, something Freire himself insisted was at the core of his
pedagogy (Chambers, 2019). Ms. Gruwell and her methods do not represent a perfect model for teaching, including, and perhaps especially, white
teachers teaching students of color. However, they do present a moving
image of a teacher having epiphany, changing her teaching for the better,
and ultimately inducing life-changing epiphanies in her students.

In the previous experiences, it is clear from the context that Ms. Gruwell needed to begin inducing epiphanies in her students in ways that went
beyond merely telling them about the virtues, or even showing them she
had them herself. Their lack of trust in her necessitated this. But eventually, once they began to trust her after the Line Game and the introduction
of the journals and her positive responses to them, and after seeing that
she no longer regarded them as just a bunch of students who needed to
quit complaining and do grammar, they began to trust her. As they did,
she could start to *show* them the virtues she hoped they would embody;
and she could start to *tell* them about the virtues she hoped they would
embody. Once the mutual trust between her and her students began, the
potential for further epiphanies increased dramatically.

In the next section, where we examine the method of producing epiphanies based on *showing*, we will return to this notion of trust. As Kenneth Strike (2014) has pointed out, helping novices have epiphanies about the goods and virtues associated with academic disciplines requires trust, which he calls an "epistemological bridge." He argues that novices do not have the cognitive and affective mental equipment to see the value inherent in the intellectual or moral virtues. Since they cannot see the value, it is very difficult to induce epiphanies in them. Trust can help in this process. Strike claims:

> My claims for trust depends on the view that the standards, goods, and virtues that are internal to intellectual practices cannot be fully cognized by the uninitiated. Hence, students cannot judge the worth of intellectual practices until they have moved some distance down the path of initiation into them. Here trust substitutes for understanding. It is an epistemological bridge. . . . Engaging students who often seem very disengaged (Steinberg 1996) in the process of initiation may be motivated through an appeal to, or manipulation of, external goods. Alternatively it can be mediated by trust. The latter approach, I argue, is more conducive to human flourishing
>
> (p. 232)

In the case of all of the examples we explore in this chapter, each of them, starting with Ms. Gruwell earlier, cultivated trust in their students and it was that trust that unlocked the epiphanies in their students. Contemporary teachers who want to induce similar epiphanies in their students would do well to first help the students trust them. Trust works better for epiphanies than trying to create them using rational or pragmatic reasons.

Epiphanies in Action: "Showing" as a Way of Inducing Epiphanies

Our second method of inducing epiphanies—*showing*—is found in Kenneth Strike's (2014) article "Trust, Tradition and Pluralism: Human Flourishing and Liberal Polity." In the article, Strike describes his high school math teacher, "Mrs Smith," who created epiphanies in her students. Unlike Ms. Gruwell, Mrs. Smith primarily creates epiphanies in her students not by what she has them do, but by *showing* them how mathematics has contributed to her life and made her life fulfilling. According to Strike, his epiphany was based not on what Mrs. Smith said or had the student do, but on her ability to reveal the beauty of mathematics through its impact on who she was. The epiphany that Mrs. Smith induces is not a moral epiphany like the kind Mrs. Gruwell induces, but the principle of how Mrs. Smith induces epiphanies could be applied to moral epiphanies as well; just as Ms. Gruwell's method of inducing epiphanies could be applied to create aesthetic epiphanies. In both Ms. Gruwell's and Mrs. Smith's cases the epiphanies induced are life-altering or trajectory-reorienting and are therefore relevant to our discussion.

In his article, Strike (2014) explains how Mrs. Smith created an environment in which mathematics was a source of beauty and inspiration. Mrs. Smith was an exemplar of the virtues required to appreciate mathematics and by being an exemplar helped her students want to cultivate the virtues necessary to see engagement in mathematics as part of the flourishing life. She was able to cultivate this desire not by "telling" students what the virtues were or why they should want them, but by "showing" them what the virtues were by her love of mathematics.

> I do not recall that Mrs. Smith used terms like elegance, simplicity, paradox or power to describe mathematics, but I do know that she *showed* us that these things were what motivated her about mathematics. These were words I acquired later for an experience to which she had pointed. . . . Mrs Smith exemplified the virtues required to realize the good of math. . . . Mrs Smith was able to *show* us what mathematics contributed to her life. . . . She could do this because she was able to point to the goods of math and because she was an exemplar of its virtues.
>
> (Strike, 2014, pp. 234–235; emphasis added)

In this image, Mrs. Smith is not making arguments; she is pointing and exemplifying. That is not to say that she could not have used words to describe the beauty of mathematics to her students—words like "power" or "elegance"—but these words would have had almost no meaning to them. They know what the words mean in the vernacular, but applying them to mathematical equations would require them to have had a certain experience with mathematics that went beyond memorizing formulae and applying algorithms. And if Mrs. Smith had tried to break down each equation and point to the specific point at which the "power" or "elegance" could be seen, it still would not have helped. Indeed, it might only make it harder for them to see, because the power or elegance of mathematics is not seen in a specific moment, but in how the whole works together. This means that even had Mrs. Smith used words like "elegance" or "simplicity," they would have had no meaning for Strike, because he could not see math in that way.

However, this does not mean that she never used words to help produce epiphanies in her students. On the contrary, Strike implies that she did use words, but that these words were meant to supplement the exemplifying and showing she used as her primary means of inducing epiphanies.

> The experience of the internal goods of a practice may often require someone who can help the learner to acquire the language necessary to articulate the goods, virtues, and standards of a practice who can

direct the attention towards the relevant features of the practice. This takes us back to the picture of the teacher who initiates by showing, helping the student to acquire the language appropriate to a practice, exhibiting the virtues, and who shows mastery through criticism of performance.

(Strike, 2014, p. 237)

Mrs. Smith used words to "help students acquire the language" of mathematics, but the words had served a support role to her exhibition and exemplification of the virtues. This leads us back to our earlier discussion about the need for explanation in the training of students in virtue that Sherman (1999), Kristjánsson (2006b), and Annas (2011) recommend. As we indicated, if it is the case that Aristotle thinks that students come to know what constitutes a virtuous act only by being mindlessly compelled to perform virtuous acts over and over again without any verbal instructions or explanations, as Curzer (2002), Vasiliou (1996), and McDowell (1996) claim he does, then we do not follow Aristotle in this. We think it is much more helpful to make students do the acts, but to also give reasons and explanations while making the students do them. These reasons and explanations will not make a great deal of sense to the student at first but as they practice the acts and hear the explanations, eventually they start to see and understand what the virtuous thing to do is in other situations.

In this way, Mrs. Smith begins the rehabituation process before the students have received an epiphany; she makes them do math problems while simultaneously explaining to them what they are doing and why it is important. But the critical component of what eventually creates the epiphany in them is that while she is having them practice, and while she is offering explanations of why she is having them practice in the way they are, Mrs. Smith is simultaneously embodying and exemplifying her love of mathematics and how mathematics is intrinsically valuable. How did she point to the goods that made math intrinsically valuable? Strike claims it was not because he could see the value at first but because he somehow trusted Mrs. Smith.

> One thing that made Mrs Smith's pointing and exemplifying successful was the integrity of her stance. It was apparent that this is how she felt about math. In effect, her message was this. "Here is what I see in math. There are goods internal to its practice. There are virtues required to realize these goods. Let me help you see them." The success of the message depended on students understanding the math well enough to have some rudiment of the experience she sought to mediate, but it also depended on our trust of Mrs Smith. She was able to point us towards these goods and virtues and show us that they enriched her life.
>
> (Strike, 2014, p. 234)

Trust is essential if the epiphany is ever to happen. As the rehabituation process starts, the students will typically be hesitant to fully engage. Teachers often leverage external compulsion (like letter grades) to engage the students in the rehabituation process, but external compulsion often fails to help students overcome the psychological barriers that would prevent them from experiencing an epiphany. The reason Mrs. Smith was successful was because she helped the students trust her by the integrity of her stance; and this trust opened their psyches up to accept the initial *aporia* of not understanding the concepts she used, and to be willing to keep "looking" for those goods that *must* exist because they saw that they existed in Mrs. Smith's life.

> The teacher can succeed only if the teacher is trusted. The teachers best "evidence" for her practice is that its values and forms of argument have been realized in her life and in the lives of others. Mrs Smith was able to show us what mathematics contributed to her life. . . . She was able to show us the beauty of a proof and the enticement of a puzzle. She exemplified the virtues of an insistence on rigour and clarity. She was not satisfied until we got to the bottom of things. She was able to show us that these goods and virtues enriched her life. (Strike, 2014, p. 235)

She was able to show these things because the students trusted her. These epiphanies came later in the class, once the students trusted her, and saw that she must be telling the truth because they could "see" it in her actions and classroom comportment.

To sum up, the trust Mrs. Smith gained by her students came not from her being able to prove through cogent argumentation and rational explanations, but through the integrity of her stance and the ways mathematics contributed to her life. The words Mrs. Smith might have used, words like the ones Socrates used in his dialogues, would at best be mere signs and symbols that suggest something beyond them, just as Alcibiades told us. Strike argues that words are modes of initiation but not argument. "They constitute an initiation, not an argument. They do not make sense as attempts to persuade students of the goods of mathematics" (p. 235). In order for a person to persuade students of the goods of mathematics, a teacher must gesture, point, and suggest, and in so doing can only hope that eventually their students will come to see mathematics correctly. Indeed, if they see math in this way, they will, in a sense, *see* math for the first time.

Epiphanies in Action: "Telling" as a Way of Inducing Epiphanies

As we have argued several times in this chapter, when epiphanies happen they can never *fully* be explained in words or arguments. That does not mean, however, that they cannot be *induced* by means of words and arguments. For example, Mrs. Smith probably said many things over the course of the school year that reflected the things she wanted her students to *see* in mathematics, and Ms. Gruwell helped prepare the ground for her student's epiphanies by the verbal conflict she had with them prior to it. In this section, we will examine a teacher who places a greater emphasis on *telling* students what epiphanies they should have. Our example is found in Mr. Keating, who is an English teacher in the movie *Dead Poets Society* (Weir, 1989). In the movie, Mr. Keating uses words and arguments to try to induce epiphanies in his students. Of course, like Mrs. Smith, Mr. Keating does a great deal of *showing* too, but his *explanations* of what he hopes his students will experience in his classroom is essential to creating epiphanies in his students. It is important to note, however, that even though Mr. Keating relies heavily on explanations of the virtues about which he wants his students to have epiphanies, his words do not literally produce them. They are verbal approximations of an experience he has had (and continues to have) and can only stand in for the experience he hopes his students will eventually have. As Strike argues, students like Mr. Keating's are novices in understanding the virtues associated with poetry, and as novices they do not have the cognitive equipment necessary to understand what Mr. Keating is talking about. As we shall see, early on the students are perplexed and confused by Mr. Keating's words and behaviors, but eventually one or two of them begin to experience what Mr. Keating is talking about. The epiphany they experience is not caused because Mr. Keating makes good arguments or helps them see the pragmatic value of his claims; rather his explanations of the value of poetry and the virtues necessary to realize those values are based on aesthetic, moral and spiritual claims that induce an inchoate longing. Like Mrs. Smith, Mr. Keating does not try to convince his students of the logic of his position, or the material advantages his students will experience if they come to see the world the way he does. He appeals to something they cannot understand; so even when Mr. Keating offers reasons, their persuasive force is not in the logic of the reasons, but in their ability to evoke something that the students long for but do not understand.

From the very first moments of his class, Mr. Keating sets the stage for students to experience an epiphany. Nothing is accidental for him. We see this in the very opening scene in which, on the first day of class, his all-male students are talking eagerly and somewhat rambunctiously in their seats before class begins. Where is Mr. Keating? He is nowhere to be seen except for one point he surreptitiously peaks his head out from his office behind his desk in the front of the classroom to observe the students in the class. The students do not notice his glance, because they are occupied with themselves. His look is clearly intentional. He is not curious about what his students are doing but making sure they are doing the *right* thing. In this case, the *right* thing is acting like students who couldn't care less about the class that is just about to begin. There is nothing in them that suggests that they are actually *interested* in his English course. They are interested in joking and talking. After thirty seconds of this, Mr. Keating walks deliberately but unconcernedly out of his office while whistling nonchalantly. Without making direct eye contact, and while continually whistling, he walks in between their desks towards the back of the class (where the door is) and then gives a slightly sarcastic whistle before leaving the class. At this point all of the students are looking at one another with a mixture of shock, confusion, nervous laughter, and so on. After about two seconds, Mr. Keating pops his head back into the classroom and says, "Well, come on!" and then heads back out. The students respond with even more confused glances and gestures, until, finally, not knowing what else to do, they get up from their seats and walk out of the room.

This scene is interesting because it reflects its own version of *aporia* that is a staple of Socrates' method for producing epiphanies. While these students would not say they were in doubt about their knowledge of virtue, they certainly are perplexed, confused and full of uncertainty. Mr. Keating intentionally creates this state, and he does it for the same reason Socrates does it. He wants to create an openness in his students to the epiphany he will momentarily try to induce.

As the students file out of the classroom and into the hallway, Mr. Keating is waiting for them, standing in front of a trophy case full of memorabilia of the school, especially pictures of students from the past. Before asking them to look at these pictures, Mr. Keating first introduces himself by alternately using self-deprecating humor and false immodesty. At one point, he tells his students that they can either call him Mr. Keating, or if they are "slightly more daring, Oh Captain, My Captain" which is a reference to Walt Whitman's poem about Abraham Lincoln. When he gives them this choice, they experience perplexity again, because it is obviously an outrageous suggestion, since it is so grandiose and immodest.

Mr. Keating's point in giving them this choice is not actually that he thinks they will call him Captain, my Captain, but it is to fascinate them with his fearlessness. He knows he sounds ridiculous to them, but he seems so confident that he does not mind being considered ridiculous and being mocked by his students with embarrassed snickers or, later, behind his back. This, of course, makes him seem all the more confident because it suggests that even though he knows he will be mocked, he is confident that they will find him fascinating.

But he is not finished with them. He goes to greater heights in his grandiose and over-the-top persona. After having them read a few lines of poetry about the concept of *carpe diem* and seizing the day, he asks them to look closely at the faces in the trophy cases. He encourages the students to put their faces right up close to the glass, so they "can hear their legacy whispered to you." The students are so befuddled that they actually lean in towards the glass, as if the boys in the photographs are really going to speak out loud to them. On the one hand, this is an absurd scene since every student and the viewers know that the photographs cannot talk, and yet the strange grandiose sincerity of Mr. Keating makes the students and the viewers want to believe him. As the students lean towards the glass, Mr. Keating whispers in a slow, very low, almost croaking, voice "Carrrrpeeee diem, boys, seize the day; make your life extraordinary." The students closest to Mr. Keating turn to look at him with awkward glances (but he just ignores them and keeps on slowly speaking), but the students are listening, and so are the viewers.

Immediately following the trophy case moment, the scene cuts to five of the students leaving the building caring armfuls of books from their classes. They all have stunned looks on their faces, and one boy says, "That was weird"; but another boy says, "but different"; to which another boy says "spooky, if you ask me." These comments are important for several reasons. The first is that clearly the boys have *not* had an epiphany of the sort we saw in Alcibiades or Glaucon. Most of them are slightly disturbed and uncomfortable. The second reason the comments are important is that even though they have not received an epiphany, they are *struck* by what happened in the classroom—they are surprised, a bit confused, perhaps scared but also, in a way, interested. This is exactly what Mr. Keating expected—this is the effects he hoped would come from their *aporias*. He knew that there was little chance of actually inducing a significant epiphany on the first day, given the psychological barriers the students came to the class with, but he knew that if he could create *aporia*, if he could get the boys thinking and talking about the class, even in confused ways, then they would be more open on the second day of class. And, indeed, the second day of class ends up being even more memorable than the first.

Before turning to the second day of class, it should be mentioned that the reason Mr. Keating wants to cause *aporia* in his students is because, as the background scenes make clear, the students are simply going through the academic motions. They do not expect anything out of school except long hours of required drudgery so that they can get accepted into an Ivy League college. They are not interested in seizing the day or reading Walt Whitman. In this sense they are just like Lysis, Alcibiades, or Glaucon. They are the young Aristocracy of America in the late 1950s, and like the ancient Athenian aristocracy, they are taught to be interested in prestige, power, and pleasure. But, just like Socrates, Mr. Keating believes that these young men may have souls that long to live differently than their culture dictates. Most of them do not know they have these longings, but Mr. Keating believes they do have them, and he knows that they must be shaken out of their routines if he is ever going to induce epiphanies in them. Just like Socrates, Mr. Keating aims first at creating *aporia*, which is what his first day of class was mostly about.

He deepens the *aporia* on the second day in a dramatic fashion. It is hard for the viewer to imagine how Mr. Keating might follow up on his unusual first day—his students were surprised, confused, even a little spooked, but because of this, they left the class thinking that the course might be different. The second day is meant to follow on the heels of this confusion, by adding more confusion and the first attempt at an incipient epiphany.

The second day begins with the students sitting quietly at their desks, while Mr. Keating sits at his own desk and dryly asks one of his students to open their massive textbook on poetry. Mr. Keating asks Mr. Perry to turn to the introduction and "read the opening paragraph of the preface entitled 'Understanding Poetry.'" Interestingly, Mr. Perry was the student who claimed at the end of the first class that at least it was "different." But as Mr. Perry starts reading, any hope that he had that the class might be different is lost as he reads a dull and pedantic explanation of how to analyze poetry. As he reads, his reading voice gets slightly less enthusiastic as the reading goes on. While Mr. Perry is reading, Mr. Keating is at first reading along in apparent earnestness, but after a few seconds he glances up from the book and surveys the class with a wry smile on his face. It is clear that he is up to something, although the viewer is not sure what.

While Mr. Perry continues to read, Mr. Keating eventually gently taps his fingers a few times on his desk and then walks up to the chalkboard, grabs a piece of chalk and starts to follow Mr. Perry's reading by making a rating-graph that parallels the one being described in the textbook. As he does this, he betrays nothing of his true intentions, but merely appears to be taking the textbook's rating method seriously. As Mr. Perry finishes the paragraph, Mr. Keating finishes his graph and then turns around and looks gently at his students for a second or so and then says just one word: "Excrement." At this point all of the students stop and look up at him. He walks around his desk to get closer to his students and then says: "That's what I think of Mr. J. Evans Pritchard. We're not laying pipe, we're talking about poetry." He then goes on to compare Mr. Pritchard's rating method to American Bandstand, where songs are rated on how well one can dance to them. The students are surprised and laughing as he does an impersonation of the host of American Bandstand, but what comes next causes them to stare in totally confused disbelief. He tells them "to rip out" the page that has just been read. As they stare—without ripping—he keep urging them with increasing feeling to "rip it out!" and "rip out the whole page!" As he goes on, they get more nervous—they are looking at each other trying to understand what is going on. They are shell-shocked. Finally, as Mr. Keating keeps urging them and urging them, Mr. Dalton, who seems to be the closest to a school rebel, finally decides that Mr. Keating is being serious. He gets a sly smile on his face as he sits up in his chair from the slouching, disengaged posture he had taken before. While looking intently at Mr. Keating, he opens his book, grabs the first page and slowly rips it out, while all the other students look on in amazement. Mr. Keating then thanks Mr. Dalton and says: "Gentleman, tell you what, not just rip out that page, rip out the entire introduction!" He then says things like "Be gone, J. Evans Pritchard!" and "I want to hear nothing but ripping!" At this point the boys start to rip and once they do they become excited and enthusiastic. Of course, they don't know exactly why they are ripping, but the relief from the disorientation and confusion releases itself in the laughing and ripping. They are doing something that they had perhaps always wanted to do at the subconscious level their whole lives in school—tear apart the dry textbooks that they were forced to learn without knowing or caring why they were learning them.

At this point, no epiphany has happened. There has been a release of pressure from the confusion the boys were feeling during the reading, and then Mr. Keating's rejection of the reading which followed it; but they still have no idea why Mr. Keating hates Pritchard so much and is willing to destroy his textbook in response. But what comes next, changes all that. After the students tear out the introduction, Mr. Keating carries around a waste-paper basket and begins to explain why he had them rip out the introduction to their textbook. He talks passionately about the "war" for the hearts and minds of young people and how words and language matters. The students are interested now, listening attentively, as Mr. Keating walks in between their desks towards the center of the classroom. When he arrives at the center, with students all around him, he says "I have a little secret for you," and then he squats down and tells them to "huddle-up," and then says it again until they hesitantly lean in to hear him as he almost whispers:

> We don't read and write poetry because it is cute. We read and write poetry because we are members of the human race. And the human race is filled with passion. Medicine, law, business and engineering—these are noble pursuits and necessary to sustain life. But poetry, beauty, romance, love—these are what we stay alive for.

His huddle culminates with him saying "The powerful play goes on and *you* may contribute a verse" and then he says it again with more feeling and emphasis. He ends by looking the boys in the eyes one at a time, as he scans the huddle and whispers, "What will your verse be?" The camera pans to the boys' faces and it is apparent that many of them are moved.

The question then becomes whether the epiphany actually happened. We know that it did in several of the students because in the next scene they have looked up the yearbook for Mr. Keating. They are fascinated by him—similar to the fascination young aristocrats had for Socrates and similar to the fascination Mrs. Smith's students had towards her— and want to know more about him. What they discover is that he was part of an informal literary society known as the "Dead Poets Society." When they uncover this, they immediately find Mr. Keating on campus and ask him what the Dead Poets Society was. He explains that it was a group of "Romantics" who sought to follow Thoreau and "suck the marrow out of life." The Society would meet in some Indian caves near the campus and read poetry to one another. Upon hearing this, Mr. Perry (the student who said "but different" on the first day of class) recommends to the group that they reconvene the Dead Poets Society. Mr. Dalton (the student who was willing to rip the page out of his textbook) immediately agrees to join. Following those two, the others are far more reluctant (because it could get them in trouble for leaving campus), but they finally acquiesce. At this point, the movie director makes it clear that an epiphany has happened in Mr. Perry (the clear leader of the group) and also with Mr. Dalton the rebel among the students, but for the rest, it has not happened; they agree to participate in the Dead Poet's Society out of an inkling that something important is happening, but they are still harassed by psychological barriers that prevent them from seeing what Mr. Perry is beginning to see. But, in at least two of his students, an important threshold has been crossed as an epiphany is beginning to dawn on them; and it has produced a strong desire to change their behaviors in light of the epiphany. In subsequent class sessions, the force of this epiphany is redoubled until it is clear that they want to be habituated in light of the new virtues they see as having value.

This scene represents Mr. Keating's direct attempt to create an epiphany. It shares several of the qualities of the epiphanies created in Plato's dialogues. One main feature is its use of *aporia* to set the stage for the epiphanies. Like we saw in our analysis of *Lysis*, the effect of confusion and disorientation creates a kind of openness in Keating's students. When they entered his classroom on the first day, they were expecting business as usual and none of them seemed interested in reading poetry or engaging in ideas for their own sake. They were confused—even shocked—by Mr. Keating's breaking of convention, and the shock seemed to help his belief in the importance of poetry to sink in. He was able to *tell* them what he hoped they would see, and some of them were able to see it; of course, they do not see it in its entirety, but a substantial change in the orientation towards their lives and what they value has changed.

Because of a lack of space, we do not have the room to go into the ways the epiphanies deepen for Mr. Perry, Mr. Dalton, and eventually for Mr. Overstreet and Mr. Anderson, but the rest of the movie makes it absolutely clear that these students' lives have been radically changed, and they will never be the same.[7]

Conclusion

In all of these examples, what has been created in students is the beginning of a desire to develop the virtues that might enrich their lives and might contribute to the betterment of society. In this way, they now have a growing *cognitive* awareness of what the virtue is (although that knowledge will need to grow significantly before they can become virtuous), and they have an *affective* desire to pursue that virtue. What they are still lacking, however, is a deepening of both these dimensions and also the growth in the conative dimension that will provide them with the strength of character and dispositions to follow through on those desires. All of these growth areas are developed throughout the habituation process which they must now undergo if they hope the epiphany to yield permanent change in their lives. In the next chapter, we discuss the way teachers can help start and support a rehabituation process in students who have experienced epiphanies. We will focus on the importance of one-on-one interactions between the student and teachers, the group interactions between teachers and the whole class, and the central role friendship plays in the creation of an extracurricular community of shared practice which can lead to the development of virtues.

Notes

1. The word "epiphany" has its etymology in the Greek word "*epiphaínō*," which means to show or display. In the ancient Greek context, epiphanies were associated with the appearance of gods and goddesses to mortals. Throughout the middle ages epiphanies were associated with supernatural revelations; however, beginning with the nineteenth century, and especially with James Joyce's secular retrieval of the word in the twentieth century, "epiphany" lost its supernatural or divine connotation and now means something like a moment of insight or realization that a person has about something important or personally significant.

2. One of the few exceptions might be Lawrence Kohlberg's theory of moral development and the neo-Kohlbergians who followed him. Kohlberg did not use the concept of epiphany, but he claimed that when students were asked to decide what to do in situations that involved a moral dilemma, they could spontaneously come to see that the answer they might have previously given was unjust and that the moral dilemma required a different response. When students achieved these realizations, Kohlberg claims that they had moved from one stage of moral maturity to a higher stage. On the face of it, when students' understanding of justice moves from one stage to another, it might seem like they are having an epiphany. However, in Kohlberg's (1981) theory, these insights were not necessarily supposed to be life-altering or trajectory-redefining. Typically he depicts them as being a straightforward recognition that one had come to a new moral awareness. According to Kohlberg, there was not necessarily any need to alter one's life or reorient one's moral trajectory; one simply had to follow the rational knowledge of what to do, knowledge that was clear, unambiguous, and action governing (pp. 47–48). For Kohlberg, development along the moral stages is a cognitive matter that does not involve affective or conative dimensions, like epiphanies do. For Kohlberg, a change from one stage to another was akin to an aha moment; a person who moved from one stage to another certainly was struck by a realization, but that realization did not *necessarily* include a dramatic shift in one's self-concept or alter the fundamental direction of one's life. It might include those things, but Kohlberg does not argue that it must.

3. While Aristotle is almost exclusively pessimistic about the prospects of rehabituation in adult life, there is one exceptional passage:

> The bad man, if he is being brought into a better way of life and thought, may make some advance, however slight, and if he should once

improve, even ever so little, it is plain that he might change completely, or at any rate make very great progress; for a man becomes more and more easily moved to virtue, however small the improvement was at first. It is, therefore, natural to suppose that he will make yet greater progress than he has made in the past, and as this progress goes on, it will change him completely and establish him in the contrary state, provided he is not hindered by lack of time.

Categories, 13a22–33

4. Of course, this is not to say that in other areas, Aristotle offers a more complete picture than Plato. From our point of view, what education really needs is the insights from both, which is why we are not offering an alternative to Neo-Aristotelianism, but a supplement to it. We hope that Plato's views on epiphanies and habituation can add to the neo-Aristotelian movement that is gathering steam in educational theory.

5. These moral conversions do not necessarily mean the person has completely reformed themselves—they are not fully "converted"—but these conversions reorient the mental structures of the person so that they desire to live differently.

6. Before examining Ms. Gruwell's pedagogical practice in *Freedom Writers*, it is important to address worries educationists have about using this movie (and others like it) as a model for teachers to follow. Some scholars have worried that there is a danger in over-romanticizing the experience of students and teachers in movies, which can set unrealistic (or dangerous!) expectations (e.g., Bulman, 2004). By displaying certain aspects of the teachers' professional obligations while neglecting others, depictions of teaching in movies does not provide a full account of the complexity of teaching and can lead to false expectations or ideals. There are truths to these criticisms, and it is certainly not our intention to suggest that the image of Ms. Gruwell (or Mr. Keating who comes later) and the epiphanies she creates in the classroom are to be accepted as the final word on how to teach. Nevertheless, the indisputable fact is that both adults and children have been incredibly inspired by *Freedom Writers* (which is supposed to be a fairly accurate portrayal of a true story), *Dead Poets Society*, and other teacher movies—so inspired that they have had their own life-altering epiphanies watching them. It is also true that we have seen *real* students experience epiphanies similar to the ones these Hollywood teachers produce in their students. These kinds of epiphanies happen in real life, in real schools, with real teachers who teach in ways similar to Ms. Gruwell and Mr. Keating. In fact, we have experienced life-altering epiphanies by teachers who employed methods similar to them. Teachers like Ms. Gruwell or Mr. Keating exist all over the world. But why use teachers from movies as an example rather than teachers from schools around the world? The reason is simple and straightforward: We can all watch the teachers in the movies. Unlike the hundreds, perhaps thousands, of teachers like them who have *not* been captured on film (or at least on film available to the general public), these films are widely accessible to the general public, and because they are widely accessible, and because many of our readers will have already seen the films, they can serve as examples for us to examine, and from which to draw insights about the production of epiphanies.

7. Sadly, in the case of Mr. Perry, the pressures he feels from his parents to return to his old way of life—as a dull valedictorian who is supposed to be a doctor and who only is interested in school insofar as his parents make him get straight As—and because of his epiphany he refuses to listen to them which leads to tragic consequences. Indeed, whenever a student experiences a life-altering and

trajectory-reorienting epiphany, it is not at all clear that this will make their life better or easier. On the contrary, it can open up a whole host of significant consequences which the teacher cannot anticipate from the outset. Thus, teachers need to carefully consider the ramifications of their actions and need to be as transparent as possible both with their students and with their students' parents about what they are hoping to achieve. This may not have been enough to avert Mr. Perry's tragic suicide, but it might have helped.

7 Rehabituation in the Contemporary Classroom

Introduction

Having seen the various ways teachers can produce epiphanies in their students, we now must consider the more essential component to producing virtue in students: Rehabituation in light of epiphany. Even the most powerful epiphanies are short-lived and if not acted upon very quickly, the force of the epiphany usually will slowly be lost. The *cognitive* knowledge of the epiphany may endure for some time, but the *affective* component of the epiphany will evaporate much more quickly. Because of the relative ephemerality of the affective aspect of epiphanies, long lasting moral growth is rare unless students undergo a rehabituation process in which they further refine their cognitive understanding of the virtue, begin to grow in their desire to pursue the virtue, and to grow in the strength of character needed to continue that pursuit when they encounter obstacles. According to Plato, all of these components of becoming fully virtuous cannot be in place unless the students begin a rigorous habituation process immediately following any epiphany they have.

The problem is that as difficult as achieving epiphanies in the classrooms is, helping students voluntarily undergo a rehabituation process is even more difficult. There are several problems in encouraging the rehabituation process. The first is that teachers only get to spend a limited time with their students on a weekly basis. This is especially true for secondary teachers who get to interact with their students only an hour a day on most days. The habituation process requires regular feedback between a person guiding the habituation process and the person undergoing it. Since teachers have so little time with students it is hard to provide them enough guidance. The second reason the habituation process is difficult is because students who have received an epiphany regarding virtue are surrounded by a culture that may not encourage the development of the virtues. This can happen both with respect to the friends and family that surround the students but also the broader popular culture that is always in the background (or foreground). The third reason is simply that old habits are hard to break. Even under the best circumstances, it is very difficult to change our habits. So even if it is the case that teachers could be with their students for eight hours a day; and even if it is the case that students were removed from cultural influences, it would still be hard for them to change ingrained patterns of behavior that may subvert the moral development of the student.[1]

In spite of these challenges, the rehabituation of students who have had epiphanies is not impossible. It takes a clear vision and determination by the teacher. In this chapter, we outline three ways a teacher can help students undergo a successful rehabituation process. Naturally, even the clearest vision and most tenacious determination by the teacher cannot guarantee success with every student, but a sincere effort by the teacher can have a dramatic impact on many students' lives. The three methods teachers can use to promote a rehabituation process include: one-on-one mentoring by the teacher with the students; creating a classroom culture that promotes virtue; and helping students cultivate friendships of excellence outside of the classroom.

Emulation and Role-Modeling for Rehabituation

All three of the previous methods of rehabituation rely on the time-tested process of emulation and role-modeling. Nearly every era and culture has used emulation and role-modeling as the foundations of the habituation process. Starting with the Ancients, people recognize that the formation of virtue in students was primarily achieved by having them perform certain tasks over and over again under the guidance of a mentor who was further along in the process. This is, not surprisingly, the case for Plato who argues that young people must imitate virtuous individuals. He says in the *Republic* that young people

> must imitate from childhood what is appropriate for them, namely, people who are courageous, self-controlled, pious, and free, and their actions. They mustn't be clever at doing or imitating slavish or shameful actions, lest from enjoying the imitations, they come to enjoy the reality. Or haven't you noticed that imitations practiced from youth become part of nature and settle into habits.
>
> (*Republic* 395c-d)

In the *Laws* he says similar things:

> Once again, education has proved to be a process of attraction, of leading children to accept right principles as . . . endorse as genuinely correct by men who have high moral standards and are full of years and experience. The soul of the child has to be prevented from getting into the habit of feeling pleasure and pain in ways not sanctioned by the

laws and those who have been persuaded to obey it; he should follow in their footsteps and find pleasure and pain in the same things as the old.

(*Laws* 659d)

And in the *Crito* he says,

One should value the good opinions . . . [of] those wise men. . . . of these things and before whom we feel fear and shame more than before the [majority]. If we do not follow his directions, we shall harm and corrupt that part of ourselves that is improved by just actions and destroyed by unjust actions.

(*Crito*, 47a–47d)

In all these instances, Plato articulates the view that we become who we are by the types of role-models we emulate and the actions we perform based on what those role-models recommend that we do. On the one hand, Plato's advice seems quite straightforward—emulating good people by doing things similar to what they do seems a tried-and-true method of developing habits similar to those of our role models. But, in the context of contemporary education it presents special difficulties. All of the earlier quotations from Plato more or less assume a one-on-one basis for the guidance of a role model, or at least a broader social culture in which *everyone* agreed on the values of role models and were mutually encouraging one another to emulate them. It is very different in pluralistic democratic classrooms where the teachers have limited opportunity for one-on-one mentoring and where, because of the diverse set of values represented in the schools, there is often very little common agreement about who our role models should be, or what they should encourage us to emulate. Nevertheless, we argue that the three methods of rehabituation in the classroom all rely on emulation and role modelling, even if the three modes differ in certain ways.[2]

The Teacher and One-on-One Mentoring With Students

The most intuitive form of emulation and role modeling is one-on-one conversations between teacher and pupil. For the purposes of this chapter we will be discussing the potential rehabituation and role modeling for students *who have had a moral epiphany and want to live a more virtuous life*. A student's desire to grow in virtue—which can be caused by an epiphany—is essential if the one-on-one mentoring is to be effective. If a teacher tries to provide moral advice to a student who does not desire to embody the virtue the teacher wants the student to grow in, the student will lack the motivation to follow the advice and the mentoring fails. But assuming, as we are, that the student has had an epiphany and genuinely desires to grow in the virtues, she will presumably be very *willing* to listen to her teacher's advice. The operative word here is "willing." Students who have had a genuine epiphany are eager to hear advice from their teachers, and in principle they want to follow through on that advice. However, the fact is that sometimes the advice demands that the student ignore their ingrained habits and the desires they produce, and it can be hard for the student to follow through on the advice. Examples of students who have received an epiphany and want to live their lives in light of the epiphany is found in *Dead Poets Society*, where Mr. Keating attempts to provide guidance to them, with mixed results.

The first example is Mr. Perry, who because of his new love of courageously pursuing the arts—a love gained by way of an epiphany in Mr. Keating's class—has to confront the fact that his father has expressly forbade his participation in the arts and has instead insisted that Mr. Perry exclusively focus on his academic studies. Mr. Perry does not know how to navigate this conflict of interest and appeals to Mr. Keating, who is the one role model he has in this situation. Mr. Keating listens empathetically to Mr. Perry's dilemma and gives him the wise advice not to lie to his father, but to "show your father who you are, what your heart is." This models some of the main virtues Mr. Keating has been trying to encourage in his students—honesty, authenticity, courage, and respect. After giving this advice it is clear that Mr. Perry understands that it is good advice and that he would be wise to follow his role model, but the problem is that he is simultaneously convinced that his dad will not listen to him and will dogmatically insist that he quit his passion for the arts. The conflict between Mr. Perry's desire to follow his role model's advice, and his conviction that the advice—while being sound in theory—will never work in practice, leads Mr. Perry to ignore Mr. Keating's advice, while lying to Mr. Keating by telling him he spoke with his father, and then secretly going behind his dad's back to continue, dishonestly, his involvement with the arts. The results are disastrous. Mr. Perry's father is enraged when he discovers his son's disobedience and blames Mr. Keating for the outcome. Mr. Perry's father decides to unenroll him from Welton and instead send him to a military academy for a rigorous and disciplinary education. This is so devastating to Mr. Perry that he takes his own life on the very night he learns it.

Naturally, this tragic result of one-on-one mentoring shows that such mentoring is not always effective and has the potential to be life altering in the worst ways. There are many psychological forces at work in a student who receives such mentoring and it is impossible for the teacher to know what outcome will actually occur. This is, unfortunately, the danger of any educational endeavor. As teachers, we cannot help but influence our students to behave or think in certain ways. Had Mr. Keating not been a one-on-one mentor to Mr. Perry it might have led to similar results. Students are necessarily changed by their teachers—whatever a teacher's philosophy might be—and it is impossible to predict those changes ahead of time. All a teacher can do is do their best to teach wisely and give wise advice and hope the advice will guide the student towards a more flourishing way of life.

Mr. Perry was not the only student to seek out the guidance of Mr. Keating in the film. Mr. Dalton, the rebel who experienced an epiphany earlier in the film, also looked to Mr. Keating as a role model. But unlike Mr. Perry, Mr. Dalton follows Mr. Keating's advice, even though at first he questions it.

After pulling two ill-advised pranks on the school administration, Mr. Dalton was caught and subjected to severe punishment, including the threat of expulsion. His pranks were inspired by the epiphanies he had received in Mr. Keating's classes but were actually inconsistent with the virtues upon which the epiphanies were based. Once Mr. Keating learned of the pranks, he directly confronted Mr. Dalton regarding the second one and told him that he thought it was a "lame stunt." Interestingly, Mr. Dalton is confused and surprised, and he can't believe that Mr. Keating is "siding with [the administration]?! What about *carpe diem* and sucking all the marrow out of life?" Mr. Keating responds emphatically but forcefully by saying "sucking all the marrow out of life doesn't mean choking on the bone. You see, there is a time for daring, and there is a time for caution. And a wise man knows which is called for." Mr. Dalton then gently and humbly says, "But I thought you would like that?" To which Mr. Keating replies "No, you getting expelled from school is not daring to me, it is stupid. Because you will miss some golden opportunities." Mr. Keating is, of course, appealing in essence to Aristotle's golden mean between having too much fear and too little fear—Mr. Dalton had too little fear and so his act was not courageous but reckless and foolish. He is also appealing to Plato's claim in the *Meno* that wisdom must guide the impulse to courage for it to be truly courageous.

> Courage for example, when it is not wisdom but like a kind of recklessness. . . . The same is true of moderation and mental quickness; when they are learned and disciplined with understanding they are beneficial, but without understanding they are harmful.
>
> (*Meno*, 88b)

To his credit, Mr. Dalton listens carefully to Mr. Keating's advice and for the rest of the movie attempts to make wise decisions based on the virtues in which he is being guided by Mr. Keating. This does not mean that he does not continue to suffer repercussions from his early recklessness, but he is far more thoughtful in his courage from there on out, and, as such, is slowly learning to act wisely in light of his epiphanies.

Mr. Dalton's attempt to emulate Mr. Keating and his mistaken belief that Mr. Keating would admire his pranks reflects one of the staples of the psychological process of emulation and imitation of role models that students go through. One of the foremost articulators of the role of imative, social learning, Albert Bandura, describes the natural process by which students come to gain a clearer understanding of what the *correct* imitation of role models involves.

> It is true that young children sometimes initiate an adult-child sequence by making an apparent approximation to adult behavior and the adults frequently respond by giving a demonstration of how the child should, in fact, behave. However, the child's approximation may in many cases represent an outcome of prior, though incomplete, observational learning.
>
> (Bandura, 1963, pp. 53–54)

Mr. Dalton had had numerous opportunities to hear Mr. Keating offer advice on how to be virtuous and had on many occasions seen Mr. Keating act virtuously himself, but all told, he did not have enough observational data-points to know that his behavior was not courageous but foolish. This will always be the danger with one-on-one mentoring with students after they have experienced an epiphany. They simply have not had enough experience seeing the teacher embody the virtues themselves, and as a consequence in trying to emulate the teacher, they will make mistakes until the habituation process is further progressed so that such misapplications of the virtue grow less frequent.

There are more examples in *Dead Poets Society* that illuminate Mr. Keating's use of one-on-one role-modeling to help habituate his students with epiphanies, but, on the whole, his most effective way of habituating them is not through one-on-one interactions. As we indicated earlier in this chapter, a high school teacher's opportunity to mentor her students in a one-on-one fashion is fairly limited, and we see this impact in *Dead Poets Society*. Fortunately, while this is the most direct and straightforward method of rehabituating students through emulation, it is not the only method for classroom teachers, or even perhaps the most effective method.

Creating a Culture of Emulation and Role-Modeling

The next method of emulation and role-modeling is based less on the direct comments of the teacher to *individual students* and more about how the teacher's own persona encourages a culture of virtue-emulation in the classroom. In these instances the rehabituation process is controlled only indirectly by the teacher. Rather than the teacher telling an individual student what actions she should consider doing, the teacher creates a classroom culture where certain kinds of activities are promoted by the students themselves.

There are several ways a teacher can create this classroom culture. The first and most essential thing to do is for them to model the virtues themselves, both in what they *teach* and what they do. There is a debate among Aristotle scholars about the habituation process and whether it is achieved by a parent or teacher merely telling the child what to do and making her do it, without any explanation, or whether the parent or teacher explains why they are making the child do certain actions. Interpreters like Curzer (2002) insist that there is nothing in Aristotle which suggests that he believed children should be told *why* they are being forced to perform certain actions. Other interpreters like Burnyeat (1980), claim that in the early years children should be simply told what to do and forced to do it, but at some point in their development—once they have internalized the virtues to a sufficient degree—their parents or teachers should begin to explain *why* the actions are virtuous. However, other interpreters, like Sherman (1999) and Kristjánsson (2006), claim that while Aristotle himself does not explicitly state that parents and teachers should explain *why* they are making their children perform certain actions, his theory would accommodate such an explanation. Whichever of these interpretations is more faithful to Aristotle is not a question we will seek to answer here, but what is of importance is that of the three, the belief shared by Sherman and Kristjánsson is the most appropriate for older students who have just recently had an epiphany regarding virtue.[3] It is most appropriate because the epiphany not only creates a desire to perform virtuous actions but also a desire to be the kind of person who performs them. The student having the epiphany aspires to *live* virtuously and to *be* virtuous. In many cases that desire will be kept alive longer to the degree to which they can vicariously participate in virtue by sharing in the aspiration with fellow aspirants, including the teacher who helped lead them to desire virtue. Even though the person who had the epiphany is still a novice and does not understand the virtue fully, the desire produced by the epiphany will often make them want to spend time with a person who is further along in the virtue. And usually they do not just want to spend time with the person but also to be able to discuss the virtue with them. The discussion will often be somewhat one-sided, where the teacher speaks in a language that the novice can only just barely understand, if at all. But simply being in the presence of the language of virtue can have the effect of prolonging the epiphany. The novice asks clarifying questions; she is eager to hear stories of when the teacher was a novice; she asks if the teacher has examples from other people's lives or knows of good books or films. In these instances the novice wants more than simple directions on what to do, and if that is all she is given, the effects of the epiphany can wane more quickly.

It is different for a young child who undergoes a habituation process with a parent or teacher. The child usually does not have the same aspirational identification with her mentor. She is not only a novice in the virtue that the mentor is encouraging her to perform but is also a novice in life—she does not know what kinds of questions should or could be asked; it does not immediately occur to her to ask for more examples, in most instances. The child is just too immature to understand the need for an expansion of the picture of virtue the mentor is trying to give her. This does not mean that the mentor should not provide these things without the novice asking for them; on the contrary, she should do so, even if the child does not understand them or want them. The advantage of Sherman's and Kristjánsson's advocacy of explaining virtues to students, while they are simultaneously requiring them to act virtuously, is that it builds a critical understanding that gradually creates a connection between the mentor and the child that will lead to a desire for shared aspiration more quickly than if the mentor only gives direct instructions on what to do. This sense of shared aspiration creates camaraderie, and camaraderie builds trust, which, again, creates a greater desire for emulation. Eventually, novices begin to sense that they are part of a community, which creates accountability, which further increases a desire to be virtuous.

An example of how older people often want more than mere direct instruction when they are being habituated into a new way of life can be seen in an example of an adult who decides that she wants to learn the violin later in life. The desire to do so leads the adult to start taking lessons. She remembers taking lessons in elementary school and not enjoying them. When she thinks back on those lessons she remembers many of the drills and instructions on *what* to do with her bow or her fingering. When she followed these instructions as a child, she did not take pleasure in doing so. True, the pleasure increased a little bit once she started to master the piece she was working on, but she still did not feel totally invested as a child. She was, in a sense, going through the motions, but she had no idea what it would have meant not to go through the motions. But this time, when the adult starts taking lessons as an adult, a very different experience ensues. She may find herself dissatisfied just being told what to do over and over again. Of course, she will submit to it because she knows her teacher is an authority, but she finds something missing. She wants more "information," more explanation, examples, and so on. It is not because she knows more about the violin in any technical sense than when she was in elementary school, but she realizes that part of the process of learning mastery with the violin, and part of the fun of learning that mastery, is to start to develop a language for it and a feel for it; and, importantly, but inchoately, she wants to participate in a deeper relationship with the teacher—that is, to see violin playing in the way the teacher does—so that she can more quickly learn what it feels like to play violin as a *real* violinist does. All of this contributes to the increase in her desire to learn the violin, which will make it more likely that she will gain mastery sooner than later.

Of course, it is not just in adults that we see the desire to learn more from the teacher than just requirements to perform certain tasks in school-children. Wouter Sanderse (2012) points out that students are

> impressed by teachers who were not just experts, but who were also interested, engaged and playful, who fascinated and inspired them, and who dared to show their personality and their identity as human beings . . . Timmerman's study emphasises that children appreciate teachers who show through their behavior what kind of person they are.
>
> (p. 130)

Of course, one of the most important moral "behaviors" teachers have at their disposal is the way they talk about their values and virtues. It may be unlikely for a teacher to physically model a virtue on a daily basis in their classroom, but it is much more likely that they can find opportunities to discuss times when they acted virtuously, or discuss *why* they take pleasure in acting virtuously outside of the classroom. This aspect of sharing who they are has a tendency to fascinate students (as Sanderse argues), especially if they are under the influence of an epiphany. The desire for virtue that the epiphany produces, creates a further desire to get to *know* the teachers that helped create the epiphany and who embody the virtues themselves.

With this moral psychology in place, we can see that even if the teacher does not have much opportunity to give direct one-on-one guidance to individual students she can bring her personality and her own pursuit of virtue into play in the classroom, which can further inspire those in the classroom to emulate her. We saw this in the example of Mrs. Smith in the last chapter. Strike was clearly fascinated with her as a freshman, when he did not understand the ways the virtues inherent to mathematics could contribute to his flourishing. Yet, as he observed and interacted with Mrs. Smith, he began to *sense* that perhaps mathematics could contribute meaningfully to his personal flourishing. He could not yet exactly see *how* mathematics could contribute to his life, but he was beginning to have premonitions. In the absence of that more direct seeing, his fascination with what mathematics contributed to Mrs. Smith's life kept his desire to discover the virtues of mathematics alive and growing. Mrs. Smith let her own virtues shine in the class, even when she was not giving direct guidance to Strike or other students. As such she helped create a culture that encouraged the love of the goods of mathematics and the virtues required to realize those goods. The upshot of this kind of approach is that the same means Mrs. Smith used to create epiphanies are the same means to start the rehabituation process. Indeed, in an important sense, the rehabituation process is simply the continual production of mini-epiphanies that when added together begin to form the knowledge, disposition, and character in students which are characterized by *cognitive* knowledge of the virtue, the *affective* desire to act on that knowledge, and an increasing *conative* disposition to follow through on those desires.

But it is not just the teacher who creates the culture. She is the primary initial motivator, but eventually the students begin to adopt some of the gestures, values, and vocabulary of the teacher. They begin to repeat these values and words to each other, even when the teacher is not directly listening. The fascination they feel for the teacher and the desire to share in the teacher's aspiration rubs off on the students, and they begin to see themselves as fellow aspirants who not only are emulating the teacher but also begin to emulate each other. This might be called "inspirational emulation" (Jonas and Chambers, 2017). According to this idea, a classroom culture of camaraderie develops when students begin to see each other as fellow aspirants who want to achieve their highest selves. When this happens it is not just the teacher who becomes a guide in the rehabituation process but also fellow students.

For this culture to be developed it is helpful if the teacher employs one or more of four strategies. The first one should go without saying: teachers should seek opportunities to embody the virtues in the classroom and outside of the classroom. While perfect consistency between our actions in the classroom and actions outside the classroom is impossible, teachers need to recognize that virtue is impossible without stable dispositions and character traits. The teacher must exhibit these character traits in the class *and outside the class* if she is to be a role model for her students. When teachers act virtuously in the classroom for the sake of "educating their students" but do not do so from a firm and unchanging character, a kind of moral hypocrisy is the result and students are usually aware of this moral hypocrisy. They can *sense at an intuitive level* that there is a kind of moral discrepancy in the teacher and they will soon see the role-modeling in the class as merely a show and a sham. This will, obviously, have a completely chilling effect on the desire to become virtuous in the students.

The second strategy teachers might consider employing in the classroom is that they can and should "talk out loud," as it were, about the mental processes (*phronesis*) that occur in them when they are in the midst of deliberating about the virtuous action to be pursued. As discussed earlier, older students who have a true epiphany often immediately want to be in community with the person who helped to induce the epiphany. As the teacher provides information, explanations, or analyses of the virtues or the way she thinks about them and engages in them, the more likely it is that the students will feel bonded to her, which will in turn increase their desire to embody the virtue. It is probably helpful if the teacher is not overly didactic or dry in their explanations (although sometimes, if intentionally adopted, a seemingly dry and didactic persona could be effective) but for the teacher to bring their personality and their idiosyncratic passion for the virtue to bear in the classroom. As Sanderse points out, students like it when they see the unique individuality of their teachers on display. The more individuality and idiosyncrasy teachers bring to their descriptions and explanations of the virtue, the more likely students' imaginations will be captured by it. Of course, there are exceptions—as, for example, when the teacher's persona reminds a student of their fifth-grade teacher that they hated—but often these idiosyncrasies work to help create a culture of inspirational emulation regarding virtue.

The third strategy a teacher can employ is to highlight the virtuous activity particular students perform and simultaneously remind the other students that they are capable of achieving similar levels of virtue. In bringing attention to those who act virtuously, some readers will worry that other students will feel ashamed or resentful of the student who received the praise. But if teachers continually affirm other students' ability to achieve the same virtue—and they really believe that it is possible— many of these students will start to believe in themselves and will not feel resentful towards those who are further along the road but may see themselves as partners with them in the pursuit of virtue. Elihu Baldwin (1837) describes the kind of peer-to-peer emulation that can occur in a classroom even if some students achieve at a higher level.

> Emulation is kind and charitable, and magnanimous; and finds only regret in the mistakes, the deficiencies and disappointments of others; while she sincerely rejoices in their highest attainments and most splendid success. He that is truly emulous of others, would not, were it in his power, turn them back, nor for one moment retard their progress, in the race of improvement. He only strives to excel them, and will admire and love them the more for their superiority, which may render that impossible.

(p. 6)

Naturally, if the teacher wants to create a classroom culture in which comments like this one regularly occur, she must believe that all students have the *potential* to regard themselves and their peers the way Baldwin regarded himself and his peers. Moreover, for Baldwin's experience to be a reality for the entire classroom, the teacher should weave explicit promotion of emulation into the fabric of the classroom. It is not enough for the teacher to model inspirational emulation. She must create a classroom culture that fosters emulation throughout. Whatever subject is being taught, the teacher should continually emphasize both the importance of cultivating one's highest self and the manner in which students can be inspired in this pursuit by witnessing greatness in others. This must include the reminder that comparisons are *not* zero-sum games and that the comparisons with others are not a competition with them but a competition with oneself to become as virtuous as possible.

Connected to the third strategy, the fourth is that the teacher should, to the degree that they can, genuinely believe that every student in the class could, at any moment, have an epiphany, and refuse to give up trying to induce them in students, and refuse to give up trying to rehabituate those who have already had an epiphany. Plato's theory of moral education is, as we have construed it, not elitist. Plato is a realist who thinks that it is simply a matter of fact that some people will become more virtuous than others; as a corollary, he also thinks that some people are more likely than others to have an epiphany regarding virtue, and he thinks that some people are more likely to succeed in a rehabituation process once they have had an epiphany. But what makes some people more likely to succeed is not based on a predetermined understanding in which "these kinds of people can never become virtuous"; or "these kinds of people will always become virtuous." Rather, for Plato, every person's soul is, at the level of innate quality, equally capable of desiring virtue; but some people's souls have been more corrupted by bad habituation than others. However, even people who have had bad upbringings like Glaucon, Dion, and Alcibiades did—and all of these people were habituated to crave power and give into their bodily desires—can have epiphanies; and people like Dion, at least, can undergo a rehabituation process and can be reformed. What was it about Dion that made him succeed in the rehabituation process but made Glaucon and Alcibiades fail? We don't know. All Plato claims is that Dion soul was more open, but that is just a metaphorical way of saying "for some reason Dion succeeded." Although Socrates is constantly evaluating his interlocutors for openness towards virtue, he does not know ahead of time who will succeed and who will not; and neither do we. Thus, following Plato, what is important is that teachers are always on the lookout for signs of students who are open to having epiphanies, and even those who do not seem open, to teach in a way that might open them, if, contrary to appearances, it turns out they are open.

Encouraging Friendships of Excellence Outside the Classroom

The last method of supporting students in the process of rehabituation is helping them to form friendships with other students who are virtue-seeking. Of the three strategies we recommend for teachers in the rehabituation process, the cultivation of virtue-seeking friendships is the most important, but it is also the most difficult. In what follows, we explain why cultivating friendships is the most important aspect of the rehabituation process and why friendships can have a powerful impact on the formation of virtue, and then we explain why cultivating these friendships is a two-edged sword that has almost as good a chance of failing as it does of succeeding.

It is our belief that helping students cultivate virtue-seeking friendships is the most important aspect of the rehabituation process. The reason it is so important is because "friendships of excellence" or "character friends," as Aristotle calls them, can have a profound effect on the formation of virtue in students, both with respect to fostering a continued *desire* to become virtuous and also with respect to increasing the *knowledge* of what constitutes virtue. Moreover, just being a good friend is, by itself, formative and helps produce virtues.

Following Aristotle, Talbot Brewer (2005) claims that friendships among virtue seekers can improve their ability to live virtuously in important ways.

> On this elaboration of Aristotelianism, it is precisely by being inducted into friendships and striving to perfect them that we become good or virtuous, to the extent that we do. To be sure, we cannot enter into such relationships unless we already have a glimmer of appreciation for fine action. Yet, as we kindle and deepen human relationships of this ubiquitous sort, our evaluative outlooks are reshaped so as increasingly to approximate a standard of shareability with all others. This standard of shareability does not capture the entirety of what we call morality, but it does rule out certain very common forms of immorality.
>
> (p. 723)

For Aristotle, there are several kinds of friends, including friendships of pleasure, friendships of utility, and friendships of excellence. All of these friendships have their place in the life of flourishing human beings, but friendships of excellence are the highest (and rarest) form of friendships because in them a small group of people help support each other in becoming virtuous human beings, which is constitutive of a life of *eudaimonia*, the highest form of flourishing. However, friendships of excellence do not happen by mere chance and can only form with people who are already on their own path to virtue.

Brewer (2005) goes on to explain how these friendships provide special support in mutually helping friends become virtuous. Even when friends who have had an epiphany desire virtue for themselves and each other, they are prone to deviate from virtue on their own because of their improperly habituated knowledge and desires.

> Humans are prone to deviate from what is good in itself when in the grip of certain emotions, feelings, or desires, including anger, fear, appetitive pleasures, desire for wealth, and desire for honour or public esteem. These emotions, feelings, and desires are partially constituted by a subjective outlook on the good—an impression that some end or course of action is a good one—and this subjective outlook can come loose from what is genuinely and objectively good. If one is to come to have the virtues of character, one's characteristic affects must be reshaped so that the apparent goods they bring to subjective awareness are genuine,

objectively affirmable goods and so that the objective goods we need to be aware of are in fact brought to our subjective attention.

(p. 746)

What character friends provide is a way of helping virtue seekers test their subjective perceptions of the good to make sure they are consistent with what is objectively good. They serve as a check on distortions caused by fears, angers or bodily desires—distortions that might otherwise lead the virtue seeker away from virtue not towards it. Because of the *affective* change that accompany the epiphany the virtue seeker will desire the virtue in question, but because of the *affective* and *conative* nature of her previous upbringing, a virtue seeker may, in the moment, more powerfully desire the actions that his fears, angers, and bodily pleasures recommend as the right course of action. A friend can help bring the virtue seeker back to his correct perception by helping the seeker overcome those desires. "These relationships can provide the sort of external, objectivity-tracking formative and corrective mechanism for our characteristic affects that isolated practical reflection alone is unable to provide" (Brewer, 2005, p. 749).

Moreover, friends can be windows into the objective virtues by means of role-modeling. In this case, it may not be that one friend is suffering from a distortion *per se*, but they may simply not know what to do in a situation. Yet, when they see their friend perform an action, the other person may all of a sudden see that action in a new light and see that it is indeed the correct action. This is a kind of mini-epiphany.

This is a very important function of friendship, and one that can be even more powerful than the role-modeling provided by a mentor. Friendships cause uniquely powerful bonds that can help overcome the malformed desires of a poor upbringing.

> It is not just from the friend that we learn virtue, but from the relationship itself. Character friendship is an experience which provides necessary elements for human cultivation of virtue that the mere experience of having a role-model cannot give us. The special form of sharing in which character friendship consists . . . triggers other emotions important for the process of virtue cultivation besides admiration, love, shame, trust, and hope. Character friendship is a praxis in which the mutual collaboration through actions and dialogue cultivates the friends' virtues.
>
> (Hoyos Valdés, 2017, p. 68)

Hoyos Valdés' point is clearly correct. The reality is that we often feel a greater emotional commitment to the virtues when we spend time with our character friendships than when we do with our mentors. True, sometimes the mentors can give us more *efficient* access to what actions to perform in the adult habituation process, but with friends, what is lost in efficiency is made up for intensity of desire and a deeper sense of shared commitment to the virtues. Hoyos Valdés (2017) argues that "since good friends are in a deep and close relationship characterized by mutual knowledge and appreciation, they can say and do things to one another that can make them grow, and that nobody else could say or do" (p. 76). For whatever psychological reasons, we often *feel* in greater camaraderie with our friends regarding the formation of our characters than with our mentors. For some reason there is a greater sense of *we* that occurs at the subconscious level that leads to a greater hope for the overall improvement of virtue in ourselves and our worlds. Emerson (1834) describes the connections between friends this way:

> The stimulating influence of such a friend . . . I consider one of the greatest blessings I have enjoyed. To be seated continually at his side, sometimes above him, though more frequently below him, to see his intense application, his untiring patience, his vigorous efforts for improvement, his unexceptional morals, and propriety of conduct— could not but be favorable to my progress.
>
> (p. 27)

The fact that Emerson acknowledges that sometimes his achievement was below his friend and sometimes above his friend speaks to the inefficiency of friendship as compared to hierarchical mentoring, but this is offset by the clear passion to strive with his friend that Emerson feels.

The question arises however concerning how the rehabituation process can proceed among two or more friends who are all novices with respect to virtue. Let's assume we have two friends, each of whom have experienced an epiphany in a classroom. They have both recently come to desire deeply to become more just people. Previously, they were not interested in virtue and spent most of their lives in pursuit of money and bodily pleasures. However, because of the power of their epiphanies, they are highly motivated to change their lives, and they discuss their epiphany with each other and receive encouragement that they are not alone in their newfound pursuit of virtue. One of the students excitedly reports that she has another friend who recently claimed that he also wanted to reform his life and to become a more just person. The two friends then go to the teacher in whose class they experienced their epiphany, and they ask the teacher what next steps they should take. The teacher tells them about character friends and the central role they can have in the rehabituation process. They take her advice and reach out to their other friend, and they all agree to help each other in the process of becoming more just. This sounds like the start of something good, and it seems that Aristotle would think that their friendship might be the start of a genuine friendship of excellence because all three of the students desire to mutually support one another in becoming virtuous; they are not choosing to be friends to maximize pleasure or to maximize utility.

On the face of it this seems like a promising start. However, Plato and Aristotle claim that in order for habituation to be effective the people being habituated must be instructed to perform *objectively* virtuous actions. If they perform the right actions they will, little by little, gain in their understanding of virtue and also in their desire to perform the virtue; and as they gain in their understanding and desire, they will increasingly be able to judge what the right thing to do in novel situations and want to do it, which will lead to further understanding, thus leading in an upward spiral where each student begins to help the other students better learn virtue. However, if they act wrongly in a situation, the opposite will occur. Each vicious action that is done, especially if the students think, in their novice state, that it is a virtuous action, will lead them further away from virtue; and then the next time they have to decide what to do, they will more likely make the wrong decision. They are starting to move in a downward spiral.

This leads to the problem at hand. Because the students are novices and have only experienced a glimpse of virtue, it is not at all clear that they have enough knowledge of virtue to know how to encourage each other in performing virtuous actions. Accidentally, they may very well encourage each other to perform the wrong actions. Sadly, in spite of the powerful epiphany they have just experienced, Aristotle and Plato tell us—and we see it in the examples of Alcibiades and Glaucon in Plato—these individuals have been habituated to prefer vice over virtue and this means they will have a disposition that, left to its own devices, will naturally lead them to choose wrongly. As we saw, Plato and Aristotle claim that an early upbringing in vice will corrupt a person's reason and appetites, and they will naturally enjoy performing vicious actions and will think that because they enjoy them that they must be the right actions to perform. The fact that these students' tastes and reason have all been trained in the wrong directions suggests that they will likely give each other bad advice, which will only lead them further away from virtue.

This means that in spite of how important character friendships are in the rehabituation process, these kind of friendships can also lead students away from the right form of rehabituation. Helping students develop successful character friendships is subtle and can be a two-edged sword to a student who is just starting her process of rehabituation. Friends who are virtue-seeking can dramatically increase the desire for virtue and the practices it requires in a person who has experienced an epiphany; but those who are not virtue-seeking can equally and dramatically decrease a desire for virtue and the practices it requires in a person who has experienced an epiphany.

Under both Plato and Aristotle's conception of mentoring and role-modeling and the centrality of mentoring and role-modeling for the habituation process, they both assume that the mentor and role model is virtuous and will therefore provide superior guidance for an individual who badly needs good guidance. Recurring to our imaginary students, in their previous upbringing, the students were guided by parents, teachers, friends, or a culture that was not guiding them well, which is why they needed an epiphany to create a desire for virtue. Rather than leading them towards virtue, these influences were leading them away from virtue. If the students who have received an epiphany and now want to pursue virtue, it is obvious that they cannot go back to their previous guides, since these guides had proven to be a bad influence. Who then do they turn to? Naturally, the first response would be that they should turn to the teacher, but as we discussed earlier the teacher usually does not have the time and space to give the student the amount of guidance they would need to become rehabituated. The teacher can give an occasional recommendation and can encourage the students to find guides who can spend more time with the students than the teacher can, but that is all rather limited. This is where friendships come in. If the teacher uses the previous methods for initiating the first steps for rehabituation, and if, especially, the teacher helps to create a culture of virtue-aspiration in the classroom, then the seeds for friendships outside of the classroom will have been planted.

But the problem is that, according to Aristotle and Plato, their needs to be some knowledge of virtue in at least one of the friends to ensure that the friendship leads towards virtue and not away from it. Does this mean that rehabituation cannot happen between novices who have been inspired by their teachers to pursue virtue together? We argue that it does not mean that. Whether or not Aristotle and Plato think that aspirants towards virtue can have friendships of excellence that lead them to live more virtuously, we think they can and teachers should encourage these kinds of friendships, especially where students do not have the potential for a relationship with a more experienced moral role model after which they can pattern their lives. What is to be done about this situation? Can teachers help guide students in finding character friendships that as a general rule effectively encourage genuinely objective virtue among friends? We think the answer is yes and that there are several things a teacher can do to bring this state of affairs about.

The first thing a teacher can do is the most obvious. Assuming the group of friends is interested in mentoring and role-modeling, the teacher can give advice directly to the friends as they deliberate about what the best course of action to do in a particular situation is. One of the characteristics of character friendships is that they continually *discuss* the best course of action among one another. The deliberative element of the friendship helps to create the fellow-feeling and camaraderie that makes the formation of character in the friendships so powerful.

After all, such friendships will be marked by conversation about matters of importance to them both, and these conversations will presumably help each to see a more ample range of alternative ways of being and acting and see them in a clearer and more objective light. Since such friends admire each other's sense of the good, each will give credence to the other's attempts to put their basic concerns into words. They will, in effect, be partners in the ongoing task of talking their own half-formed evaluative commitments into a full-fledged and determinate stance on the world. Their confidence in each other's outlooks will also lead them to care about each other's approval and to strive to be worthy of it.

(Brewer, 2005, p. 735)

Nevertheless, the discussions and deliberations between friends can go wrong because of their fledgling understanding of virtue, and this is where the teacher can come in to help mediate the discussion and ensure that the best course of action will take place. In this case, the teacher is a secondary check on the perceptions of the virtue-seeking friends, even though the passion and power may mostly come from the excitement about virtue developed in the discussions among the friends.

The second thing a teacher can do is to help point the group of friends towards people from the past, including philosophers, historical figures, literary characters, and so on, who were virtuous people or virtue seekers themselves and who promote aspiration in contemporary virtue seekers. The reality is that even though the pursuit of virtue across the ages has not been identical, there are certain actions, and the virtues they support, which are shared between different times and cultures. Teachers can help groups of character friends gain access to these voices, which will provide guidance to the friends when the teacher or other mentors are not around. This can be done by speaking to one or more of the friends directly or by providing guidance in the classroom that one or more of the friends attends. When a teacher introduces students to voices from the past who participate in the wisdom tradition, they will be indirectly guiding the character friendships towards new role models. The teacher's use of the wisdom tradition in guiding character friendships helps

to justify Aristotle's tentative reliance, in elaborating his account of the virtues, on received beliefs about which kinds of actions are good and fine. Such beliefs are valuable starting points precisely because they have been capable of gaining the stable affirmation of generations of people facing different circumstances and occupying a wide variety of social standpoints. Given this, they may encapsulate concrete findings not only about shareability but also about what humans need to meet their basic needs and how their projects and pleasures might be shaped in the course of socialization to render their effective pursuit compossible with the like pursuits of others.

(Brewer, 2005, pp. 749–750)

By received beliefs, Brewer does not mean the beliefs and values that characterize contemporary popular cultures, which have not stood the test of time and nor shown to contribute significantly to the flourishing of millennia. At the same time, he does not think the enduring answers to how to become virtuous in wisdom traditions are sufficient to be foolproof guides for virtue seekers. On the contrary he explicitly acknowledges that "these beliefs can yield at best a sketchy and tentative account of the substantive content of the virtues" (Brewer, 2005, p. 75). Nevertheless, sketchy as the account may be, it does help guard against radical departures away from what is objectively virtuous. Teachers can point these students towards these voices, and the voices can form a kind of litmus test, while the epiphanies are still fresh. When the epiphanies are fresh they will *see* the virtue in the authors. Once these authors are admitted by the students to be trustworthy, then they can keep one another accountable to act in the ways these authors would approve. If one of them begins to desire to go back to her old way of life, the others can remind her that this is exactly what she should expect, which is exactly what happened to Alcibiades and Glaucon.

At this critical juncture, the friends who have not slipped back into the same desires must act as the role model that none of them have (beyond the teacher who is not present often enough to know this is happening). How can they help? It seems that all they can do is remind their friend of her previous epiphany and remind her that if she can find the strength of will to overcome the desire to return to her old way of life and instead act according to the epiphany and the voices in the wisdom tradition, then she might, once again, remember the desirability of those actions and the connection they had to the epiphany she had previously experienced. In other words, if she can trust her friends and the voices that they listen to, and act upon their advice, the desires that she is being tempted by might disappear and the epiphanic desires can come back. It will be hard for her to make this choice, but her love of her friends and her trust in them may provide the strength of will that she would not have otherwise.

In this way, we can see how character friends—even though they are just novices with respect to virtue—might be able to serve as proxies for the missing role models. This is assuming of course, that they have access to the kinds of authors mentioned earlier, and that the teacher, where possible, could also provide guidance regarding the virtues. This is where the teacher becomes critical in supporting this rehabituation process. Not only can she give direct advice whenever possible to one or more of these students about which actions to perform to support the rehabituation process, but she can also guide these students to find sources besides herself who, while not being able to give direct advice about specific situations (since they are found only in books), can give general advice on what kinds of actions to pursue and what kind of actions to avoid. These books will never provide a fully adequate explanation of what to do, but the general guidance may be sufficient to help the friends know when they are on the wrong track and to encourage them when they are on the right one.

The role of the teacher in helping students form the friendships of excellence consists, most importantly, in the teachers explicitly encouraging students to develop friendships of excellence and explaining the importance of them in the reformation of their lives. From our point of view, teachers should not only, where possible, give direct one-on-one advice to students about what actions they should perform and explain the importance of those actions for the formation of the cognitive, affective, and conative dimensions of virtue, and not only should they be providing voices from the past, but they should also be giving guidance on how to form character friendships and giving advice to the group of friends about specific actions once the friendships are formed. Finally, they can and should guide students to find additional voices to speak into their lives—both from within contemporary virtue-seeking communities and among voices from the past across the intellectual and moral disciplines.

Conclusion

In this chapter, we have explored the various ways teachers can help support students in the rehabituation process after the students have had an epiphany and have a strong desire to embody the virtues to a more significant degree. We have acknowledged that the rehabituation process is difficult and that many students who begin it will fail to complete it. There are many forces—individual and cultural—that makes the process difficult. However, in spite of the difficulty, we believe that teachers can have hope that lasting change can happen in their students and that supporting them in a rehabituation process is a noble endeavor and should be done as well as possible. We have argued that teachers can provide support by being direct mentors to individual students and helping to guide them on their decision-making process about specific actions; they can also help guide the culture of the classroom as a whole both by giving direct instructions about virtue to the students but also by creating a classroom environment that encourages mutual inspirational emulation; and finally, they can help students create friendships of excellence and help guide those friendships as they progress and grow. One of the most important ways to help initiate these friendships is to discuss them explicitly in the classroom. Students who have even an inkling of a desire to become virtuous often immediately see the distinction between the three different kinds of friendships in Aristotle and are interested in cultivating character friendships. Indeed, in our own classrooms, we have seen with our own eyes that bringing up the distinction between the three kinds of friendship in Aristotle can often have an epiphanic effect on students.

With an initial framework for understanding how teachers might create the conditions for epiphanies in their classrooms, and with an initial framework for understanding how teachers might follow those epiphanies by supporting students in a rehabituation process, we will conclude this book with a summary of the practical implications for teacher preparation and why we believe that the Platonic view we are offering offers new hope for contemporary moral educators in the pursuit of encouraging moral development in their students. We then briefly conclude with a summary of how teachers might think about their practice to induce epiphanies and support the rehabituation process for their students.

Notes

1. Of course, probably the most ideal way a teacher could help support the rehabituation of her students would be to help them find a community of practice in which the virtues are exemplified by the community. Often these communities take the form of religious groups, but presumably there are secular communities who are committed to the virtues. If a teacher could help a student enter these communities—assuming the communities met many times a week and were structured to help support novices in the growth of the practices—the student would have found a way to largely circumvent the three problems listed earlier. Unfortunately, the teacher may not know whether these communities exist, or where to find them, or whether the student or her parents would want to join the communities. It also seems communities of this sort are contracting in the West, and they are few and far between and not as robust in their structure as they once were.
2. For an extended discussion of role-modeling and emulation in education, see Warnick (2008).
3. We would also argue that it is important for young children as well, even though they cannot understand the explanations the parent or teacher offer, but, over time, they will gain almost by contextual osmosis what the explanations mean. Annas (2011) argues similarly:

> Learning as complex as [virtues] requires the conveying of explanation from the parent, and upshot on the part of the child. Many people have stressed that a lot of this is not, especially with small children, explicitly articulate. We certainly don't have to imagine the parent always spelling out every time the point that acting in such and such a way is brave, generous, or whatever. . . . Nevertheless, parents are engaged, in a lot of what they do, in explaining to their children what it is that is brave in chasing off a dog or generous in spending your time for other people, in getting them to see the point of acting in certain ways and the importance of achieving that by acting differently in a different context, rather than repeating the original action.
>
> (p. 23)

For a more thorough discussion of this topic, see Annas (2011, pp. 18–32).

Conclusion

In this conclusion we will articulate why we believe that the Platonic theory of moral education presented in this book is a desirable framework for thinking about moral education in contemporary democracies. We start by comparing it to Kohlberg's historically influential theory and then connect it to the more contemporary moral education theory articulated by the neo-Aristotelians. After making this case, we will offer some final thoughts on the way teachers might approach their classrooms if they want to implement some of Plato's insights.

Plato's Improvements on Kohlberg and Aristotle

There were several aspects of Kohlberg's theory of moral education that made it extremely attractive to educators and contributed to its significant influence. The first was its universality. Kohlberg's theory was founded on a belief that all human beings innately desired justice as a universal virtue and that whatever stage of development the student was in, she was attempting to act justly. Kohlberg argued that all peoples from all cultures had an inborn desire for justice and that even though expressions of justice differed somewhat between cultures, they shared certain fundamental characteristics. According to Kohlberg, justice was a universal virtue that accommodated for cultural difference without being totally relativistic. This appealed to educators because it offered them a framework for encouraging the proper treatment of others that seemed to transcend cultural differences and yet also seemed sensitive to cultural differences at the same time.

The second reason Kohlberg's theory was attractive was its optimism and belief in students. Because he believed the desire for justice was universal, Kohlberg also believed that every child, no matter what their background or upbringing, could develop the virtue of justice and had the potential to keep progressing through the stages of moral development. This optimism was furthered by his claim that all that was necessary for students to move up the stages of development was to be asked questions and provided with opportunities to gain insights about justice by trying to resolve moral dilemmas. It was refreshing to have a new perspective on moral education in which students were seen as young people who had agency in their moral development and who had an innate desire to act justly. Similar to the much-lauded "asset mindset" in contemporary schooling, Kohlberg's theory reoriented teachers' perspectives on their students, encouraging teachers to think of their students as people who were already on their way to moral development and not as students who were lacking morality and must have in forcefully implanted in them. This provided a new hope for the moral fabric of democratic societies.

The third reason Kohlberg's theory was attractive was because it provided a theory of moral education that avoided indoctrination. When Kohlberg was developing his theory of moral development, the horrors of World War II and the moral indoctrination that helped to spawn it were still very fresh in educators' minds. And even more fresh was the specter of nuclear war and the indoctrination that was being used by the Soviets to support an ever deepening cold war. Kohlberg provided a plan to help students become more just and avoid indoctrination. He argued that students went through six stages of moral development and that the movement from one stage to the next happened in the students spontaneously and naturally. The teacher did not have to force her students to believe certain things or act certain ways, but merely needed to provide an environment in which students could move up the stages of development. The teacher's role was to facilitate discussion of moral issues and questions, posing problems and asking students to think through solutions. This came as a relief to educators because (1) it was straightforward and relatively simple. All teachers had to do was ask questions, pose problems, and facilitate discussions and students would grow morally. There was no need to be an expert in morality or know the answer to all morally difficult questions. The teacher could simply provide an environment to discuss these things. This relieved teachers of a great burden of moral responsibility. However (2), it also relieved them of the nagging issue of indoctrination. If they had to provide the moral code the students were to follow and if they were expected to make students follow it, then they had to answer the question for themselves, whether they were not participating in the same kind of educational indoctrination that the Nazis and Soviets participated in. Kohlberg's theory dispensed with the need to force students to obey an external mandated moral code, but, again, without resorting to relativism.

For these reasons (among others) Kohlberg's theory enjoyed tremendous success for many years. However, eventually his theory was called into question from a number of different camps, like, for example, feminist-inspired care theorists who argued that Kohlberg's theory over-prioritized reason and logical thought as the basis for justice. Similarly, character educators also thought Kohlberg over-prioritized reason and logic and believed that there was more to moral development than the cultivation of justice through a cognitive lens. What both criticisms pointed to in slightly different ways was the radically intellectualist nature of his theory—the belief that moral knowledge and moral action were ultimately cognitive in nature and the role of the moral educator was to focus exclusively on the cognitive dimensions of justice.

Part of the optimism of Kohlberg's theory was that it centered on the belief that "he who knows the good, chooses the good" (1981), which is the fundamental tenet of intellectualist views of moral development. The belief that knowing the good is doing the good sounds great in principle, but, eventually, becomes extremely dubious in practice. Not only do kids (like adults) often claim to know what the right thing to do is, and yet fail to do it, it is hard to believe that knowledge is sufficient for virtuous actions. Of course, at first we can write off the discrepancy between the claims of knowledge and subsequent action by thinking that the students "must not have *really* known what they claimed they knew." But when this happens over and over again, and especially when we inquire into the knowledge that the students claim they have, only to discover that the students really do seem to know, then doubt starts to creep in about the intellectualist optimism. This suspicion is further augmented when the teacher begins to reflect on her own moral failings and how, in spite of her certainty that she knows what the right thing to do is, she does not follow through as her knowledge should dictate.

On top of these morally psychological concerns, several critics in the 1970s and 1980s raised suspicion regarding the validity of Kohlberg's "scientific" approach and his claim that rational knowledge was the key to progress in moral areas. Neo-Kantians like Korsgaard (1996) were and are, to be sure, still committed to the belief that moral action can be governed by purely rational principles, but the rise of neo-Aristotelianism (starting with Anscombe's (1958) groundbreaking article "Modern Moral Philosophy" and continuing to gain momentum through the 1960s, 1970s, and 1980s) and the Aristotelian belief that the moral virtues can *not* be cultivated through rational arguments alone added to doubts about Kohlberg's intellectualist project.

Ultimately, Kohlberg's theory fell out of fashion. And beyond the fact that educators still find his stages of moral development interesting to think about, it has tacitly been largely rejected as a viable theory of moral education at the level of practice.

And this finally leads us back to Plato's theory of moral development offered in this book. While Kohlberg claimed to be inspired by Plato's theory of moral development and the intellectualism that he claimed formed the basis of it, he actually significantly misinterpreted and misapplied Plato's educational principles. The fact is, as we have shown in the pages of this book, Plato's theory of moral education is, contrary to popular belief, patently *not* intellectualist. Rational, cognitive knowledge is not sufficient for virtue according to Plato. Rather, students must also have the right desires and the right dispositions to be fully virtuous. There is, to be sure, a *cognitive* dimension to his theory, insofar as students must know what the right thing to do in a given situation is, but there is an *affective* and *conative* dimension that is equally important if students are going to have *full* knowledge of virtue, which means they will consistently act in light of that knowledge. Without the *affective* and *conative* dimensions, students will not consistently act virtuously whatever their cognitive status is with respect to the knowledge of virtue.

Plato has given us two methods of cultivating the affective and conative dimensions of virtue development—epiphanies and rehabituation. In this sense, our Platonic theory of moral education is a significant departure from Kohlberg's cognitivist theory. However, we believe that the three reasons discussed earlier as to why Kohlberg's theory was attractive to educators are as important today as they were half a century ago. To recall, Kohlberg's theory argued first that there was a universal set of principles (which all were various instantiations of justice) that all humans share at the most innate and intuitive level, and that these principles protect students from simple-minded relativism. Relativism can lead to an "anything goes" mentality or paralysis about how we should grow as a moral community and communicate with each other about how to best pursue a flourishing life with each other. We believe that human beings do share a great deal of core principles about justice and mutual respect and toleration, and if students could sufficiently see the value of them, they could be persuaded of them for the importance for their own lives.

Second, we agree with Kohlberg's optimism for the potential of students to see the value of virtuous actions and can be led to desire to perform these actions. Naturally, our optimism is tempered by the fact that epiphanies are often hard to achieve and that the rehabituation process to follow can often fail to yield lasting change if not carried through. But, like Plato we are firmly convinced that epiphanies can and do happen, and that when they do they can profoundly change the life trajectory of the person having them. Of course, we can never predict whom in our classrooms will have these epiphanies, but in principle we believe that it could happen for *every* student no matter what their background or what their previous moral status is. This optimism provides energy and hope to continue to try to induce these epiphanies and, when they do not work, not to assume that the students somehow are not capable of achieving them, but somehow that we, the teachers, have failed to induce them in a way that is effective. It is the same with the rehabituation process. In spite of the reality that not every attempt at rehabituation will succeed, we believe the teacher can grow as a mentor, can learn better how to create a culture of greater inspirational emulation, and can improve her ability to support the formation of character friendships in her students.

The third aspect of Kohlberg's theory that our Platonic view shares is his concern for indoctrination. Like Kohlberg, we not only agree that simply telling students what the moral thing to do is, and making them perform those actions without them understanding why we are having them perform them, are both practically ineffective, it is also far too heavy handed (for older students especially) to be desirable, even if it did work. Even though we believe that teachers should believe in the universality of the virtues (while understanding that each culture will manifest them somewhat differently), we believe that if the virtues are truly universal the students will see that they are by having an epiphany about them. Put differently, the advantage of the Platonic theory of moral education we have laid out is that it neither requires that the teacher insist that their students agree with the teachers' moral commitments, nor does it require that students act on the teachers' commitments. Rather, it expects that students will, if they have had an epiphany, want *to act on the epiphany on their own* and will not need the teacher to insist on anything. And if a student does not have an epiphany, our theory allows that they should not feel obligated to change their students thinking or their behavior. That does not mean that the teacher will not try to figure out ways to better induce epiphanies in her classroom, but she knows that ultimately it is only the epiphany. This puts the ultimate agency for growth back in the student's hands and therefore mitigates accusations of indoctrination. Of course, it is very important that the teacher to admit they are trying to create these epiphanies so that students have the opportunity to challenge them and not be subtly manipulated into having them.

In sum, the Platonic theory of education offered in this book takes what is best about Kohlberg's theory and leaves aside the worst. It does a similar thing with neo-Aristotelian approaches to moral education. As we have made clear throughout this book, Plato and Aristotle agree on nearly everything regarding the early education of young children. They both agree on the centrality of habituation, imitation, and role-modeling, if youngsters are to become virtuous human beings—which means to have the cognitive, affective, and conative capacities necessary to act consistently virtuous from a firm and unchanging character. Neo-Aristotelians depart significantly from cognitivists like Kohlberg because Kohlberg does not have an adequate explanation of how students are supposed to develop the desires and dispositions to perform virtuous actions. Aristotle was not an intellectualist with respect to virtue and like Plato insisted on a method for cultivating the affective and conative dimensions of moral behavior.

The Platonic vision of moral education differs in one significant regard, however. Aristotelians argue that the *affective* dimension of moral understanding is formed almost exclusively in a child's early development, and if a child is badly raised and misses the critical formation of their desires, there is almost nothing teachers or even parents can do to change their desires later. At best they can be given societal laws that, under the threat of punishment, they will be compelled to obey. In obeying these laws, adults can come to a modicum of appreciation for the law, but they will not desire to become virtuous to a significant degree. Thus, these adults and young adults are more or less incurably vicious, or at least not virtuous. It is different for Plato. He believes in the power of epiphanies and that young adults can have a radical reorientation of their desires and discover a new vision of what human flourishing is. True, these epiphanies only provide a temporary glimpse of virtue, but if they are sufficiently strong, they can lead the individuals to undergo voluntarily a rehabituation process, and not just undergo it but *want* to undergo it. Here again, the teacher is not compelling the students to undergo the process, but the students desire it for themselves, and the teacher merely helps support them in this process. Thus, while a Platonic theory of moral education is, at its foundations for early education, nearly identical to neo-Aristotelian theories, it includes a method of virtue development for adult or young adults that is absent in Aristotle.

In the previous section we have argued for the ways our Platonic theory takes what is best from the tradition of Kohlberg's theory and takes what is best from the ever growing neo-Aristotelian movement and combines it into a more comprehensive theory of moral education—comprehensive in the sense that it accounts for what we know about realistic virtue development in young children *and young adults* and puts it into one theory. However, it is not comprehensive in other ways, insofar as it does not provide a foolproof way to ensure the development of the virtues in every student. Nonetheless, we will briefly outline some strategies teachers can use to improve their ability to morally educate their students using a Platonic framework.

Some Concluding Remarks on Using a Platonic Theory in the Classroom

In Chapter 5, we discussed three dimensions of Socrates' practice of inducing epiphanies: the philosophical, the psychological, and the pedagogical dimensions. The *philosophical* dimension is based on Socrates' understanding of the virtue he wants to impart to his students. In each of the epiphanies we saw him generating, Socrates entered the conversation with a virtue in mind. The *psychological* dimension of Socrates' method is found in his practice of evaluating his students psychological openness to an epiphany. While Socrates was willing to have conversation with nearly anybody, and while he was willing to use that conversation to undermine false beliefs in his interlocutors who were not open to epiphanies (like Callicles, Thrasymachus, or Protagoras), he reserved his epiphanic experiences for those who were psychologically open to them (like Lysis, Glaucon, or Alcibiades). He would assess the psychological barriers of all his discussion partners to determine the suitability of engaging in the induction of epiphanies. Once Socrates assessed his interlocutors' psychological openness, he would then employ a *pedagogical* strategy meant to overcome the residual barriers to generate an epiphany. Often, these strategies were indirect. Socrates would help his discussion partners come to an epiphany about virtue without directly telling them what the virtue was or why they should want it for their lives. He considered indirection necessary because he believed that many young people become defensive if their beliefs or values are challenged directly. By using a more circuitous route, he would protect them from their own defensiveness, which thereby help to further open them to an epiphany. Yet, at other points in the conversation he becomes more direct, as when he is coming to the end of his dialogue with Glaucon in the *Republic*. By this point, he can see that Glaucon is ready to hear the truth, and so he becomes direct.

We saw these same principles at play in the examples of Ms. Gruwell, Mrs. Smith, and Mr. Keating in Chapter 6. In each of those cases, it was clear that the teacher had a definite philosophical and ethical vision about what they hoped their students would see in their epiphanies. In the same way it is important for contemporary teachers to enter their classrooms with at least a sense of the virtues they hope to promote in their classrooms—a sense about which they feel very strongly and confidently, even if they do not have full knowledge and may even be unsure to the degree to which they consistently embody the virtues. Of course, they must embody them consistently enough that they are not in a position of significant moral hypocrisy.

We also saw in the examples of the teachers in Chapter 6 that they each seemed to understand the psychological barriers in their students that might stand in the way of their ability to induce epiphanies. This does not mean they all came to the first day of class with this knowledge. In the case of Ms. Gruwell, for example, early on she had a very badly mistaken view of what she thought the students should learn in the classroom, and an even more badly mistaken view of what the psychological barriers were for her students. It was only after *they helped her* to experience an epiphany that both her philosophical vision and her psychological acuity came into play. But once she realized that she had as much to learn from them as they had to learn from her, she began to figure out ways to overcome their barriers and help them to discover for themselves the value of empathy, respect and understanding—things she learned with them. It is the same with Ms. Smith and Mr. Keating. While they began their class with a better philosophical understanding of the virtues they wanted to promote and the psychological barriers that would stand in the way of their students coming to embrace those values, they also had to learn from their students along the way to better help them induce epiphanies and follow up with their support of a rehabituation process.

We also saw in the previous examples, the pedagogical dimension of how each teacher induced epiphanies. Unlike Socrates and Plato who use primarily a form of dialogue, Ms. Gruwell, Mrs. Smith, and Mr. Keating each employed their own distinctive pedagogical methods to bring about epiphanies. Ms. Gruwell primarily induced epiphanies by having students perform certain actions; Mrs. Smith primarily induced epiphanies by showing the students the virtues by her exemplification of them; and Mr. Keating primarily induced epiphanies in his students by using words to explain the value of the virtues, even if the students did not understand at first what he was talking about. As we discussed, these teachers not only used these methods—they employed all of them to some degree including dialogue—but they each had their own idiosyncratic *style* of applying them. To sum up, In each case, the teachers came to their students with (1) a philosophical vision of the virtue they want to inculcate, (2) a psychological understanding of the barriers that would impede their students' ability to desire the virtue, and (3) a pedagogical plan to create an epiphany that would induce a desire to embody the virtue. Each of these three teachers employ indirect modes of teaching as preparation to induce the pursuit of virtue. However, they will, at times, be more direct in their teaching. In each case they rely on what Aristotle calls *phronesis*, which is the practical wisdom to deliberate about how to act virtuously. In the case of these teachers, they all use pedagogical *phronesis*, which helps them know when to be indirect and when to be indirect.

It is our opinion that to the degree to which teachers carefully use philosophical reasoning, psychological reasoning, and pedagogical reasoning in their classrooms, they have the potential to create life-altering and trajectory-reorienting epiphanies in their students. And if they use similar reasoning regarding the rehabituation of students, they might be able to improve dramatically the moral lives of their students and perhaps improve the overall moral character of the communities the students live in. Understood correctly, Plato offers us a theory of moral education that is entirely appropriate for twenty-first-century democracies.

Appendix
Appetite, Reason, and Education
in Socrates' "City of Pigs"

Introduction

Early in Book II of the *Republic* (370c–372d), Socrates briefly depicts a city where each inhabitant contributes to the welfare of all by carrying out the role for which each is naturally suited. Citizens of the city are happy and contented, having all their basic needs met and enjoying simple pleasures in peace and safety. Socrates calls this city the "true city" and the "healthy one"; but Glaucon objects, calling it a "City for Pigs" because it lacks the luxuries and conveniences to which he has grown accustomed. Socrates responds by claiming that it is not a "healthy" city that Glaucon desires, but instead a "feverish" and "luxurious" one. Interestingly, rather than furthering his case for the healthy city, Socrates acquiesces to Glaucon and begins the process of constructing the luxurious city Glaucon desires. The result is, eventually, the *kallipolis*, which stands as the centerpiece of the *Republic*.

The fact that Socrates does not press the issue further, and the fact that he never explicitly returns to the First City,[1] raises the question of whether Socrates' praise of the First City should be taken at face value. Nearly all commentators argue that it should not, claiming that the First City does not represent Socrates' preferred community (Reeve, 1988; Barney, 2001; Cooper, 2000; Nettleship, 1901; Devereux, 1979; Annas, 1981; Crombie, 1962; McKeen, 2004).[2] The point of this appendix is to argue the contrary. The claim is that Socrates straightforwardly believes the First City is a healthy and desirable city. His reason for not pursuing the point with Glaucon is not because the First City is somehow deficient but rather because Glaucon is. It will be argued that Socrates willingly constructs the feverish city so that Glaucon can come to recognize that the First City is the desirable city. According to this interpretation, the purging of the feverish city and turning it into the *kallipolis* is a way for Socrates to help Glaucon purge himself of his own fever. After making this argument, some of the prominent interpretations against the straightforward reading of Socrates' praise of the First City will be examined. These interpretations assume that Socrates' willingness to follow Glaucon in the construction of the *kallipolis* indicates that his praise of the First City was not genuine.

To support the view that his praise was not genuine, interpreters offer theoretical and exegetical evidence that purportedly demonstrates the inferiority of the First City. But the evidence they offer, and the arguments they make, are not tenable, and, in fact, only serve to strengthen the straightforward reading.

The Exegetical Case for the First City

The exegetical evidence in favor of the straightforward reading of Socrates' praise of the First City is simple and direct: Socrates states plainly (although briefly) at 372e–373c that he considers the First City to be the "true" and "healthy" city. The members of this city, Socrates says, "live in peace and health" without "falling into either poverty or war," and they will "bequeath a similar life to their children." He contrasts this society with the luxurious society Glaucon wishes to construct, calling the latter a "city with a fever."[3] Socrates argues that the city Glaucon seeks requires a "multitude of things that go beyond what is necessary for a city"; and rather than living in peace and health (as the citizens of the First City do), the citizens' "next step will be war," and they will "have a far greater need for doctors" because of the unhealthy lifestyles they live. If we take him at his word, Socrates' explicit praise of the First City, and the nearly opposite contrasts he draws with the luxurious city, should leave little doubt that he considers the First City the superior community, especially because, as all commentators are compelled to admit, Socrates never rescinds his praise of the First City. However, while it seems clear that Socrates prefers the First City to the luxurious city that Glaucon desires, the question becomes whether he prefers it to the *kallipolis*, which has been purged of the "fever" found in the luxurious city. At first glance, it would appear that he must not prefer the First City because of the obvious fact that he acquiesces to Glaucon's desire to construct a different city and never explicitly returns to the First City at all. The thought is that if Socrates genuinely believes that the First City is the true and healthy city, it seems plausible that he would refuse to be diverted from elaborating its truth and health at Glaucon's bidding. In other words, it seems doubtful that Socrates would have bothered to spend hours of his time in dialogue with Glaucon, supposedly attempting to construct a just city, when he believes that a just city had already been established.[4]

It is Socrates' willingness to be diverted from the First City that has led most commentators to either gloss over his praise of that city or to interpret that praise as ironic (Rowe, 2007, pp. 43–45). But all of these responses miss the significance of Socrates' praise, however. The straightforward reading of Socrates' praise of the First City is not only exegetically simpler—insofar as it does not require an explanation of why he bothered praising the city at all—it is essential to understanding the purpose of the dialogue.

The ultimate goal of the dialogue between Socrates and his interlocutors is to discover justice in the soul, and to show the superiority of justice over injustice. Socrates claims that in order to discover justice in the soul, it will be helpful to construct a just city, as justice will be easier to "see" since a city is a larger thing than a person (368d–369a). The reason for wanting to discover justice in a city is ultimately to discover justice in the soul. Thus, whatever reason Socrates has for allowing himself to construct the *kallipolis*, we can be sure the ultimate reason is to assist him, Glaucon and Adeimantus in the discovery of justice in the soul and to show justice's superiority over injustice. Unfortunately, after the interlocutors construct a city that, as we shall argue, Socrates takes to embody justice (the First City), Glaucon is unable to see the justice of that city and demands a different type of city, namely a luxurious one with a fever. Consequently, in order for Socrates to fulfill his goal of the dialogue he must provide an image that better assists Glaucon in seeing justice.[5] Since Glaucon has failed to see justice and its superiority, Socrates must make a second attempt. The second attempt he makes is to create a longer and more graphic image that he believes will more effectively achieve the goal of helping Glaucon see the superiority of justice. This goal is achieved through the construction of the *kallipolis*. It is therefore consistent for Socrates to maintain that the First City is the true and healthy one and, nevertheless, go on to construct a new city. On this interpretation, it is not surprising that Socrates should give in to Glaucon's wishes.

The interpretation that Socrates is willing to construct the *kallipolis* to help Glaucon see justice, rather than because Socrates thinks the *kallipolis* is superior to the First City, is further supported when we consider Socrates' response to Glaucon's desire to construct the luxurious city. After Glaucon makes his request construct a luxurious city, Socrates concedes that this "may not be a bad idea, for by examining it, we might very well see how justice and injustice grow up in cities" (372e).[6] This response is important because it gives no indication whatsoever that Socrates desires to construct the new city because it is a superior city, but because through the examination of it they might be able to better "see" how justice and *injustice* come to be in a city. The language illuminates the heuristic purpose of the new city. He does not indicate that they are creating a better city, but a city by which they can *better see* the nature of justice. Glaucon does not yet recognize that the desire for immoderate pleasures is a feature of injustice (something he will eventually see near the end of the dialogue at 591c–592a); and so Socrates suggests that constructing a luxurious city may be necessary in helping Glaucon to see justice by way of contrast with injustice.

The appetitive desire for luxury found in the producers in the *kallipolis* reveal injustice to Glaucon as he witnesses the ways in which their desire for wealth leads individuals to "luxury, idleness, and revolution" (421d–422a). In order to control these desires, Socrates articulates the tripartite division of society (which turns out to be analogous to, or structurally isomorphic with, the soul): the philosopher-kings, auxiliaries, and producers. The desire for wealth is controlled when the philosopher-kings moderate the desires of the producers through the agency of the auxiliaries. In other words, the producers, who have appetitive desires that would lead to injustice in the society, are given restrictions (e.g., laws) by the philosopher-kings (who determine the best way to structure society). Once these restrictions are in place, the auxiliaries ensure that the producers obey them. And once this system is in place, Socrates claims that justice has returned to the society. Thus, the transition from the feverish city to the *kallipolis* allows Glaucon to see "justice and injustice" coming into being in a city, whereas the First City did not. This fact alone justifies Socrates' willingness to construct the *kallipolis* with the care and complexity that he does. Hence, it does not follow from the care and complexity with which the *kallipolis* is constructed that Socrates must therefore prefer it.[7] Even though he considers the First City to be the superior city, he was willing to take great care in constructing the *kallipolis* because it would help Glaucon come to see the nature of justice and injustice. However, the *kallipolis* does not merely help Glaucon "see" what justice is—as we saw in Chapter 5, it teaches him to desire it for himself.[8]

Through the construction of the *kallipolis*, Glaucon comes to understand justice, and affirms it as authoritative in his life. He is purged of his fever as the *kallipolis* is purged of its own. This is seen towards the end of the dialogue, where Socrates summarizes what he and his interlocutors have learned from the *kallipolis* what justice is (618c–619a). Instead of an encomium on the beauty, virtue, and justice found in the *kallipolis* (which is what we might expect after constructing a just city), Socrates backs away from any talk of the *kallipolis* whatsoever.[9] Instead he ends with an exhortation to take what they have learned from the *kallipolis* and apply it to their lives. Socrates claims that they must

> learn those [subjects] that will enable him to distinguish the good life from the bad and always to make the best choice possible in every situation. He should think over all the things we have mentioned and how they jointly and severally determine what the virtuous life is like. That way he will know what the good and bad effects of beauty are when it is mixed with wealth, poverty, and a particular state of the soul. . . . And from all this he will be able, by considering the nature of the soul, to reason out which life is better and which life is worse and to choose accordingly.
>
> (618c–619a)

The injunction to use what they have learned about justice and virtue in the preceding dialogue gestures to the pedagogical character of the dialogue, but what is additionally important is the last sentence in which Socrates implicitly denies the necessity of the philosopher-kings to determine virtuous action. This is important because Socrates' statement directly contradicts his earlier, seeming insistence that only the philosopher-kings are able to reason correctly about "which life is better and which life is worse" (505e–506e).[10] As such, if we argue that Socrates prefers the *kallipolis* to the First City as a political society, as most commentators do, then his remarks to Glaucon earlier are negated, because Socrates repeatedly indicates that he and Glaucon are not philosopher-kings (402b-c; 416b-c; 505a). His remarks to Glaucon earlier make sense only if he denies the position that the philosopher-kings alone can apprehend virtue.[11] Why then does he posit the philosopher-kings in the *kallipolis* and insist that only they can apprehend virtue? Socrates' supposed requirement that the philosopher-kings be necessary for the apprehension of virtue is revealed to be what it is: A metaphor for the *faculty of reason*, the virtue apprehending aspect of the human soul, which all individuals have to one degree or another. The philosopher-kings are, in other words, idealized representations of the rational part of the soul. The reason Socrates argues that only the philosopher-kings can apprehend virtue is because only the rational part of the soul can apprehend virtue so conceived (but this does not mean that reason is sufficient for the *acquisition* of virtue; for that, obviously, a body and desires and so on are needed). His goal in making such a sharp distinction between the philosopher-kings, the auxiliaries, and the producers in the *kallipolis* is not to establish a political ideal but to establish an ethical one. As Julia Annas (1981) correctly argues, the goal is to

> grasp the *ideal* of virtue, which is presented via the picture of the ideal state. The message, however, is not the simple-minded one that he should wait for some philosopher-kings to come along, or try to become one himself. Rather, he should internalize the ideal of virtue as a 'city of himself' (592A7)—that is he should internalize in his soul the structure pictured in the ideal city
>
> (p. 81)[12]

If Glaucon and Socrates can use reason to apprehend the just life, the question then becomes what that life looks like. As it turns out, it is the life of moderation that Socrates had earlier attributed to the inhabitants of the First City.[13] Socrates argues that the virtuous person is one who

> will not entrust the condition and nurture of his body to the irrational pleasure of the beast within or turn his life in that direction, but neither will he make health his aim or assign first place to being strong, healthy, and beautiful unless he happens to acquire moderation as a result. Rather, it's clear that he will always cultivate the harmony of his body for the sake of the consonance in his soul. . . . [And he will] look to the constitution within him and guard against disturbing anything in it,

either by too much money or too little. . . . And he'll do the same thing where honors are concerned. He'll willingly share in and taste those that he believes will make him better, but he'll avoid any public or private honor that might overthrow the established condition of his soul.

(591c–592a)

This description could be a description of the inhabitants of the First City. Concerning the question of health, they live happy and healthy lives but do not seem to care about the strength and beauty of their bodies except insofar as taking care that they are well fed and adequately clothed. Concerning the issue of having too little or too much money: While it may appear that the First City has too little wealth (at least to Glaucon), we must remember that Socrates condemns Glaucon's desire for it to have more wealth, claiming that Glaucon desires a "luxurious" and "feverish" city. This is a condemnatory remark since Socrates explicitly states later on that "luxury and softness [are] condemned because . . . [they] produce cowardice" (590b). From the interchange between Glaucon and Socrates we see that the First City embodies the moderate position between poverty and wealth. Based on the First City's avoidance of luxury, we see that it does not suffer from an inordinate desire for wealth; and we see that it does not suffer from poverty, for Socrates claims that the citizens of the city will not bear more children than they can afford, "lest they fall into either poverty or war" (372b). Finally, concerning the (acquired) desire for honor, the inhabitants of the First City do not seem to pursue any honor other than the knowledge that each of them performs a valuable task for the city based on their skills and abilities, and the honor of being part of a community and family that gets to "feast with their children, drink their wine, and [be] crowned with wreaths [while they] hymn the gods" (372b).

This interpretation is supported by the fact that the definition of justice that Socrates propounds at 443b (and throughout the rest of *Republic* never rescinds or substantially modifies) can be read as the fundamental basis of the First City: Namely, that each member of society will only do the job that they are naturally suited for and, in so doing, will provide for the other inhabitants of the city. Indeed, Socrates points back to the First City when he explains the definition of justice at 443b–c:

Then the dream we had has been completely fulfilled—our suspicion that . . . we had hit upon the origin and pattern of justice right at the beginning of the founding of our city. . . . Indeed, Glaucon, the principle that it is right for someone who is by nature a cobbler to practice cobblery and nothing else, for the carpenter to practice carpentry, and the same for the others is a sort of image of justice—that's why it's beneficial.

Socrates' insistence that they had hit on the "origin and pattern of justice right at the beginning of the founding of our city" indicates that the First

City embodied justice. But because the First City lacked the dissonance found in a feverish city, where the inhabitants have desires that are at odds with the stability of the society, Socrates saw the benefit of constructing a city that embodied injustice (the feverish city), so that the contrast between it and the justice found in the *kallipolis* could be better observed. To recall, his *ultimate* goal is not merely to establish what justice is in a city but to use the city to establish *justice in the soul*. Thus, Socrates takes Glaucon's demand for luxuries in stride and begins to construct the feverish city, not because he ultimately desires to construct the *kallipolis* for its own sake but because the feverish city, and the purified *kallipolis* that follows it, will open Glaucon's eyes to the nature of justice and injustice.

The tripartite structure of the *kallipolis* is therefore meant to represent the elements of the human soul that must be harmonized if it itself is to *become* just. But Socrates' concern here is not merely to describe abstractly the nature of justice to Glaucon but to help Glaucon *desire* it for himself. He will not be able to fully accept the "truth" and "health" of the First City until his soul is conformed to that same image of justice. This is apparent at 443b–444a, where Socrates explains that merely doing one's job for the sake of the community is not enough to count as justice, even if it supports civic unity—the work must issue from an *internal* disposition towards harmony in the individual. Justice is not fulfilled in a mere political arrangement but requires the internal conformity in the souls of the individuals who make up that political arrangement.

> Indeed, Glaucon, the principle that it is right for someone who is by nature a cobbler to practice cobblery and nothing else, for the carpenter to practice carpentry, and the same for the others is a sort of image of justice—that is why it is beneficial. . . . And in truth justice is, it seems, something of this sort. However, it isn't concerned with someone's doing his own externally, but with what is inside him . . . He puts himself in order . . . and harmonizes the three parts of himself like three limiting notes in a musical scale—high, low, and middle. He binds together those parts and any others there may be in between, and from having been many things, he becomes entirely one, moderate and harmonious. Only then does he act. And when he does anything, whether acquiring wealth, taking care of his body, engaging in politics, or in private contracts—in all of these, he believes that the action is just and fine that preserves this inner harmony and helps achieve it, and calls it so, and regards as wisdom the knowledge that oversees such actions. And he believes that the action that destroys this harmony is unjust, and calls it so, and regards the belief that oversees it as ignorance.

From this analysis we see that through the device of the *kallipolis*, Socrates is able to help Glaucon apprehend what it is to be just. This being the case, the account given previously, of why Socrates constructs the *kallipolis* if he believes the First City is the healthy and just city, is rendered even more plausible. Since Socrates' goal was ultimately to locate justice in the soul, it should not surprise us if, after constructing the *kallipolis*, we find that he has accomplished that ultimate goal. While only Socrates was able to recognize justice in the First City, Glaucon has come to recognize justice in the *kallipolis* and through the construction of it.

But why then should we assume that Socrates prefers the First City to the *kallipolis* if they both depict justice? The answer is, quite naturally, because Socrates himself states that he prefers it when he calls it *the* true and healthy city.

Objections to the Straightforward Reading

With the exegetical case for the straightforward interpretation of Socrates' praise of the First City in place, it may be helpful to address two of the dominant objections to it. In broad strokes, both objections attempt to demonstrate that Socrates' praise of the First City cannot be taken as genuine because he indirectly repudiates his praise by making statements during the construction of the *kallipolis* that are inconsistent with, or in contradiction to, the qualities of the First City. In other words, while Socrates never *explicitly* rescinds his praise of the First City, he *indirectly* does so in later passages of the *Republic*. However, through an analysis of these objections it will be shown that Socrates' later statements are not inconsistent with his praise of the First City but actually support it.

There are two lines of reasoning that commentators have used to demonstrate the inconsistency between Socrates' praise of the First City and his description of human nature in the construction of the *kallipolis*. The minority position is that Socrates does not consider the inhabitants of the First City to be fully human in the relevant sense (Cooper, 2000, pp. 13–14; Crombie, 1962, pp. 89–90; Nettleship, 1901, p. 72). On this reading, the inhabitants are in some fundamental sense subhuman and thus are not meant to be representative of a plausible human community. The majority position, on the other hand, argues that it is precisely because the inhabitants are fully human that the First City cannot be Socrates' preferred community. The claim is that because the inhabitants are human they have *pleonectic* desires to want more than the need: As such, the city will eventually devolve into chaos since the first city has no method of social control, like laws and government, to suppress them (Barney, 2001, pp. 217–220; Reeve, 1988, pp. 171, 176; Devereux, 1979, pp. 38–39; Annas, 1981, pp. 76–78; McKeen, 2004, pp. 70–72; DesLauriers, 2001, pp. 228–235). On both lines of reasoning, Socrates' praise of the First City cannot be taken at face value because the city is an impossible city in some way. Both of these lines of reasoning will be examined in turn, and it will be argued that neither provide sufficient evidence to warrant the rejection of Socrates' praise.

The First Argument for the Rejection of the 'City of Pigs': Appetitive Desires and Justice

The first argument that Socrates' praise of the First City ought not to be taken at face value is based on a reading according to which the inhabitants do not have the full range of human desires. The argument is that they lack the appetitive desires that constitute both *pleonexia* and the drive that leads to human civilization (Cooper, 2000, pp. 13–14; Crombie, 1962, pp. 89–90; Nettleship, 1901, pp. 69–72).[14] According to this interpretation, the inhabitants of the First City are motivated only by the desire to satisfy their minimal needs; they do not have those other, "unnecessary" human desires to want more than they need, nor to desire pleasure for pleasure's sake. Commentators who hold this view do not see the presence of these kinds of appetitive desires in the First City and therefore argue that justice must necessarily be absent from it. For these interpreters, justice is absent because they ascribe to Socrates a definition of justice as the willingness to do the right thing *in the face of* a desire not to do it. On this view, "justice requires not merely fair taking of turns, so to speak, but doing so with some countervailing motivation *not* to do it, or at least while recognizing that one might get something quite nice if one shirked" (Cooper, 2000, p. 14). Accordingly, because the inhabitants of the First City only desire what they need, and because the society is set up in a way that everyone's needs are met, there will never be an occasion when members of the First City are forced to overcome their desires; therefore, justice never comes into play. If they had appetitive desires, however, they would occasionally desire something beyond their needs and in opposition to the public good; and on those occasions, they would be required to overcome those flagrant desires so as not to harm their fellow inhabitants, the overcoming of which would lead to acting justly. But since this state of affairs will never obtain (they will not have desires that need to be overcome), the First City cannot be a truly just city and therefore cannot be desirable to Socrates. Its inhabitants do not have the kind of desires which would necessitate justice at all, nor make justice possible.

This line of thinking is logically valid. If the inhabitants of the First City do not have desires to act badly, and if Socrates defines justice as the willingness to act rightly in the face of desires to act badly, and if Socrates only desires a just city in this sense, then it follows that the First City is not just, and therefore Socrates cannot desire it. Unfortunately, while the argument is valid, it is unsound, as its premises are false.

The first premise is demonstrably false as Socrates explicitly affirms the view that all human beings have appetitive desires and must master those desires if they are to be in harmony with themselves (see, e.g., Barney, 2001, p. 218). Socrates claims that it is "clear that there is a dangerous, wild, and lawless form of desire in *everyone*, even in those of *us* who seem to be entirely moderate and measured" (572b, emphasis added), but that these desires can be "held in check by the laws and by the better desires in alliance with reason" (571b). And as Glaucon indicates (echoing Socrates' claim) *all* individuals desire to acquire more wealth and luxuries, even if they do not appear to desire it: "the desire to get more . . . is what *anyone's* nature naturally pursues as good, but nature is forced by law into the perversion of treating fairness with respect" (557c, emphasis added).

Of course, it could be the case that—as the minority position claims—the inhabitants of the First City are not to be included in Socrates' and Glaucon's "everyone," "us," and "all individuals" because they lack the relevant human characteristics. But, as has been previously indicated, there is no evidence for this view, and commentators who hold it do not offer any evidence either.[15] Unfortunately, while it *seems* to the minority position that Socrates does not consider the inhabitants of the First City to be human, it seems otherwise to most commentators—and for good reason, for Socrates repeatedly identifies himself with the inhabitants in the same way that he identifies himself with "everyone" in the previous passage about wild and lawless desires. Thus, without evidence demonstrating the inhabitants' lack of relevant human characteristics, the view that the First City lacks justice because the inhabitants do not have desires to act upon appetitive desires should be rejected, since Socrates claims that "everyone" has such desires, even those who seem to lack them.

Thus, the first line of reasoning that Socrates' praise of the First City cannot be taken at face value is shown to be false. On the basis of Socrates' identification of himself and his interlocutors with the inhabitants of the First City and his subsequent admission that "everyone" has lawless desires, it is necessary that the citizens of the First City do have appetitive desires, and that justice is present in the First City because each member of the city is doing his or her own job and exercising moderation with respect to his or her desires.

The Second Argument for the Rejection of the 'City of Pigs': Appetite, Reason and Civic Devolution

Now that we have seen the first kind of argument that interpreters have employed to reject the First City and Socrates' praise of it, there remains the second. The second line of reasoning also concerns appetitive desires and a particular definition of justice but draws different conclusions about them: Namely, that the citizens of the First City are fully human and therefore appetitive desires are present in them, and, because they are present, the First City will eventually fall into injustice and will be torn apart. This interpretation has the advantage over the first interpretation in that it rightly argues that appetitive desires are present in the First City (Barney, 2001, pp. 218–219; Reeve, 1988, p. 178; McKeen, 2004, p. 90); however, it too has a serious flaw, which renders it ultimately untenable.

The second line of thinking rejects the First City less on theoretical grounds and more on practical grounds. The argument runs something like this: the inhabitants of the First City have what appears to be a just and healthy city, but the justice and health of that city cannot be maintained for long because the appetitive desires of the inhabitants will eventually come into conflict with their better judgment. When this inevitable conflict comes along, chaos will naturally ensue, as there are neither *internal* nor *external* constraints established to mediate the conflict on behalf of justice.[16] These interpretations raise the legitimate issue of rational regulation in the First City. If, as argued previously, Socrates conceives the members of the First City as having appetitive desires, then what would prevent the inhabitants from following those desires that would lead to injustice?

Now if Socrates genuinely believes that the First City is a healthy city, it seems safe to assume it must be a city that will not devolve into chaos shortly after it is founded. Yet, according to commentators, Socrates has given us no indication of the presence of rational rule, and therefore we should be worried that the city *will* devolve into chaos, especially when we consider that Socrates explicitly indicates that the appetitive part of the soul is the largest and that in most people the rational part of the soul does not have the resources to control it (Barney, 2001, p. 219) By this reasoning it would seem that Socrates cannot really mean that the First City is the true and healthy city because of its (unacknowledged) tendency to devolve into chaos.

On the face of it, it is potentially worrisome that Socrates does not provide explicit stopgap measures to protect the First City from degenerating into chaos, and indeed commentators have taken this as evidence to warrant an ironic reading of Socrates' praise.[17] While it is true that Socrates does not provide explicit "external" measures to protect the First City from appetitive desires, it is not true that he does not provide any measures. Socrates clearly indicates that there is rational control in the First City, contrary to what the previous commentators would have us believe.

To observe the rational control in the First City, it will be helpful to quote Socrates' description of it at length.

> First, then, let's see what sort of life our citizens will lead when they've been provided for in the ways we have been describing. They'll produce bread, wine, clothes, and shoes, won't they? They'll build houses, work naked and barefoot in the summer, and wear adequate clothing and shoes in the winter. For food, they'll knead and cook the flour and meal they've made from wheat and barley. They'll put their honest cakes and loaves on reeds or clean leaves, and, reclining on beds strewn with yew and myrtle, they'll feast with their children, drink their wine, and, crowned with wreathes, hymn the gods. They'll enjoy sex with one another but bear no more children than their resources allow, lest they

fall into either poverty or war . . . they'll obviously need salt, olives, cheese, boiled roots, and vegetables of the sort they cook in the country. We'll give them desserts, too, of course, consisting of figs, chickpeas, and beans, and they'll roast myrtle and acorns before the fire, drinking moderately. And so they'll live in peace and good health, and when they die at a ripe old age, they'll bequeath a similar life to their children.

(372a–372d)

After offering this description, and before Socrates can elaborate his theory of justice found therein, Glaucon interrupts him, claiming that the city is only fit for pigs, and that it does not compare to what "people have nowadays" (372d). In Socrates' description of the First City, and in Glaucon's rejection of it, we see evidence that the citizens of the First City do have appetitive desires, which is what we would expect to see considering Socrates' claim (quoted earlier) that "everybody" has lawless desires. The existence of appetitive desires is seen in Glaucon's claim that merely having the pleasures of sex, and wine, and beds, and homes, and feasts, and desserts, and salt, and cheese, and other accouterments of human civilization will not satisfy people "nowadays." That Socrates offers no provision for these desires bothers Glaucon because he is convinced that people should not have to forgo such desires.

So far, then, this description provides us with even more evidence that the rejection of the First City based on the absence of appetitive desires is fallacious. Unfortunately, the description of the First City and Glaucon's response only magnifies the seeming plausibility of the second kind of argument for the rejection of the First City. Since Glaucon could never be satisfied in the First City because of his appetitive desires, it seems reasonable to suppose the inhabitants of the First City, who would have appetitive desires themselves, would not be any more satisfied.

However, as we have noted earlier, while it is true that Glaucon would not be satisfied in the First City, it does not necessarily follow that all individuals would not be satisfied. Socrates, for instance, does not require such luxuries.

Socrates is . . . an erotic man, but his *eros* does not lead him . . . to injure others or take what belongs to them. In order to satisfy his *eros*, he need not compete with other men to their detriment. He has no wealth and no honor; in fact, he is despised and believed to be unjust. Yet he is happy. . . . He does not live without the ordinary pleasures because he is an ascetic, but because the intensity of the joy in philosophy makes him indifferent to them.

(Bloom, 1968, p. 347)

Interestingly, this might be a suitable description of an inhabitant of the First City. The question then becomes: What causes Socrates to have such desires?

As we have seen, the one thing we know with certainty is that Socrates must, because he is human, have appetitive desires (572b). What then keeps these desires in check? Socrates offers two possibilities: (1) they are "held in check by the laws [governing society]," or (2) they are held in check "by the better desires in alliance with reason" (571b). With these as the only two options Socrates offers, it is clear in his case that it is the latter possibility and not the former that governs the inhabitants of the First City. Socrates, all the way up to his execution, obeys the edicts of justice because they are reasonable and never because the laws of the state demand them.[18]

Like Socrates, the inhabitants of the city are motivated by the edicts of reason and thus do not need the external compulsion of the state to moderate their desires.[19] Again like Socrates, they have the potential for lawless desires but have moderated them "by the better desires in alliance with reason." That rational moderation must be governing their actions is seen clearly in their "drinking moderately," and most strikingly in their ability to "enjoy sex with one another but bear no more children than their resources allow, lest they fall into either poverty or war." This is a striking example of rational moderation in the First City because Socrates later claims that there is no "greater or keener pleasure than sexual pleasure" (403a), and that it is therefore an especially dangerous passion when it is not properly moderated. Importantly the inhabitants' ability to moderate their passions means that the inhabitants of the First City must have been educated to do so. That is, the fact that the citizens have learned to moderate their unhealthy desires is a sure sign of a robust education; for Socrates claims that the only way to overcome those desires is to be governed by the rational self (571c-d), and the only way to develop the rational self is to be educated into it (401d–402a). Additionally, Socrates overtly states that those who live in peace and are gentle with one another must be lovers of learning and wisdom.[20] It is the love of wisdom and learning that allow the citizens to "live in peace and good health" and protects them from falling "into either poverty or war" (372a–372d).

With this interpretation in place, we are now in a position to address some of the practical concerns of the second line of reasoning that rejects the First City. To recall, the argument of the second line was that there was nothing to protect the inhabitants of the First City from the chaos that would ensue once their appetitive desires began to outstrip their better, more simple desires. From the proceeding analysis it should be clear that the inhabitants do have a safeguard against civil chaos—namely, reason and education. This fact directly repudiates the assertions of the second rejection of the First City, like the claim that the "inhabitants of the First City are . . . ruled by the appetitive part of the soul" (Barney, 2001, p. 218), and that "the First City very strikingly lacks any such rational control" (p. 219). In light of the preceding analysis, these claims seem misplaced. Rather, what is clear is the fact that the first inhabitants are not ruled by their appetitive desires because they embody an *internal* rational control provided by their education. The inhabitants of the First City do not need an *external* system of rational control (i.e., laws and punishment)[21] because they have an *internal* system of rational control. Their appetitive desires are controlled by their educated rational selves.[22]

To sum up the case against both lines of reasoning that deny the straightforward interpretation: neither line of reasoning provides compelling evidence that Socrates' claims about human nature that he makes during the construction of the *kallipolis* are inconsistent with, or in direct contradiction to, his praise of the First City. On the contrary, his description of human nature fits perfectly well with a straightforward reading. Contrary to the minority position, the inhabitants of the First City do have appetitive desires; and contrary to the majority position, the inhabitants of the First City have rational capacities to moderate those desires, and thus the First City need not necessarily devolve into chaos.

Education in the First City

Having established the exegetical plausibility of the straightforward reading, and having demonstrated the weakness of the principal objections to the straightforward reading, it is necessary to conclude with a brief explanation of the way moderation is cultivated in the First City. If, as has been shown, the health of the First City relies on the rational moderation of its members, the question arises of how this moderation is to be cultivated in subsequent generations, especially since Socrates explicitly states that the inhabitants will "bequeath a similar life to their children." How are these inhabitants to ensure that the next generation will live lives of just moderation, if there is no centralized governmental control to ensure fidelity to justice?[23] This is an issue because Socrates admits that the appetitive desires are usually the most powerful aspects of the soul and are stubbornly resistant to the governance of reason, and, moreover, Socrates also states that it is only the few, best natures that can obtain moderation at all: "But you meet with desires that are simple, measured, and directed by calculation in accordance with understanding and correct belief only in the few people who are born with the best natures and receive the best education" (431c). As such, the average citizen of the First City must have two things if they are to be moderate: a proper nature and a proper education. Unfortunately, Socrates is clear that he does not believe that average individuals have the natures necessary for cultivating moderation on their own, and thus we are left with the question of how the average individual in the First City can ever be taught to moderate their desires and follow virtue.

This is the decisive issue for Barney (2001) in her criticism of the First City. She believes that, unlike the *kallipolis*, the First City does not have a mechanism for helping average individuals overcome their unruly desires, and that "in the absence of such careful 'cultivation' by an external reason, the typical state of most people would be the intemperate and irrational pursuit of pleasure" (p. 219). While it is true that "careful cultivation" is necessary to help the average individual become moderate, Barney assumes too much when she assumes that there is no such "careful cultivation" in the First City. From Socrates' admission, we can infer that "careful cultivation" must be present in the First City, otherwise they would have never been able to obtain the moderation that they are said to have in the first instance. In other words, that there *is* moderation in the First City—to such a degree that Socrates' describes it as the "true" and "healthy" city—entails that there must be a good education present in it. As for why Socrates does not mention the education system in his short description of the First City is because, as the dialogue goes, he is interrupted by Glaucon—but this does not warrant the interpretation that it lacks any kind of education. Indeed, the thought that the First City is "spontaneously" moderate in the absence of a virtuous education is not plausible. Insofar as there is moderation, moderation which is not only being exercised by its citizens but is being passed along to their children, we can infer the presence of an education that is aimed at the careful cultivation of virtue.[24]

Education alone does not suffice to ensure moderation, however. As Socrates claims earlier, for moderation to exist in an individual, one must have a *nature* suitable for it. As we have seen, the First City is stable and just, and therefore it will not self-destruct as some of the previous interpreters suggest. Nevertheless, for the First City to be considered a viable political option, it must welcome a range of human beings and not only those whose natures are the "best." It would seem that if only the best natures can be educated to be moderate, then the First City must be made up only of those with the best natures. If that is so, then the First City is not a realistic city at all since the best natures are so incredibly rare, according to Socrates. Fortunately, a few lines after seeming to claim unequivocally that only the best natures can be moderate, Socrates modifies his position, arguing instead that moderation is possible for all people no matter their nature.

> Unlike courage and wisdom, each of which resides in one part, making the city brave [auxiliaries] and wise [philosopher-kings] respectively, moderation spreads throughout the whole. It makes the weakest, the strongest, and those in between—whether in regard to reason, physical strength, numbers, wealth, or anything else—all sing the same song together.
>
> (431e–432a)

On this account, moderation is the one virtue that can be embodied (assuming they have a proper education) by all individuals. This does not mean, however, that moderation will be inculcated identically among all individuals. Socrates argues that those individuals who do not have the best natures must be taught to trust the wisdom of those who have the best natures (431c-d). They must be able to affirm the guidance of the wise themselves and not be compelled merely to obey the laws through force, which, importantly, entails a well-regulated education system. The moderation of the First City is therefore more complex than was suggested earlier. All individuals must be moderated by an internal rational rule. For those whose natures are not the best, their internal rational rule does not originate with themselves, and necessitates an education of a kind that inculcates and propagates the wisdom of the few. Thus, in a sense, the *internal* rational control of the inhabitants of the First City has an *external* dimension.

The newly born inhabitants of the First City must, in other words, be trained to cultivate their reason so that they can develop a virtuous constitution that values moderation and thereby comes to have it. This training comes through a habituation into the reason of the best natures (518e). As it turns out, Socrates later insists that it is only after an individual person has demonstrated that they can live virtuously and moderately that they should be allowed to become a full-fledged member of a community. Unlike contemporary Western cultures, a person does not become a full-fledged citizen based on the arbitrary criterion of age but on a rite of passage in which they demonstrate their ability to use reason to govern their unruly passions. Individuals who never develop the ability to live moderately must be governed by their parents until they behave in ways consistent with the values of the community. This imposition is necessary to protect the peace and longevity of the community.

> When [reason] is naturally weak in someone, it can't rule the beast within him but can only serve them and learn to flatter them. . . . Therefore to ensure that someone like that is ruled by something similar to what rules the best person, we say that he ought to be the slave of that person who has a divine ruler within himself. It isn't to harm the slave that we say he must be ruled . . . but because it is better for everyone to be ruled by divine reason, preferably within himself and his own, otherwise imposed from without, so that as far as possible all will be alike and friends, governed by the same thing. . . . But it's also our aim in ruling our children, we don't allow them to be free until we establish a constitution in them, just as in a city, and—by fostering their best part with our own—equip them with a guardian and ruler similar to our own to take our place. Then, and only then, we set them free.
>
> (590d–591a)[25]

This passage is important for several reasons. The first is that it again denies the strong demarcation between philosopher-kings, auxiliaries, and producers, which is a hallmark of the *kallipolis*. For Socrates, any healthy community is one in which "as far as possible all will be alike and friends, governed by the same thing," which is reason. The First City better approximates the egalitarian strain of Socrates' statement.

The second important idea in the passage is that in his requirement to give children an education that maximizes their potential to develop reason, he affirms the egalitarian posture of the First City. While it is true that he claims that there may be individuals who are born without the capacity to reason, he also claims that anyone who can be educated into the capacity will be made free. This means that individuals should never be subject to the control of others based on accidental characteristics like background, heredity, and so on, but only on their ability to behave in accordance with virtue. It would then seem that, given Socrates' insistence on providing children with an education that aims to develop reason, and given the emphasis in the culture on living peacefully and virtuously, the vast, vast majority of the community would not need to be enslaved.

The third reason is that it demonstrates the way the First City would be protected from internal threats. Children within the community will not be given freedom to make decisions for themselves until they can demonstrate that they are able to moderate their appetitive desires and act virtuously. As such, the city will be protected from individuals who could threaten its peace and harmony. Presumably, in the case that a child pretends to follow virtue and moderate her desires, but, once freed, behaves badly, this individual would be "put in chains" again, either by her parents or her parents in conjunction with the rest of society as a way of protecting the society and indeed herself.

With this process of education in mind we are now in a position to better understand what it is about the First City that is true and healthy. It is true and healthy insofar as all of its members have been educated to live moderately and virtuously, and as such have a form of equality even if they have a diversity of skills, interests, and talents. They are not ascetic but seem deeply to enjoy the simple pleasures found in their individual work and in their life as a community. Neither are they philistine, as they enjoy a variety of foods, wine, and poetry. Each of them obeys reason and therefore they have no need for laws or government, beyond those few who must be governed by their parents because they cannot moderate themselves. Moreover, they appreciate and honor one another's skills, interests, and talents because each member contributes to the good of the whole. This appreciation provides them with a sense of honor but does not encourage the invidious desire to outdo others with respect to honor since they are each honoring and being honored equally. They are also not consumed with wealth but have enough to live pleasurable and peaceful lives.

Conclusion

It has been argued that the First City embodies the justice that Socrates desires, and thus we have no reason to doubt his sincerity when he praises it. The question then is whether he considers the First City superior to the *kallipolis* which also embodies justice. In one sense it seems clear that it is not, namely in the sense that the First City fails to depict justice to those whose souls have not been conformed to it. The *kallipolis* is superior *pedagogically*. As the stated goal of constructing a just city in the first place was to establish justice in the soul and to show its superiority, then the *kallipolis* would seem to be the superior city. But in another sense, it is clear that Socrates thinks the First City is the superior city, in so far as he calls it the "true" and "healthy" city. In what way, then, is the First City the superior one? A plausible answer is that it is *politically* a superior city. Indeed, as was indicated earlier, Socrates is surprisingly silent in his praise of the *kallipolis* once it is completed. Rather than offering superlative comments on the political perfection of the city—like the ones he offers regarding the First City—he abruptly leaves off discussing the *kallipolis* as a political entity and focuses instead on the way it reveals justice in the soul. Were he to consider it his political ideal, we would expect him to say so. The fact that he does not is suggestive, especially in light of his previous praise of the First City.

The *kallipolis* serves an important purpose, but its purpose seems less political than pedagogical: It is primarily to help Glaucon see what justice is, and so too the superiority of the just life to the unjust life. The *kallipolis* is a city that has been purged in order to become just, and thereby it is instrumental in educating Socrates' interlocutors. The *kallipolis* is not the *true* and *healthy* city but one that has become a heavenly city in the course of a dialogue that has helped Glaucon find justice in his soul. And its pedagogical value need not stop at Glaucon. Socrates claims that it is a model for "anyone who wants to look at it" and be transformed by it. But it would seem that the *kallipolis* is not Socrates' preferred city *qua* city. And now that Socrates' praise of the First City can be taken sincerely and straightforwardly, the important question of what it is that makes it the healthy and true one can be further investigated.

Notes

1. Although Socrates never *explicitly* revisits the First City, he *implicitly* revisits it in several places throughout the *Republic*, for example at 420b and 443. See, also, Rowe (2007a).

2. The one exception is Rowe (2007a, pp. 43–45; 2006b, p. 15), who argues in numerous places that Socrates is in earnest regarding his praise of the First City, in spite of the fact that commentators ignore or dismiss Socrates' praise.

3. Importantly for the thesis of this appendix, Socrates' claim that Glaucon desires a "city with a fever" seems, at least at first, unfounded; for all that Glaucon has requested is that the inhabitants "recline on proper couches, dine at a table, and have the delicacies and desserts that people have nowadays." This is important because it suggests that Socrates sees something amiss in the *tone* of Glaucon's complaint rather than merely in the luxuriousness of the *items* he requests. Couches and tables and desserts hardly represent gluttony. Indeed, Socrates grants the inhabitants of the First City "feasts" and "sex" and "desserts" and

"wine," all of which seem more in keeping with a commitment to luxury and gluttony than the fairly modest requests that Glaucon makes. Why then does Socrates react so strongly to Glaucon's requests? It is not because the items themselves are overly luxurious but because Glaucon's desire for them betrays his lack of moderation, and moderation is the virtue Socrates later claims forms the basis of a just soul (443b–444a). Glaucon's insistence that individuals should not have to moderate their desires demonstrates that Glaucon's soul is not in a healthy state (or better, not in a *just* state). In this moment, the fever that Socrates is referring to can only be the fever in Glaucon's soul, since a city with couches, tables, and desserts certainly does not entail, nor does it even suggest, a city with a fever. This line of interpretation will be crucial in the coming discussion.

4. That the First City is *just* and not merely "true" and "healthy" is evidenced by the fact that the city is patterned on the definition of justice that Socrates offers at 443b-c:

> Then the dream we had has been completely fulfilled—our suspicion that . . . we had hit upon the origin and pattern of justice right at the beginning of the founding of our city. . . . Indeed, Glaucon, the principle that it is right for someone who is by nature a cobbler to practice cobblery and nothing else, for the carpenter to practice carpentry, and the same for the others is a sort of image of justice—that's why it's beneficial.

5. While an analysis of Glaucon is central for the purposes of this appendix, it can be argued that Socrates begins to construct a new city because the challenge posed by Socrates' interlocutors was to show that the just life is a better life than the unjust one *tout court*. This, too, is evidently not sufficiently shown by the First City. In other words, the First City is apparently insufficient to persuade those who do not already share Socrates' view that the just life is better than the unjust one. This reading, however, still does not warrant interpreting Socrates' praise of the First City as disingenuous.

6. Importantly, a few lines earlier (371e), Socrates had asked Adeimantus where justice and injustice were to be found in the outline of the just city that immediately preceded Socrates' description of the First City. Adeimantus claims he does not exactly know how to identify them. Socrates responds that while justice and injustice may be hard to see, the interlocutors must "look into it and not grow weary" (372a). Then he immediately launches into his description, thus indicating that he considers justice and injustice to be present.

7. The fact that commentators have not recognized the pedagogical purpose have led them to assume that the care and complexity must be evidence of Socrates belief in the *kallipolis*' political superiority. This assumption is unwarranted.

8. The difficulties of this project are well known. Though we do not have the space to pursue this topic here, we are inclined to think that a straightforward reading casts a different light, as it were, on the infamous banishment of the poets: namely, enabling us to ask its pedagogical role with respect to purging Glaucon's immoderate soul—or, perhaps, restructuring Glaucon's moral psyche.

9. The fact that Socrates offers no such encomium bears on the argument of this appendix and will be discussed in the conclusion that follows.

10. See Iakovos Vasiliou (2008), who engages with this puzzle.

11. Thus the straightforward reading of Socrates' praise has the added benefit of reconciling Socrates' inconsistencies between his discussion of the philosopher-kings and himself and Glaucon.

12. Annas argues that, at 592A7, the phrase "city of himself" is significant because it better establishes the fact that the *kallipolis* is not meant to be a political city

to be lived *in* but an idealized city that represents justice in the soul. The fact that many translators have opted for an interpretation that suggests that Glaucon should find the real *kallipolis* reflects one of the biases that this appendix is attempting to dislodge.

13. Socrates equates justice and moderation at 443b–444a.

14. The reason so few commentators share Cooper (2000), Crombie (1962), and Nettleship's (1901) assumption—that the inhabitants of the First City are not fully human in the relevant sense—is that Socrates gives no indication whatsoever that they are not fully human. Indeed, during the construction of the First City, Socrates repeatedly identifies himself and his interlocutors with the inhabitants of the First City (369c, 369d, 370a), and when Glaucon suggests that modern people would not be content in the First City, Socrates retorts only that some people would not be satisfied. The burden of proof therefore lies on the aforementioned commentators to adduce evidence that Socrates does not think the citizens are fully human in the relevant sense, since there is evidence that he thinks they are. Unfortunately, they do not offer the exegetical evidence of Socrates' denial of the humanity of the inhabitants of the First City; and, as will be shown, the theoretical evidence they offer instead is not convincing either.

15. The closest these commentators come to offering evidence is the exegetically unsupported statement that the inhabitants lack these characteristics. Cooper (2000) argues,

> [Simplicity] is all the people actually want. That is because . . . they are assumed not to be motivated at all by any of that open-ended desire for pleasurable gratification that was the hallmark of human life. . . . So, at any rate, Socrates *seems* to argue.
>
> (pp. 13–14; emphasis added)

The fact that Cooper acknowledges that Socrates only "seems" to argue for the citizens lack of open-ended desires is telltale. There is no direct evidence whatsoever that he regards these citizens to be unlike other human beings; indeed, as argued earlier, the direct evidence is on the side of their inclusion in the human community by Socrates' repeated identification of himself and his interlocutors with the inhabitants of the First City, like when he claims

> I think a city comes into being because none of *us* is self-sufficient, but *we* all need many things. Do you think a city is founded on any other principle? . . . Come, then, let's create a city in theory from its beginnings. And it's *our* needs, it seems, that will create it.
>
> (369c; emphasis added)

Socrates' repeated use of the first person plural in his description should not be ignored here; from the very beginning of the founding of the First City (which, importantly, also remains the basis of the *kallipolis*), Socrates indicates that the city will be made up of people like him and Glaucon and Adeimantus. There is no suggestion whatsoever in these lines that he imagines these inhabitants to be different in their basic nature from him or his interlocutors. Indeed, Socrates' identification of his needs and the needs of the inhabitants of the First City continue when he says "surely *our* first and greatest need is . . . food. . . . *Our* second is for shelter" (369d; emphasis added). And, "It occurred to me that, in the first place, *we* aren't all born alike but each of *us* differs somewhat in nature from the others, one being suited to one task, another to another" (370a; emphasis added). In fact, it would require much more from these commentators to explain the point, for Socrates, in filling an imaginary city with subhumans or nonhumans in the first place. Glaucon's impassioned response is odd, too, on this view.

16. Reeve (1988) puts it this way: "It should be obvious, however, that the First Polis is no more self-sufficient than its members. For . . . it lacks the means of defending itself against such consequences of unnecessary appetites as war and civil strife" (p. 178). Echoing similar ideas, Barney (2001) claims that

> the problem with the First City is not just that it would be unstable from one generation to the next. . . . Rather, the city is not a genuine possibility at all: for it embodies the hypothesis that a city without rational rule could be moderate in its appetites, and that hypothesis is false.
>
> (p. 220)

17. Naturally, it could be argued that Socrates would have provided such measures had not Glaucon interrupted him and demanded a luxurious city. Nevertheless, because he does not provide stopgap measures, we must determine whether they can be found implicit in the later chapters of the *Republic*.

18. This is the case even in *Crito* where Socrates argues that an individual should obey the laws of the state, even if those laws unjustly condemn the individual to death. His reasons for obeying his own execution are not because he kowtows to the state out of fear of punishment but because obeying the laws of the state conform to the edicts of reason.

19. Suggesting that the inhabitants of the First City follow reason to moderate their desires will seem to some to be an illicit introduction of philosophical reasoning into the city. On the basis of Socrates' own words about moderation, and on the basis of the identification of himself with the inhabitants of the First City, the inhabitants must exercise some level of reason. Thus, even though the inhabitants of the First City may seem like simple rustics, Socrates' words entail that they must also exercise reason. See, also, Rowe (2007a, p. 44).

20. "Then . . . we [can] confidently assume in the case of a human being, too, that if he is to be gentle towards his own and those he knows, he must be a lover of learning and wisdom" (376c).

21. As we shall see, while Socrates does not seem to envision a system of laws in the First City, he later claims that for moderation and reason to be established in a community, children should not be freed from their parents' rational control until they have demonstrated their internalization of it. Thus, while there may be no formal laws or formal policing of those laws, it does seem that Socrates advocates an informal agreement between community members requiring the control of members of the community who have not demonstrated their embodiment of reason.

22. This passage is significant because it repudiates McKeen's (2004) claim that the First City is a mutual benefit society and does not value justice for its own sake (pp. 89–90). Even if it were the case that the inhabitants of the First City valued peace and good health, and eschewed poverty and war, *as individuals* and for their own benefit, as McKeen argues, we would not be able to conclude that they did not value justice for its own sake. To know whether justice is valued for its own sake, we must determine whether the benefit the individual seeks is based on her own moderation and harmony (justice), or in the fulfillment of her unnecessary appetitive desires. In either case, the individual will perform his role "because each believes that this is better for himself," but in the case of the just individual, the seemingly self-interested action includes an orientation towards justice.

23. Naturally, Socrates does not have time to elaborate on this point in his brief description of the First City, as he is cut off by Glaucon's objection. Nevertheless, based on what Socrates claims later in the *Republic*, we can infer a great deal about the cultivation of moderation that must be present in the First City.

24. This interpretation is to be preferred to Barney's (2001), for it does not commit Plato or Socrates to the view that people can be spontaneously moderate: Indeed, the view is rather that where there is moderation there was an appropriate kind of education.
25. This discussion takes place after Socrates and Glaucon have ceased talking specifically about the *kallipolis* as a political entity. They are general conclusions about the training of individuals that follow from the establishment of the tripartite structure of the soul, conclusions that would apply to any community organization.

References

Albert Bandura. (1963). *Social Learning and personality Development*. New York: Holt, Rinehrt and Winston.

Aldridge, D. (2013). Three epiphanic fragments: Education and the essay in memory. *Educational Philosophy and Theory, 46*(5), 512–526.

Annas, J. (1981). *An introduction to Plato's Republic*. Oxford: Oxford University Press.

Annas, J. (1999). *Platonic ethics, old and new*. Ithaca, NY: Cornell University Press.

Annas, J. (2011). *Intelligent virtue*. Oxford: Oxford University Press.

Anscombe, E. (1958). Modern moral philosophy. *Philosophy, 33*(124), 1–19.

Barney, R. (2001). Platonism, moral nostalgia, and the "city of pigs". *Proceedings of the Boston AreaColloquium in Ancient Philosophy, 17*, 207–227.

Barrow, R. (2008). *Plato*. London: Continuum.

Benson, H. (2000). *Socratic wisdom: The model of knowledge in Plato's early dialogues*. Oxford: Oxford University Press.

Bloom, A. (1968). *The republic of Plato*. New York: Basic Books.

Bobonich, C. (2002). *Plato's utopia recast: His later ethics and politics*. Oxford: Clarendon Press.

Bobonich, C. (2008). Plato's politics. In G. Fine (Ed.), *Oxford handbook of Plato*. Oxford: Oxford University Press.

Boghossian, P. (2012). Socratic pedagogy: Perplexity, humiliation, shame and a broken egg. *Educational Philosophy and Theory, 44*(7), 710–720.

Bolotin, D. (1979). *Plato's dialogue on friendship*. Ithaca, NY: Cornell University Press.

Brewer, T. (2005). *Virtues We Can Share: Friendship and Aristotelian Ethical Theory*. Ethics, *115*(4), 721–758.

Brickhouse, T., & Smith, N. (1994). *Plato's Socrates*. New York: Oxford University Press.

Brickhouse, T., & Smith, N. (2000). *The philosophy of Socrates*. Boulder, CO: Westview Press.

Brickhouse, T., & Smith, N. (2009). Socratic teaching and Socratic method. In H. Siegel (Ed.), *The Oxford handbook of philosophy of education*. Oxford: Oxford University Press.

Brickhouse, T., & Smith, N. (2010). *Socratic moral psychology*. Cambridge, MA: Cambridge University Press.

Brown, E. (2012). The unity of the soul in Plato's Republic. In R. Barney, T. Brennan, & C. Brittain (Eds.), *Plato and the divided self* (pp. 53–74). Cambridge: Cambridge University Press.

Bruell, C. (1999). *On the Socratic education: An introduction to the shorter Platonic dialogues*. Lanham, MD: Rowman and Littlefield.

Bulman, R. (2004). *Hollywood goes to high school: Cinema, schools, and American culture*. New York: Worth Publishers.

Burnyeat, Myles F. (1980). *Aristotle on learning to be good*. In Amélie Oksenberg Rorty (ed.), Essays on Aristotle's Ethics. University of California Press. pp. 69–92.

Burnyeat, M. (1990). *The Theaetetus of Plato*, translated by M. J. Levett. Indianapolis, IN: Hackett Publishing Company.

Burnyeat, M., & Frede, M. (2015). *The pseudo-Platonic seventh letter* (pp. xv + 224), edited by Dominic Scott. Oxford: Oxford University Press.

Chambers, D. (2019). Is Freire incoherent? Reconciling directiveness and dialogue in Freirean pedagogy. *Journal of Philosophy of Education*, *53*(1), 21–47.

Clay, D. (2000). *Platonic questions: Dialogues with the silent philosopher*. University Park, PA: The Pennsylvania State University Press.

Cooper, J. (1997). Introduction. In J. Cooper (Ed.), *Plato: Complete works*. Indianapolis, IN: Hackett.

Cooper, J. (2000). Two Theories of Justice. *Proceedings and Addresses of the American Philosophical Association*, *74*(2), 3–27.

Crombie, I. (1962). *An examination of Plato's doctrines* (Vol. I). London: Routledge

Curren, R. (2000). *Aristotle on the necessity of public education*. Lanham, MD: Rowman & Littlefield.

Curren, R. (2013a). A neo-Aristotelian account of education, justice, and the human good. *Theory and Research in Education*, *11*(3), 231–249.

Curren, R. (2013b). Aristotelian necessities. *The Good Society*, *22*(2), 247–263.

Curzer, H. (2002). Aristotle's painful path to virtue. *Journal of the History of Philosophy*, *40*, 141–162.

Deane, P. (1973). Stylometrics do not exclude the seventh letter. *Mind, LXXXII*(325), 113–117.

De Marzio, D. (2006). The care of the self: Alcibiades I, Socratic teaching and ethics education. *Journal of Education*, *187*(3), 103–127.

DesLauriers, M. (2001). Commentary on Barney. *Proceedings of the Boston Area Colloquium in Ancient Philosophy*, *17*, 228–235.

Devereux, D. (1978). Nature and teaching in Plato's Meno. *Phronesis*, *23*(2), 118–126.

Devereux, D. (1979). Socrates' first city in the republic. *Apeiron*, *13*, 36–40.

Devereux, D. (1995). Socrates' Kantian concept of virtue. *Journal of the History of Philosophy*, *33*(3), 381–408.

Devereux, D. (2008). Socratic ethics and moral psychology. In G. Fine (Ed.), *The Oxford handbook of Plato*. New York: Oxford University Press.

Ebert, T. (1968). Plato's theory of recollection reconsidered: An interpretation of Meno 80a–86c. *Man and the World*, *6*(2), 163–181.

Ebrey, D. (2014). Meno's paradox in context. *British Journal for the History of Philosophy*, 22(1), 4–24.

Elihu Baldwin. (1837). "Address on Encouragement of Emulation in the Education of Youth Delivered before the Education Convention of Indiana" Indianapolis, Indiana: Douglass and Noel.

Ferrari, G. R. F. (2007). The three-part soul. In G. R. F. Ferrari (Ed.), *The Cambridge companion to Plato's Republic* (pp. 165–201). New York: Cambridge University Press.

Gadamer, H. (1980). *Dialogue and dialectic*. New Haven, CT: Yale University Press.

Gallagher, R. L. (2004). Protreptic aims of Plato's Republic. *Ancient Philosophy*, 24(2), 293–319. Retrieved from https://doi.org/10.5840/ancientphil 200424241.

Gary, K., & Chambers, D. (forthcoming). Educating for moral epiphany. *Educational Theory*.

Gary, K., & Yacek, D. (2020). Transformation and epiphany in moral education. *Jubilee Centre for Character and Virtues*. Retrieved from www.jubileecentre. ac.uk/userfiles/jubileecentre/pdf/conference-papers/VirtuesFlourishingLife/ Gary_Yucek_Full.pdf.

Gibson, A. B. (1957). Change and continuity in Plato's thought. *The Review of Metaphysics*, 11(2), 237–255.

Gonzalez, F. J. (1995). Plato's Lysis. *Ancient Philosophy*, 15(1), 69–90.

Grote, G. (1875). *Plato, and the other companions of Sokrates*. London: John Murray.

Haden, J. (1983). Friendship in Plato's *Lysis*. *Review of Metaphysics*, 37(2), 327–356.

Hadot, P., & Davidson, A. I. (1995). *Philosophy as a way of life: Spiritual exercises from Socrates to Foucault*. Malden, MA: Blackwell.

Hall, R. (1971). Techne and morality in the *Gorgias*. In J. Anton (Ed.), *Essays in ancient Greek philosophy*. Albany, NY: State University of New York Press.

Hansen, D. T. (1988). Was Socrates a "Socratic teacher"? *Educational Theory*, 38(2), 213–224.

Haroutunian-Gordon, S. (1986). The teacher in question: A study of teaching gone awry. *Teachers College Record*, 88(1), 53–63.

Haroutunian-Gordon, S. (1987). Evaluating teachers: The case of Socrates. *Teachers College Record*, 89(1), 117–132.

Haroutunian-Gordon, S. (1988). Teaching in an "ill-structured" situation: The case of Socrates. *Educational Theory*, 38(2), 225–237.

Haroutunian-Gordon, S. (1990). Statements of method and teaching: The case of Socrates. *Studies in Philosophy and Education*, 10, 139–156.

Hernandez-Santamaria, N. (2006). How are epiphanies sparked by adult educators translated? *Adult Learning*, 17(1–4), 27–28.

Higgins, C. (1994). Socrates' effect/Meno's affect: Socratic elenchus as cathartic therapy. In M. S. Katz (Ed.), *Philosophy of education 1994* (pp. 307–315). Urbana, IL: Philosophy of Education Society.

Howland, J. (1991). Re-reading Plato: The problem of Platonic chronology. *Phoenix*, 45(3), 189–214.

Howland, J. (2005). Storytelling and philosophy in Plato's *Republic*. *American Catholoic Philosophical Quarterly*, 79(2), 213–232.

Howland, J. (2014). Glacuon's fate: Plato's *Republic* and the *Drama of the Soul*. *Boston Area Colloquium on Ancient Philosophy*, 29(1), 113–124.

Howland, J. (2018). *Glaucon's fate: History, myth, and character in Plato's "Republic."* Philadelphia: Paul Dry Books.

Hoyos Valdés, Diana. (2017). The notion of character friendship and the cultivation of virtue. *Journal for the Theory of Social Behaviour.*

Irwin, T. (1977). *Plato's moral theory: The early and middle dialogues.* Oxford: Oxford University Press.

Irwin, T. (1979). *Plato's Gorgias.* Oxford: Oxford University Press.

Jarvis, A. (1996). *Taking a break: Preliminary investigations into the psychology of epiphanies as discontinuous change experiences.* PhD Diss., University of Massachusetts.

Jenkins, M. (2015). Early education in Plato's *Republic. British Journal for the History of Philosophy*, 23(5), 843–863.

Jonas, M. (2015). Education for epiphany: The case of Plato's Lysis. *Educational Theory*, 65(1), 39–51.

Jonas, M. (2016). Three misunderstandings of Plato's theory of moral education. *Educational Theory*, 66(3), 301–322.

Jonas, M. (2018). Plato on the necessity of imitation and habituation for the cultivation of the virtues. In D. Carr, J. Author, & K. Kristjánsson (Eds.), *Varieties of virtue ethics.* London: Palgrave.

Jonas, M. E., & Chambers, D. W. (2017). *The Use and Abuses of Emulation as a Pedagogical Practice.* Educational Theory, 67(3), 241–263.

Jonas, M., Nakazawa, Y., & Braun, J. (2012). Appetite, reason, and education in Socrates' city of pigs. *Phronesis*, 57(2012), 332–357.

Kahn, C. (1996). *Plato and the Socratic dialogues: The philosophical use of a literary form.* Cambridge: Cambridge University Press.

Klosko, G. (1981). Implementing the ideal state. *The Journal of Politics, 43,* 365–389.

Kohlberg, L. (1970). *Education for justice: A modern statement of the platonic view.* Cambridge, MA: Harvard University Press.

Kohlberg, L. (1981). *The philosophy of moral development.* New York: Harper & Row Publishers.

Korsgaard, C. (1996). *Creating the kingdom of ends.* New York: Cambridge University Press.

Kristjánsson, K. (2005). Can we teach justified anger? *Journal of Philosophy of Education*, 39(4), 671–689.

Kristjánsson, K. (2006). Habituated reason: Aristotle and the 'paradox of moral education'. *Theory and Research in Education*, 4(1), 101–122.

Kristjánsson, K. (2006a). Emulation and the use of role models in moral education. *Journal of Moral Education*, 35(1), 37–49.

Kristjánsson, K. (2006b). Habituated reason: Aristotle and the 'paradox of moral education.' *Theory and Research in Education* 4(1), 101.

Kristjánsson, K. (2007). *Aristotle, emotions and education.* Aldershot: Ashgate.

Kristjánsson, K. (2014a). On the old saw that dialogue is a socratic but not an aristotelian method of moral education. *Educational Theory*, 64(4), 333–348.

Kristjánsson, K. (2014b). There is something about Aristotle: The pros and cons of aristotelianism in contemporary moral education. *Journal of Philosophy of Education*, 48(1), 48–68.

Kristjánsson, K. (2014c). Undoing bad upbringing through contemplation: An aristotelian reconstruction. *Journal of Moral Education*, *43*(4), 468–483.

Kristjánsson, K. (2015). *Aristotelian character education* (Routledge Research in Education, 138). London: Routledge.

Kristjánsson, K. (2016). Flourishing as the aim of education: Towards an extended, "enchanted" Aristotelian account. *Oxford Review of Education*, *42*(6), 707–720.

Lagravenese, R. (Director). (2006). *Freedom writers*. Paramount Pictures.

Lear, J. (1992). Inside and outside the Republic. *Phronesis*, *37*(2), 184–215.

Ledger, R. (1989). *Re-counting Plato: A computer analysis of Plato's style*. Oxford: Oxford University Press.

MacKay, D. S. (1928). On the order of Plato's writings. *The Journal of Philosophy*, *25*(1), 5–18.

McCormack, D. (2015). A poem points, a thesis explains: Pedagogic epiphany and liminal disposition in adult education. *The Adult Learner: The Irish Journal of Adult and Community Education*, 1, 75–87.

McDavid, B. (2019). On why the city of pigs and clocks are not just. *Journal of the History of Philosophy*, *57*(4), 571–593.

McDonough, Richard. (2013). Referential Opacity and Hermeneutics in Plato's Dialogue Form. *Meta: Research in Hermeneutics, Phenomenology, and Practical Philosophy*, *5*(2), 251–278.

McDowell, J. (1996). Deliberation and moral development in Aristotle's ethics. In S. Engstrom & J. Whiting (Eds.), *Aristotle, Kant, and the Stoics: Rethinking happiness and duty*. Cambridge: Cambridge University Press.

McKeen, C. (2004). Swillsburg city limits (The "City of Pigs": *Republic* 370c–372d). *Polis*, *21*(1–2), 71–92.

McPherran, M. L. (1992). Socratic piety in the *Euthyphro*. In H. Benson (Ed.), *Essays on the philosophy of Socrates*. Oxford: Oxford University Press.

McPherran, M. L. (2012). Socrates' refutation of Gorgias: *Gorgias* 447 C-461 B. In *Oxford studies in ancient philosophy: Virtue and happiness: Essays in honour of Julia Annas* (pp. 13–29). Oxford: Oxford University Press.

Mintz, A. (2006). From grade school to law school: Socrates' legacy in education. In S. Ahbel-Rappe & R. Kamtekar (Eds.), *A companion to Socrates* (pp. 476–492). Malden, MA: Blackwell Publishing.

Mintz, A. (2007). The midwife as matchmaker: Socrates and relational pedagogy. *Philosophy of Education Yearbook 2007*, 91–99.

Mintz, A. (2011). Four educators in Plato's Theaetetus. *Journal of Philosophy of Education*, *45*(4), 657–673. https://doi.org/10.1111/j.1467-9752.2011.00828.x.

Mintz, A. (2014). Plato the teacher: The crisis of the Republic. *Journal of Philosophy of Education*, *48*(3), 507–509.

Mintz, A. (2018). *Plato: Images, aims, and practices of education*. London: Springer.

Morgan, M. (1992). Plato and Greek religion. In R. Kraut (Ed.), *The Cambridge companion to Plato*. Cambridge: Cambridge University Press.

Morrow, G. (1929). The theory of knowledge in Plato's seventh epistle. *The Philosophical Review*, *38*(4), 326–349.

Nails, D. (1994). Plato's "middle" cluster. *Phoenix*, *48*(1), 62–67.

Nehamas, A. (1999). *Virtues of authenticity: Essays on Plato and Socrates*. Princeton, NJ: Princeton University Press.

Nettleship, R. L. (1901). *Lectures on the Republic of Plato*. New York: St. Martin's Press.

Nichols, M. (2009). *Socrates on friendship and community*. Cambridge: Cambridge University Press.

Nietzsche, F. (1997). *Daybreak* (R. J. Hollingdale, Trans.). Cambridge: Cambridge University Press.

O'Brien, M. (1967). *The Socratic paradoxes and the Greek mind*. Chapel Hill, NC: University of North Carolina Press.

Pekarsky, D. (1994). Socratic teaching: A critical assessment. *Journal of Moral Education*, 23(2), 129.

Penner, T. (1992). Socrates and the early dialogues. In R. Kraut (Ed.), *The Cambridge companion to Plato*. Cambridge, MA: Cambridge University Press.

Penner, T. (1997). Socrates on the strength of knowledge: *Protagoras* 351B–357E. *Archiv für Geschichte der Philosophie*, 79, 117–149.

Penner, T. (2000). Socrates. In C. J. Rowe & M. Schofield (Eds.), *The Cambridge history of Greek and Roman political thought*. Cambridge, MA: Cambridge University Press.

Penner, T., & Rowe, C. (2005). *Plato' Lysis*. Cambridge: Cambridge University Press.

R. W. Emerson. (1834). Life of Reverend Joseph Emerson, Pastor of the Third Congregational Church in Beverly, M. S., and Subsequently Principal of a Female Seminary, Boston, MA: Crocker and Brewster.

Reeve, C. D. C. (1988). *Philosopher-kings: The argument of Plato's Republic*. Indianapolis: Hackett.

Reeve, C. D. C. (1989). *Socrates in the apology* (pp. 37–53). Indianapolis, IN: Hackett.

Reich, R. (1998). Confusion about the Socratic method: Socratic paradoxes and contemporary invocations of Socrates. *Philosophy of Education*, 68–78.

Rider, B. (2011). A Socratic seduction: Philosophical protreptic in Plato's Lysis. *Apeiron*, 44(1), pp. 40–41.

Roochnik, D. (1992). Socrates' use of the techne-analogy. In H. Benson (Ed.), *Essays on the philosophy of Socrates*. Oxford: Oxford University Press.

Roochnik, D. (1996). *Of art and wisdom: Plato's understanding of techne*. University Park, PA: Pennsylvania State University Press.

Rowe, C. J. (2006). Socrates in Plato's dialogues. In S. Ahbel-Rappe & K. Rachana (Eds.), *A companion to Socrates*. Oxford: Blackwell.

Rowe, C. J. (2007). *The Cambridge companion to Plato* (C. R. F. Ferrari, Ed.). Cambridge: Cambridge University Press.

Rowe, C. J. (2012). Socrates on reason, appetite and passion: A response to Thomas C. Brickhouse and Nicholas D. Smith, *Socratic Moral Psychology*. *Journal of Ethics*, 16, 305–324.

Rud, A. G. Jr. (1997). The use and abuse of Socrates in present day teaching. *Education Policy Analysis Archives*, 5(20).

Rudebusch, G. (2009). Socrates, wisdom, and pedagogy. *Philosophical Inquiry*, 31(1–2), 153–173.

Sanderse, W. (2011). Review essay of Kristján Kristjánsson's "Justifying emotions: Pride and jealousy," "Justice and desert-Based emotions," "Aristotle, emotions, and education" and "The self and its emotions". *Theory and Research in Education*, 9, 185–196.

Sanderse, W. (2012). *Character education: A neo-aristotelian approach to the philosophy, psychology and education of virtue*. Delft: Eburon.

Sanderse, W. (2013). The meaning of role modelling in moral and character education. *Journal of Moral Education*, 42(1), 28–42.

Sanderse, W. (2015). An aristotelian model of moral development. *Journal of Philosophy of Education*, 49(3), 382–398.

Santas, G. (1979). *Socrates: Philosophy in Plato's early dialogues* (p. 194). Boston, MA: Routledge.

Schneider, J. (2013). Remembrance of things past: A history of the Socratic method in the United States. *Curriculum Inquiry*, 43(5), 613–640.

Scott, G. A. (2000). *Plato's Socrates as educator*. Albany, NY: State University of New York Press.

Seeskin, K. (1987). *Dialogue and discovery: A study in Socratic method*. Albany: SUNY Press.

Sherman, N. (1999). The habituation of character. In N. Sherman (Ed.), *Aristotle's ethics: Critical Essays*. Lanham, MD: Rowman and Littlefield.

Shorey, P. (1903). *The unity of Plato's thought*. Chicago, IL: University of Illinois Press.

Shorey, P. (1933). *What Plato said*. Chicago, IL: University of Chicago Press.

Singpurwalla, R. (2006). Reasoning with the irrational: Moral psychology in the *Protagoras*. *Ancient Philosophy*, 26, 243–258.

Smith, R. (2011). The play of Socratic dialogue. *Journal of Philosophy of Education*, 45(2), 221–233.

Stauffer, D. (2006). *The unity of Plato's* Gorgias: *Rhetoric, justice, and the philosophic life*. Cambridge: Cambridge University Press.

Strike, K. (2014). Trust, traditions and pluralism: human flourishing and liberal polity. In D. Carr & J. W. Steutel (Eds.), *Virtue ethics and moral education*. London: Routledge.

Strong, M. (1996). *The habit of thought: From Socratic seminars to Socratic practice*. Chapel Hill, NC: New Views Publications.

Taylor, C. (1989). *Sources of the self: The making of the modern identity by Charles Taylor*. Cambridge: Harvard University Press.

Taylor, C. C. W. (2000). *Socrates: A very short introduction*. Oxford: Oxford University Press.

Tessitore, A. (1990). Plato's *Lysis*: An introduction to philosophical friendship. *The Southern Journal of Philosophy*, 28, 115–132.

Thesleff, H. (1989). Platonic chronology. *Phronesis*, 34(1), 1–26.

Tindale, C. (1984). Plato's Lysis: A reconsideration. *Apeiron: A Journal for Ancient Philosophy and Science*, 18(2), 102–109.

Vasiliou, I. (1996). The role of good upbringing in Aristotle's ethics. *Philosophy and Phenomenological Research*, 56, 771–797.

Vasiliou, I. (2008). *Aiming at virtue in Plato*. Cambridge: Cambridge University Press.

Versenyi, L. (1975). Plato's "Lysis". *Phronesis*, 20(3), 185–198.

Vlastos, G. (1978). The virtuous and the happy. *Times Literary Supplement Feb* (3961), 232–233.

Vlastos, G. (1985). Socrates' disavowal of knowledge. *Philosophical Quarterly*, *35*, 1–31.

Warnick, B. (2008). *Imitation and education: A philosophical inquiry into learning by example*. New York: State University of New York Press.

Weir, P. (Director). (1989). *Dead poets society*. Touchstone Pictures.

Wilberding, E. (2014). *Teach like Socrates: Guiding Socratic dialogues and discussions in the classroom*. Waco, TX: Prufrock Press.

Wilberding, J. (2012). Curbing one's appetites in Plato's Republic. In R. Barney, T. Brennan, & C. Brittain (Eds.), *Plato and the divided self* (p. 137). Cambridge: Cambridge University Press.

Wolfsdorf, D. (2007). Φιλία in Plato's "Lysis". *Harvard Studies in Classical Philology*, *103*, 235–259.

Woodruff, P. (1992). Plato's early theory of knowledge. In H. Benson (Ed.), *Essays on the Philosophy of Socrates*. Oxford: Oxford University Press.

Woolf, R. (2012). How to see an uncrusted soul. In R. Barney, T. Brennan, & C. Brittain (Eds.), *Plato and the divided self* (pp. 150–173). Cambridge: Cambridge University Press.

Yacek, D. (2020). Should anger be encouraged in the classroom? Political education, close-mindedness and civic epiphany. *Educational Theory*, *69*(4), 421–437.

Yacek, D., & Ijaz, K. (2019). Education as transformation: Formalism, moralism and the substantivist alternative. *Journal of Philosophy of Education*, *54*(1), 124–145. https://doi.org/10.1111/1467-9752.12366.

Index